THE WORD-HOARD BEOWULF

The Word-hoard Beowulf

A
TRANSLATION
with COMMENTARY

PETER RAMEY

Angelico Press

For information, address:
Angelico Press, Ltd.
169 Monitor St.
Brooklyn, NY 11222
www.angelicopress.com

paper 978-1-62138-912-5
cloth 978-1-62138-913-2

Cover image: The Fuller Brooch, a ninth-
century Anglo-Saxon silver and niello
brooch depicting the five senses

Book and cover design
by Michael Schrauzer

CONTENTS

INTRODUCTION

I. BEOWULF, CHRISTIANITY, AND TOLKIEN'S THEORY OF LANGUAGE

The role that Christianity plays in *Beowulf* has long perplexed scholars. Although the story takes place in pagan Scandinavia around AD 500, the poem has been shaped by a profoundly Christian imagination. Throughout the text God is continually invoked by the narrator, while the two major characters, Beowulf and Hrothgar, refer to God frequently in their speeches. Although no mention is made of specific Christian doctrines, the poem nevertheless speaks in generic terms about God in all the decisive moments of the text.

Early scholars dealt with the poem's Christianity by simply dismissing it. For 19th-century philologists like Jacob Grimm, *Beowulf* was an essentially pagan Germanic epic; any religious sentiments in it must represent added incrustations of a later Christian age and could be safely ignored—or even edited out. Critics like F. A. Blackburn would argue that the early medieval monks who copied the text likely added a "Christian coloring" to it, which therefore plays no part in the authentic poem. Eventually these views would be discredited. Conducting a more thorough examination, J. R. R. Tolkien and others showed that theological ideas are so deeply woven into the story that they can only be part of the text as originally written. Yet the notion that Christianity is extraneous to *Beowulf* persists to this day. How, after all, could orthodox Christian values sit side-by-side with the glory-seeking heroics of the pagan world that the poem celebrates?

In fact, the same question troubled the Anglo-Saxons themselves. Were the old heroic tales compatible with the new faith, or must they be rejected? The question was similar to one that had troubled classically trained Christian authors of late antiquity such as St. Jerome and St. Augustine. Could the classical pagan literature they had studied and come to love be reconciled with their Christian faith? For some, the answer was decidedly negative. "What has Athens to do with Jerusalem?" the second-century Church Father Tertullian famously thundered. Jerome, too, was vexed by the question throughout his life: in a dream Christ appeared before Jerome accusing him of not being a Christian but a "Ciceronian" due to his fondness for the Roman orator Cicero. But others such as Augustine saw value in the pagan writings. He declared, "Let every good and true Christian understand that wherever truth may be found, it belongs to the Lord"—even if found in pagan literature.

The same question confronted the Christianized Anglo-Saxons with regard to their own pagan past. *Quid Hinieldus cum Christo?* "What has Ingeld to do with Christ?" the Anglo-Saxon churchman Alcuin, echoing Tertullian, demanded in an angry letter to an Anglo-Saxon bishop in AD 797. Reports had reached Alcuin that ecclesiastics were in the habit of listening to "the songs of heathens" at mealtimes instead of reading Sacred Scripture. For Alcuin, the tales of Ingeld—a legendary warrior who appears in *Beowulf*—were incompatible with devotion to the Christian faith. "The house is narrow," Alcuin declares; "it cannot contain both. The celestial king wishes to have nothing in common with lost and pagan kings whose names are rattled off; for the eternal king rules in heaven, while the lost pagan king howls in hell."

If Alcuin followed Tertullian's footsteps in repudiating the pagan tradition, the *Beowulf* poet seems to have followed Augustine's in his willingness to redeem it. The poem he composed can be seen as rising to the challenge laid down by Anglo-Saxon churchmen like Alcuin. What does Ingeld have to do with Christ? For the *Beowulf* poet, the answer seems to be: quite a lot. Indeed, the question of God's involvement in the action of the heroes of old is where its chief interest lies; God's mysterious role in the pagan past stands at the heart of the text.

Rather than merely defending the stories of old, the *Beowulf* poet goes further: he theologizes them, imbuing the legendary events and figures with a spiritual dimension while at the same time carefully preserving their authentic traditional character. The nonhuman creatures acquire a metaphysical quality: the Dragon is a creature of flesh and blood, but also an incarnation of gold-hoarding avarice. Grendel is an *eoten*, a trollish creature, but he is also Cain's *cynn*, a demonic being and God's foe. Grendel's Mere is a spooky pool; it is also a space of evil that goes all the way down to the infernal depths, an image of hell in the tradition of the *Visio Pauli*, a medieval vision of the damned. The poet takes a *both/and* approach. Beowulf is a fierce warrior, eager for praise; he is also the "mildest of men and the most gracious, / the kindest to his people" (3181-82). Within the bounds of the poem, the poet can reimagine the heroic past and preserve it, but now framed within a Christian theological perspective. The heroic deeds of Beowulf are attributed to God, and also to Fate, and also to his own prowess—sometimes all within the same sentence. This *both/and* approach generates tension, but it is a productive tension. When the poet declares that Beowulf destroyed Grendel with his great strength, and in the same breath declares it was God, and then also Wyrd (fate), it doesn't make the poem inconsistent; it makes it *interesting*. We intuit a mystery at work. Within the frame of the poem there opens up a profundity in which all three statements are true at once. It is the same world where a warrior can be fierce, violent, and vaunting—and also a self-sacrificing savior figure. *Beowulf*, in other words, is fascinating not in spite of its Christianity, but precisely because of it. The encounter between Christianity and the Germanic heroic tradition lends the poem its particular dynamism. As Tolkien explains, the poet's "imagination, pondering old and new, was kindled. At this point new Scripture and old tradition touched and ignited." Their combustible combination is the source of *Beowulf*'s enduring power.

But how does this happen? The poet's great feat was to imbue his poem with a sense of the sacred without undercutting its traditional heroic ethos. He achieves this result by theologizing the story in three ways.

The first way is to place special emphasis on God's universality, while avoiding reference to overtly Christian doctrines. The poet reminds readers again and again that the same God who is known and worshiped by Anglo-Saxon Christians was also at work in times past, even among their heathen ancestors, for God is present in all places and at all times, working to carry out his will. Just as he controls the seasons, so he governs the lives of human beings, now and in the pagan past, since "mighty God has ruled / over the race of men always" (701–2). Tolkien summed up the poet's perspective neatly:

> There is One God, supreme ruler of the world, and true King of all mankind. In Him all events (*wyrd*) are governed.... From Him proceed all good things and gifts (including courage and strength). This has always been so. It was so in the days of your fathers' fathers. What is more, they knew it, even as all the descendants of Adam, unless seduced by the Devil, or falling into despair in evil times. Good wise men of those days feared God and thanked him. (2014: 273)

The second way is to utilize the principle sometimes termed "double determination." Beowulf killed Grendel, the poet states, but he also insists God defeated the monster. In Thomistic terms, God acts as the primary cause, while his human agents serve as the second-ary cause. The value of courage is upheld, but ultimate control and victory are attributed to the Ordainer of all. God's will is at work in and through his human agents—a point that the narrator, as well as Beowulf and Hrothgar, makes explicit.

The third way is to discover in the old tales echoes of redemptive history. Although the heroes of the past like Scyld, Hrothgar, and Beowulf fall outside of scriptural revelation, their lives nonetheless recapitulate sacred narrative. Scyld Scefing arrives as a child alone in a boat to become the savior of his people, echoing the Moses story. Scyld's son Beow is sent by God, who has perceived the people's great distress; Beow will overcome the surrounding nations, much like the God-sent champions in the book of Judges. Beowulf is portrayed as a savior whose sacrificial death recalls Christ's. More generally, kings, who receive a special emphasis, function as images of divine kingship in their protection, authority, and distribution of rewards. In several other traditional-heroic ideas and institutions, to be discussed below, the poet finds points of contact between the new faith and the old Germanic world. His theological vision brings an added depth to *Beowulf*. Among scholars, Tolkien was one of the few to grasp this quality: the poet, drawing upon the old legends, "has used them afresh in an original fashion, giving us not just one more, but something akin yet different: a measure and interpretation of them all."

Here the question might arise: If this metaphysical vision is indeed central to *Beowulf*, why have so many failed to see it? Despite the work of scholars like Tolkien, readers today frequently dismiss the poem's religiosity, particularly non-specialists who are unable to read it in Old English. All too often the religious references are explained away as a sop thrown to the poet's more devout early medieval audi-ence—or even as a tactic used to sneak an essentially pagan poem past the ecclesiastical censors.

One reason for this dismissive attitude is the language used in modern English translations. Put simply, most renderings of *Beowulf* flatten its metaphysical elements, what Tolkien calls its "mythical mode of imagination." This flattening is not entirely the fault of translators. Modern English has nothing like the Old English poetic vocabulary, or "word-hoard," to draw upon to describe the mythical and mysterious world of *Beowulf*. Without the specific names for its nonhuman creatures, the titles for God, or the expansive language of fate, the poem's metaphysical vision is severely diminished, or even distorted, in modern English. The enigmatic gigantic beings who lumber through the poem, the ents and eotens (*entas* and *eotenas* in their Old English plural forms), are reduced to homely "giants" and "ogres." *God*, in the role of mysterious measurer or ordainer of fate, whom the poet calls the *Metod*, is frequently mistranslated as "Maker" or even more blandly and impersonally as "Providence."

Such colorless translations do not merely diminish the power of the poem; they have also led generations of readers to assume the supernatural and theological elements are no more than embellishments, a "Christian coloring" to a story centered on human heroism. But the Old English vocabulary helps to reveal that the reverse is true: human action in the poem takes place as only one part of a vast cosmological drama. Mythical creatures, hidden spells, curses, dragons, gigantic beings, magical pools, mysterious artifacts, God, fate, and individual doom—all are in play, as the poet probes again and again the question of the workings of the Divine Will among the heroes of old. But in the hands of modern translators, the rich riddle-like world of *Beowulf* often comes out looking like a comic book.

The Word-Hoard Beowulf has been devised to address this issue. To give non-specialists access to the poem's "mythical mode of imagination," this version of *Beowulf* brings to light the essential Old English vocabulary, incorporating into the main text of the translation titles used for God and specific names for evil and nonhuman creatures, as well as terminology for kinship and heroism. This method is informed by Tolkien's theory of language as the repository of myth. For Tolkien, the belief systems and stories of a culture are embedded in its words. Because, as Tolkien maintains, "the incarnate mind, the tongue, and the tale are . . . coeval" (1936: 122), thought, language, and belief interpenetrate one another. Words encode particular ways of seeing, and come to us freighted with a unique history or "etymology," that is, layers of earlier meanings. The work of philologists like Tolkien is to uncover the earlier meanings and reconstruct the worldview they once expressed. The same linguistic principle lies at the root of Tolkien's own mythmaking, which begins with the invention of his own languages and from there grows into narrative.

Words, in Tolkien's view, are not value-neutral tools for communication; they are carriers of culture. They come to us freighted with history and myth. This is true even though language continually

changes, with the result that speakers may be unaware of the etymology of a given word. Rarely, for instance, do we stop to ponder
the pantheon of gods that populate our days of the week. *Wednesday*
is the day of the deity Woden (Odin in Norse myth), a god associated with a once-dominant Germanic warrior cult, while *Tuesday*
preserves the name of the god *Tiw,* cognate with the Latin *deus* and
Sanskrit *deva,* all of whom descend from a paternal sky-god whose
protection was invoked over the villages of Proto-Indo-European-
speakers some six millennia ago. Oblivious as we may be to such
etymologies, they are present in the words we use and are part of
the story of our words and, for speakers of the language, our own
story. The same is abundantly true of the language of *Beowulf,* the
site of many unique and sometimes indecipherable word-artifacts.
By attending closely to its language, we come to better understand
the mythology, metaphysics, and ethical values underlying the poem.

II. THE EARLY GERMANIC WORLD OF THE POEM

To make sense of *Beowulf* and the poet's theological project, it is
necessary to first understand the world in which the story takes place.
This section will give an overview of the early Germanic milieu that
provides the poem's setting, and then sketch out how the poet imbues
early Germanic customs and concepts with new Christian significance.

The Anglo-Saxon society in which the *Beowulf* poet lived should
not be confused with the world the poem describes. The poem we
have was probably composed sometime around 725 —there are some
who argue for a century or more later—while the events that occur
in the poem take place centuries earlier, around AD 500. The story is
set not in Anglo-Saxon England but in southern Scandinavia during
the age of the great Germanic Migrations (approximately 375–550).
During this time, Germanic peoples moved into territories formerly
controlled by the Roman Empire, and these migrations included the
arrival of Angles and Saxons to Britain. It was a period of upheaval and
continual conflict, as Germanic peoples fought one another as well as
Roman armies and invading Huns. Yet in later centuries it would be
remembered as the age of heroes; stories of great warrior-kings like
Hygelac and Theodric were retold and reshaped in the oral tradition
until they were transformed into legends. In this respect the Migration
Age functioned much like the Old West in the American imagination.
It provided a powerful cultural memory and sense of identity. Later,

Anglo-Saxon kings would claim to descend from heroes like Scyld, Ingeld, Offa, and other figures who appear in *Beowulf,* listing the names of these warrior-kings in their royal genealogies.

Though steeped in legend, the world depicted in *Beowulf* has a basis in history. Most of the names mentioned harken back to historical figures, however shrouded in myth, and most of the Germanic tribal groups named in the text are attested in other sources. At least one event from the poem, Hygelac's disastrous raid in Frisia, was a historical event, recorded in the Latin Chronicles, that took place between the years 516-531. Most of the historical personages and events, however, have been reshaped into legends, so now provide little trustworthy historical information. Yet "while the poem does not offer reliable historical fact, it does yield a great deal of information about early Germanic culture" (Klaeber 4th ed.; li, note 6). It is above all the distinctive vocabulary of *Beowulf* that evokes the earlier Germanic world from which the poem derives. The vocabulary of *Beowulf* has its roots in the Common Germanic culture that predates the Migration Age, a people group who inhabited southern Scandinavia—a region the poet calls the *Scede-lands*—and who spoke a language we now call Proto-Germanic or Common Germanic. Over time the Common Germanic speakers began to split into separate linguistic groups, some of which would eventually make their way, centuries later, to Britain, bringing with them a language they called *Anglisc.* But the early Germanic peoples left no written account of themselves; the few early runic inscriptions they left tell us very little. Nonetheless a picture of their vanished culture can be pieced together by reconstructing the language that they spoke. Through what is called the Comparative Method, linguists have used the surviving Germanic languages to re-create the ancestor language, Common Germanic.

This reconstructed linguistic evidence can be further supplemented by the testimonies of Roman writers who encountered the people they called the Germani in the centuries following the breakup of Common Germanic into separate groups. Caesar fought against some of these Germanic peoples in the 50s BC during his military campaigns in Gaul. In his *De Bello Gallico* he described them as a tall, warlike people who inhabited the forests east of the Rhine River. Over a century later, the Roman historian Tacitus gives a much more detailed picture in his *Germania.* The accounts by Caesar, Tacitus, and others are colored by their own concerns and biases, and their accuracy is sometimes questionable; nevertheless, they are valuable witnesses to early Germanic culture, and many of the details have been confirmed by linguistic and archaeological evidence. The following paragraphs will sketch out the picture of the early Germanic society that this combined evidence reveals, with particular attention to customs, beliefs, and warfare. Though *Beowulf* was composed many centuries later, it corroborates features depicted in the *Germania*, and its vocabulary recalls this earlier Germanic world, if dimly.

Early Germanic culture reckoned time in terms of *nights* rather than days, and measured years in *winters.* Years were divided into two seasons (called *missera* in *Beowulf*) rather than four. This time-reckoning system is still evident in *Beowulf;* the hero declares he was on the waves for a space of "five nights" as he battled sea-monsters, and the dragon's treasure is said to have lain in the earth for "a thousand winters" before the hoard is opened. The year was divided into lunar months, but months were not initially divided into weeks (the seven-day week, which derives from ancient Hebrew culture, was introduced with the coming of Christianity). They inscribed objects with runes, a writing system that had alleged magical properties as well as ordinary uses. Beowulf presents King Hrothgar with a giant sword hilt "rightly marked in rune-letters"—the sole reference to writing in the poem. The diet of early Germanic people consisted heavily of meat and dairy, at least relative to Roman standards, and they drank fermented beverages made of barley and honey they called *alu* and *meduz.* At ceremonial drinking banquets they imbibed these beverages from cups fashioned from the horns of the aurochs, a massive wild ox now extinct, which Caesar says they hunted in the thick forests that covered much of Germania.

But the central and defining feature of early Germanic life was warfare. Much like *Beowulf,* Tacitus and Caesar depict a society centered around a warrior elite. This all-encompassing military focus no doubt reflects the tumult leading up to the Migration Age, in which war was the dominant fact of life, as well as the particular social arrangement of the inhabitants of Germania. Unlike the Roman Empire, which employed a professional army to guard its borders, in Germanic lands every freeborn male was a warrior by default. According to Caesar, Germanic youths were given weapons at an early age to begin their training, and Tacitus observes that the men would carry their weapons with them at all times. Both writers comment on the reputation of the Germani as ferocious fighters. This war-centered identity is reflected in Germanic naming conventions. Names of both men and women typically include words for war, weapons, and fierce animals, and terms denoting power and renown. Wulfgar (wolf-spear), Æschere (ash-spear-army), and Hildeburh (battle-stronghold), to pick just three examples from *Beowulf,* are broadly representative of this naming practice, which continued among the Anglo-Saxons even after their conversion to Christianity, and only died out after England was conquered by the French-speaking Normans.

The ferocity of the Germani was encouraged by their distinctive military arrangement, the dright (OE *driht* or *gedryht; druhtiz* in reconstructed Common Germanic), which meant "troop, following." The dright was a war-band made up of followers who had voluntarily attached themselves to a particular war-leader and fought on his behalf. Tacitus labeled this troop with the Latin word *comitatus,* "armed escort, retinue of warriors." The leader of this body of warriors was called the drighten (*drihten* in Old English; the *-en* suffix means "leader of," so drighten means "leader of the dright"). The relationship between dright and drighten was marked by reciprocal bonds of loyalty; the warriors fought on behalf of their drighten, and the drighten rewarded them with gifts of treasure won from battle or raiding. According to Tacitus, this relationship inspired the warriors to fight with extraordinary intensity:

> When they go into battle, it is a disgrace for the chief to be surpassed in valor, a disgrace for his followers not to equal the valor of the chief. And it is an infamy and a reproach for life to have survived the chief, and returned from the field. To defend, to protect him, to ascribe one's own brave deeds to his renown, is the height of loyalty. The chief fights for victory; his vassals fight for their chief. (Tacitus, *Germania and Agricola,* trans. A. J. Church and W. J. Brodribb, 1877)

The war-leader led by example, and the warriors who followed him did so by choice, not compulsion. Their personal dedication to the war-chief distinguished the Germani from soldiers in the Roman army: "If any word sums up the relationship between Germanic leader and follower," D. H. Green writes, "it is the concept of loyalty rather than obedience, two concepts which sum up the difference in military control between the Romans and their opponents" (69). The same reciprocal bonds of loyalty characterize Beowulf's relationship to his thanes (OE *thegn* is the term for the individual follower of a leader or king); his men follow him to Daneland to face Grendel, none of them expecting they will return home (lines 690–95). So powerful was the bond of loyalty between dright and drighten that, following the conversion to Christianity, Anglo-Saxon authors composing religious verse drew upon dright-drighten terminology to portray the relationship between Christ and his disciples.

To Romans like Tacitus, the Germanic warriors appeared not only fierce, but fearless. The bond between dright and drighten inspired acts of daring, called *ellen* in Old English, and cultivated a disdain for death. Deeds of *ellen* on the battlefield resulted in *dōm*, heroic renown, lasting glory. As an early 8th-century Old English proverb declares, "Often the man slow to act puts off *dōm*, every victorious exploit; therefore he dies alone." Far better to hazard one's life on the battlefield than to die alone, cut off from joys of fellowship of dright and drighten. Disgrace, not death, was the enemy most to be feared. As Beowulf will remind Hrothgar, because all face death eventually, "let he who can win *dōm* before death," for that is best for a warrior after he is gone (1384–89). Heroic defiance in the face of death and defeat are a hallmark of Old English and Norse literature. J. R. R. Tolkien labeled this "creed of unyielding will" the theory of "Northern courage." In early northern European literature "a hero," Tom Shippey explains, "is defined not by victory but by defeat." Heroic defiance in the face of defeat gave warriors something even more prized than victory: *dōm*. (This mentality may account for Beowulf's much-debated decision to face the dragon alone.)

But courage brought warriors more tangible rewards as well. Common epithets for the war-leader include *beag-gyfa*, ring-giver, and *gold-wine*, gold-friend, and the poem lavishes attention on scenes of gift-giving in the hall as the leader distributes rich gifts among his followers. Treasure-giving often occurs in the context of the *symbel*, usually translated "feast," although food is never mentioned in these scenes. Instead, a drinking cup, typically bestowed first by the lady of the house, is passed around the hall in a communal drinking ceremony. Here drinking and gift-giving are accompanied by speeches of praise and warriors' *bēots*, heroic vows. Tacitus describes these "banquets," which lasted days at a time, as occasions during which crucial decisions were made, such as alliances, pacts of peace, and even marriage pledges: "At no other time, they think, is the heart so open to sincere feelings or so quick to warm to noble sentiments." Rejoicing together in the hall, the warriors experience what in *Beowulf* is called *drēam*, the communal joy of the war-band, which in the poem represents the height of human happiness; in the presence of the drighten, the warriors rejoice in the communal cup, in the heroic tales recited by the singer, or *scop*, and words affirming their own worth as warriors. The same word, *drēam*, is employed in Old English religious poems to describe the rejoicing of the saints in heaven. This word, derived from the same source as *dright*, originally meant "the communal rejoicing of the dright." Later it developed the very different meaning of modern English *dream*.

Germanic peoples worshiped an array of gods and goddesses in sacred groves and at shrines made of piled stones called a *hearg* in Old English (Proto-Germanic *harugaz*), although these details of heathen religion are all but absent from *Beowulf.* Sacrifices were offered to the gods, consisting of weapons, animals, and human victims. Of these gods, the most prominent were the two war gods Tiw and Woden, along with the fertility god Thunor ("thunder"), still present to us in our days of the week. In Norse they are known as Tyr, Odin, and Thor, and their Proto-Germanic forms have been reconstructed as *Tiwaz, Wodanaz,* and *Thunraz*. Like Latin *deus*, Tiw derives from Proto-European *deywos*, the chief sky god; Tiw was apparently the ruler of the gods until later displaced from this position by Woden. But both Tiw and Woden were linked with warrior cults. The name Woden derives from "leader of the *wod*, the frenzied," the *-en* suffix denoting "leader of," as in *drighten*. Woden would inspire his followers with frenzy in battle, akin to the berserkers of later Viking-age Scandinavia, who were thought to be invulnerable in battle.

The ferocity of the Germani in battle compensated for their marked disadvantages in weaponry. Tacitus noted that unlike the Romans, the Germani possessed few iron weapons. Their primary weapon was the wooden spear, which was accompanied by a wooden shield covered with leather and brightly painted. Although iron was used for the spear tip and the shield boss, the sword, made completely of iron, was a much rarer, high-status weapon. The same was true of iron protective gear—the helmet (*helm*) and ring-mail shirt (*byrne*), which in most cases were possessed only by high-ranking warriors. To the heavily armored Romans, the Germanic peoples were shockingly lightly armed—Tacitus exclaims they went into battle *nudi*, naked, by which he means they were without protective armor, and Roman reliefs depict Germanic warriors in battle as shirtless, wearing only the tightly bound breeches (*brec*) that were the distinctive garb of northern barbarians in colder climes. Even late in the Anglo-Saxon period, rank-and-file warriors went into battle with nothing more than a spear and a shield. This explains the particular fascination with weapons and armor in *Beowulf*. When Beowulf and his men arrive at Heorot, for example, the Danes marvel at their impressive iron weapons — helmets, mail-coats, iron-tipped spears — as they jingle and flash in the sun; these warriors, the Danes remark, are indeed "ennobled by their weapons." It is the sword, however, that holds the highest place of honor in the poem. The astounding proliferation of terms for this weapon shows in what awe it was held. More common was the long knife or *seax* which warriors carried with them, to be used in battle as well as for everyday uses.

For all the importance of the war-band, it was the kin-group that was the fundamental social unit in early Germanic societies. This aggregate of relatives was the basis of one's identity and security, which is why individuals in *Beowulf* are invariably defined in terms of kinship relations and why the word *cynn* recurs with such frequency — 27 times as a single word and many more times in compounds. In a society without any centralized authority — no police, no law courts, no formal political representation — the kin-group afforded individuals their only measure of protection and social status. It was also a means of maintaining social stability. It is telling that in Old English *sibb* means both "kinship" and "peace," so closely intertwined were the two notions. But achieving and maintaining peace paradoxically involved the use of controlled violence, called *fæhth*. This word, typically translated "feud," refers to a state of declared and sanctioned violence between groups. "Feud" today has associations of lawlessness and disorder — gangland killings or Hatfields and McCoys. But in a tribal, pre-state society, the kin-group *was* the law; the threat of retaliation was the only means of maintaining the social order and defending oneself against injury. Alliances were another means of establishing order. Sons were therefore obligated, Tacitus explains, "to take up both the feuds and the friendships of a father or kinsman."

Tacitus mentions another means of settling conflict: "But feuds do not continue forever unreconciled. Even homicide can be atoned for by a fixed number of cattle or sheep, the compensation being received by the whole family." Tacitus is referring to the *wergild*, "man-price," in which compensation would be paid out to the family of one killed or injured. Settlements could be made at a regular formal assembly, or *thing*, where all freeborn males gathered to make judicial and political decisions, and where assent to a proposal was signaled by the clashing of weapons. Such assemblies were especially significant in the absence of centralized authority.

Because one's protection depended on the strength of the kin-group, it was in the interest of its members to extend kinship ties, and this could be achieved though intermarriage with other tribal or kinship groups. The term "peace-weaver" is used in *Beowulf* to describe the practice of using marriage to settle inter-tribal conflicts—sometimes with disastrous results. Because marriage was exogamous, with the bride moving into the household of her husband, a special relationship developed between the *eam* (maternal uncle) and his nephew, in order to strengthen ties with the bride's relatives, the in-laws. Tacitus remarks that in some cases the relationship of *eam* and nephew was stronger than that of father and son: "The sons of sisters are as highly honored by their uncles as by their own fathers. Some tribes even consider the former tie the closer and more sacred of the two." We see these close ties between Beowulf and his *eam*, King Hrethel, who fostered him as a child—fosterage being another means of strengthening kinship.

Because of its all-encompassing importance, no fate was worse than the loss of one's kin-group, whether through war, bloodfeud, or exile. Without status, identity, or protection, an individual suffered a kind of social extinction, and was highly vulnerable. A collection of short Old English lyric poems known as the Elegies give poignant expression to this plight, a situation that was probably a common enough occurrence during the upheaval of the Migration Age. The place that exile holds within the Anglo-Saxon imagination is rather like the fixation on heartbreak in popular music and movies today. In place of the idealization of romantic relationships, what we see in this early literature is the celebration of kinship ties, along with the intimate bond warriors felt for their war-leader.

The conversion of the Germanic peoples to Christianity was culturally transformative. It brought a new set of ethical principles that challenged traditional mores; it introduced what has been called a "guilt" culture that over time replaced the "shame" culture, making individuals morally responsible in a way that the collective identity of the kin-group did not (guilt is a sensation one can feel all alone; shame generally requires other people). The Church supported the ending of feuds. Christianity also introduced an entirely new class of people — monastics — who lived communally, did not beget children or fit within the traditional kin-group structure, and brought literacy and classical learning everywhere their communities spread. Yet Christianity also absorbed a great deal of Germanic culture. The Lord God was called *Drighten*; the pagan holidays of Easter and Yuletide became Christian festivals. Sacred sites were rebuilt as churches. The special blessing of health and safety that was conferred by the gods, *hāl*, became the basis of the word *hālig*, holy. Traditional folklore was subsumed within biblical narratives, so that Grendel is a descendent of Cain, and the Germanic *eotens* and *ents* are linked to the giants of the Bible. Traditional heroic vocabulary and themes were recycled to tell the stories of saints and biblical figures. And of course it was this Christian culture that created, copied, and carefully preserved the extraordinary poem we today call *Beowulf.*

It will be helpful to conclude this section by sketching out a few of the ways in which the poet of *Beowulf* reimagined the Germanic past through the lens of Christianity. Clearly the poet saw great value in the heroic tales of old. Not only were these tales central to Anglo-Saxon identity, they also had, in the poet's eyes, theological merit. Looking back at the traditional heroic narratives, the poet recognized points of contact between the Germanic world of legend and the Christian faith. By highlighting these, the poet was able to recuperate the heroic tradition, preserving its essential features while imbuing them with spiritual significance. Several Germanic notions readily lent themselves to his theologizing imagination.

The most important of these was the reciprocal bond between *dright* and *drighten*. This configuration offered an image of devoted, disciple-like followers, as well as a picture of a ruler personally committed to his men. The giving of treasure in recognition of heroic deeds was easily recast as an image of God's kingly rewards.

Another important point of contact for the poet is the *symbel*, the joyous sharing of the cup, which recalls the Eucharistic communion and the heavenly communion the Eucharist presages. It is in the ceremony of the cup that the war-band experiences *drēam*, the communal joy and oneness of the war-band in the hall. This joy in the hall presents an image of Eden-like paradise, as well as of heavenly bliss. It is this *drēam* that the Satanic figure of Grendel cannot abide and sets out to destroy.

The monstrous figures also take on a theological cast. The creatures of folklore and Germanic myth are drawn by the poet into a cosmic battle—the Great Feud—in which they are depicted as the diabolic adversaries of God and the human beings who bear God's image. Although we can no longer be certain, aspects of this cosmic battle were probably already in place in Germanic myth, especially since the much later Norse myth depicts the Giants as the perennial foes of the Æsir, the gods of Asgard.

Dōm, the glory earned by heroic action, is another feature of the heroic world that the poet seeks to recuperate. The root sense of the word is "judgment," which is still evident in "Doom" and "Doomsday" (Judgment Day). But when used in heroic contexts in Old English *dōm* has also the sense of "positive judgment, public approbation, glory." It is the work of warriors to seek *dōm*, Beowulf declares, and the poet appears to agree. While a reputation for aggression, vaunting, and violence might seem at odds with Christian values of humility, meekness, and turning the other cheek, the figure of Beowulf has been deliberately fashioned by the poet to challenge this assumption. As Tolkien has noted, Beowulf demonstrates the self-sacrificing dimensions of warfare: "He may earn glory by his deeds, but they are all in fact done in the service of others. Beowulf does not come first with Beowulf." In this way the *dōm* of the warrior (glory) and the *dōm* of God (judgment) gradually merge, so that when the hero dies near the end, it is ambiguous whether the *dōm* Beowulf's soul is said to seek after death is "judgment" or "glory." Perhaps both are meant.

III. TRANSLATION METHOD AND FORMAT

Apart from the Bible, *Beowulf* may well be the text most translated into modern English. There are rhyming *Beowulfs*, prose *Beowulfs*, experimental *Beowulfs*, feminist *Beowulfs*, graphic-novel *Beowulfs*, and nearly every other kind of *Beowulf* conceivable. But none of them affords access to the rich and multilayered vocabulary of the original. Even Tolkien's posthumously published translation does not do so, never having been intended for publication, and written in loose prose style. It is impossible, Tolkien declared, for translations of *Beowulf* to "indicate all the possibilities or hints afforded" by the poem's original language. "For many Old English poetical words there are (naturally) no precise modern equivalents of the same scope and tone: they come down to us bearing echoes of ancient days beyond the shadowy borders of Northern history" (1940: x; xi). Tolkien gives the example of the adjective *eacen*. "Huge," "broad," "mighty" are all serviceable translations of this word. "But an enquirer into ancient beliefs, with the loss of *eacen*, will lose the hint that in poetry this word preserved a special connotation. Originally it means not 'large' but 'enlarged,' and in all instances may imply not merely size and strength, but an *addition* of power, beyond the natural" (xi). The reader of a modern English translation, coming across a "large" sword or "huge" treasure in *Beowulf*, will never guess that these items are charged with supernatural properties. As noted above, the limitations of modern English are especially problematic for representing metaphysical and mythical elements.

Because the power and poetry of *Beowulf* are deeply embedded in its language, the present version takes a more radical approach. Key Old English terms, sometimes in slightly modified form, are included in the main text of the translation, followed by explanatory notes at the bottom of the page. While this method results in a less fluid text, it has the benefit of giving readers contact with some of the actual language of *Beowulf*. Most who read *Beowulf* in translation have no inkling that a rich and arresting word-hoard lies hidden beneath the smooth modern English surface. *The Word-Hoard Beowulf* is designed to bridge the gulf between specialists and non-specialists. Here readers enter a world of curious linguistic artifacts, mysterious spiritual forces, unresolved textual cruxes, and polysemous vocabulary. Here they encounter a poem of unfathomable depths; like Grendel's Mere, it can be said of the poem that "there lives none so frōd [wise and ancient] / among the sons of men that knows its bottom" (1366-67).

To be sure, there are considerable obstacles to this translation strategy. The English language has undergone seismic shifts in the centuries since *Beowulf* was composed, changes not merely in vocabulary, but in grammar, sound structure, and syntax. Representing even a sampling of Old English requires flexibility and a willingness to make modifications, especially with inflections—the word endings that indicate grammatical function. I have added modern plural (-s) endings to nouns where Old English uses various endings; sometimes I use a later (Middle or Early Modern English) form of a word where the Old English phonology or spelling would pose an insurmountable barrier to pronunciation. The same goes for the now-defunct verb endings. But wherever modifications occur, the original Old English form has been supplied in the accompanying note.

In a few instances a modern English version of the Old English word has been provided, but with its earlier meaning (such as "mere-wife" for OE *mere-wif*)—always with explanatory note. In order to make the translation as intelligible as possible without requiring constant recourse to the notes, I have "doubled up" some terms so that the Old English word appears first, followed by a modern rendering within the same sentence, especially when an Old English word makes its first appearance ("His hand-slayer...was a wandering wæl-gæst, a slaughter-spirit," 1330–31). My aim is to keep the main text understandable with only minimal help from the notes, especially as the reader grows familiar with recurring terms.

Early medieval scribes used four written characters no longer found in modern English. Two of these, called eth [ð] and thorn [þ], represent the "th" sound and were used interchangeably. Another, called wynn [ƿ], is the equivalent to our *w*. Because these characters are unfamiliar to readers today, they have been replaced with "th" and "w," respectively. A fourth special character, known as *ash* [æ], which makes the *a* sound in *apple* and *cat*, has been retained, since there is no other written character available to represent this specific sound (*a* can indicate a range of sounds, not just this precise sound). Thus, *þrym* becomes *thrym*, and *Beopulf* becomes *Beowulf*, but *gæst* (pronounced like the first syllable of *ghastly*) remains *gæst*. Old English, like Latin, also distinguishes between long and short vowels, and editors sometimes mark long vowels with a line over the vowel called a *macron*. Macrons are used in this version only where the word might be easily mistaken in its pronunciation or meaning, such as *drēam* (pronounced *dray-ahm*, not *dreem*), "communal joy," or *dōm* (pronounced *dome*, not *dahm*), "judgment, glory."

So much for method. Equally difficult is the matter of word selection. Which Old English words ought to be retained in the main text? The decision to include specific Old English terms has been based on four criteria:

1) *Keywords*. Words have been retained that are theologically, thematically, or cultural essential, such as *wyrd, dōm, Metod* (loosely, "fate," "glory," "the Ordainer," respectively), as well as language conveying insight into early medieval material culture, warfare, and psychology.

2) *Recurrence.* Much of the vocabulary consists of poetic formulas which recur so often that they will quickly become familiar. It is therefore convenient to retain many of them, such as *mære, cynn, mathel* (respectively, "renowned," "kinship group," "to give a speech").

3) *Elusive language.* Words that are ambiguous, contested, or uncertain — or simply untranslatable — are left unaltered, with notes discussing them below.

4) *Alliterating words.* Wherever feasible, the alliterative patterns of the original text have been preserved. While this is not the primary aim of this translation, and no attempt has been made to maintain alliteration in every line, it is an additional consideration. The original music of the poem is part of its power and meaning — "the verses fall like sword-strokes in the thick of battle," one keen observer has remarked (Green 53) — so even a trace of it is worth preserving.

These four criteria provide the basis for the translation method. But they have been applied with the flexibility necessary to make the translated text as readable as possible, in the hope that the translation can be at least partially understood without constant recourse to the explanatory notes. All the same, a smooth, fluent translation is by no means the ultimate objective. To the contrary, the purpose of this rendering is to introduce readers to the difficulties, debates, polysemous meanings, and complex theological language of the original, in the belief that these will stimulate interest rather than smother it.

Apart from the original vocabulary, the translated text is a literal, line-by-line representation of the Old English. In only a few exceptional instances have the lines been reordered to provide clarity. The translated text is based on Klaeber's standard edition of *Beowulf* (4th edition).

Tolkien provides the theoretical approach to language that has guided the development of this text. He has also supplied two masterful works of *Beowulf* criticism: his landmark lecture, "*Beowulf: The Monsters and the Critics*" (1936), and the notes in *Beowulf: A Translation and Commentary* (2014). Quotations from these two texts are woven regularly into the commentary.

By drawing upon Tolkien's vision and insight, *The Word-Hoard Beowulf* will enable readers to more fully experience the poem's metaphysical vision, affording direct access to what Tolkien called its "mythical mode of imagination."

The Word-hoard
Beowulf

THE PROLOGUE: *The Rise of Scyld and His Ship Funeral*

Hwæt—

We have heard of the power of the Gar-Danes,
the thrym of the people-kings in days of old,
how those æthelings carried out courageous deeds.

Often Scyld Scefing deprived enemy armies,
5   a great many mægths, of their mead-settles;
he struck terror into eorls, after he was first

Prologue Synopsis. The poet begins by recalling the heroes of old among the Danish kings, and describes the rise of one of them, Scyld Scefing ("Shield, son of Sheaf"). Although he was a foundling who arrived mysteriously as a child alone in a boat, Scyld would rise to prominence as ruler of the Danes, conquering the surrounding tribes by destroying their halls (thus "depriving them of their mead-settles") and forcing them to pay tribute. Scyld also founds the Scylding dynasty when he fathers a son, Beow, to whom God grants widespread fame and glory. Then in his old age Scyld dies; his men, following his instructions, load his body into a ship filled with treasures and weapons and push it out to sea. The poet depicts the rise of the Scylding Dynasty as divinely ordained.

Hwæt signals the start of a poetic discourse or speech. It has is no exact modern English equivalent; attempts by translators include "Behold!," "Lo!," "Hear!," and "So." (The special character *æ* makes the sound of the *a* in *cat*.)

1. *Gar-Danes* (OE *Gar-Denas*). A now-obsolete term for spear, *gar* survives only in *garlic* (called "spear-leek" on account of its shape) and the pointy-nosed *garfish*. It is one of many compounds used in *Beowulf* for the Danes. Spears were the primary weapon of early European warfare and feature prominently in *Beowulf.*

2. *thrym*, "power, force, greatness, glory." This word is the centerpiece of the poem's opening sentence as well as the poem as a whole. It is what makes these heroes of old matter and the reason we are hearing about them. Typically translated "glory," *thrym* involves not just a notion of splendor but also power—the noun can also refer to the collective power of a troop of warriors, "a multitude." It is a keenly admired quality: heroes and kings with *thrym* are those who can impose their will upon the chaotic world around them, investing it with order. In Old English texts the word is also applied to the majesty of God and the power of His heavenly host. Unlike modern notions of power as a corrupting force, *thrym* is celebrated in the poem as an unmitigated good that is bestowed upon mortals by God.

3. *æthelings* (*æthelingas*) are noblemen, members of the warrior class. Persons of the lower classes are all but absent from the poem.

4–5. *Scyld Scefing... mægths.* Scyld is a mythical foundling who establishes the great Scylding dynasty in the land of the Danes (Zealand, in modern-day Denmark). With the introduction of Scyld, the poet harkens back to a foundational north Germanic myth, connecting the tale of Beowulf to

found destitute. He experienced comfort for that,
grew mighty under the clouds, increased in honors,
until all the surrounding peoples
10   over the whale-road had to obey him,
give him gomb. That was a good king.

Afterwards an offspring was born to him,
a young one in the courtyards, whom God sent
as a comfort to the people. He had seen their dire distress,
15   how they suffered earlier, lordless,
for a long while. For this the Lord of Life,
the Waldend of Glory, gave them worldly honor.

---

this more primeval figure. Scyld arrives mysteriously all alone in a boat
as a child and grows up to rule the Danes, eventually subduing all the
neighboring tribes. Although these events occur in northern Europe, it is
clear from their poetry that Anglo-Saxons linked their own identity to the
heroic world of their ancestral homelands; indeed, the West Saxon kings
traced their line back to Scyld and other legendary figures in their royal
genealogies. In the *Beowulf* poet's hands, however, the story takes on a
deeper theological dimension. Using language that recalls the Moses story
as well as the book of Judges, the poet subtly recasts Scyld as a deliverer
sent by God. This theologizing impulse will continue throughout the
epic, introducing what was in all likelihood a daring idea: that God was
actively—if mysteriously—involved in the pre-Christian Germanic past,
working his will through heroes like Scyld and Beowulf.

7. *comfort* (OE *frofor*), "consolation, comfort, relief, help"; the term recurs
throughout the poem and here indicates divine favor.

10. *whale-road* (*hron-rad*) is a *kenning*, or metaphorical compound, meaning "sea." Tolkien describes kennings as "pictorial descriptive compounds
or brief expressions which can be used in place of the normal or plain word"
(2014: 141). They are a salient feature of Old English and Old Norse poetry.

11. *gomb* (OE *gombe*): "tribute." An archaic and remarkably rare word,
gombe occurs only here and in one other Old English poem; it has been
taken as evidence for the early date of *Beowulf.* Scyld subdues the surrounding tribes (*mægths;* pronounced *MYE-ths*) by destroying their seats
of power, their mead halls, which contain long wooden benches or *mead-
settles.* Though Scyld is legendary, his conquests may reflect a historical
reality. Widespread hall-destruction is attested by the archeological record
of pre-Viking Scandinavia.

15. *lordless* (OE *aldorleas*). The birth of Scyld's son Beow, portrayed as a
divinely ordained action in response to the people's helplessness, ensures the
continuation of the Scylding dynasty and the Danes' political predominance.

16-17. *Waldend,* ruler, one who wields power and enjoys dominion. The
poet depicts God as a Germanic ruler *par excellence* — or to put it the other
way around, human rulers mirror God in their function to the people. A
parallel thus runs throughout the poem between God and human lords,
with most of the terms for the deity also being used for human rulers.

Beow was renowned: far and wide spread the glory
of Scyld's offspring in the Scede-lands.
20   So shall a young man by good deeds,
by bold gifts of wealth in his father's bearm,
bring it about that afterwards, when old, there will remain
willing companions with him when war comes,
his people will stand by him. With praiseworthy deeds
25   shall a man prosper in every mægth.

Then at his appointed hour Scyld departed,
full of vigor, to journey into the Lord's wær.
They bore him then to the edge of the sea,
his dear companions, as he himself had commanded
30   while he, the friend of Scyldings, still ruled with words.
Long had that beloved lord of the land had its possession.

There at the hythe stood the ring-prowed ship,
icy and outbound—the ætheling's vessel.
They laid their beloved lord,
35   their ring-giver, in the ship's bearm,

---

18. *Beow.* The name that occurs here in the manuscript is "Beowulf,"
but most editors believe it to be a scribal error and emend it to *Beow*, the
name given for Scyld's son in West Saxon genealogies and one better suited
to the meter. The meaning of *Beow* ("grain, barley"), along with Scyld's
father's name, Sheaf, may indicate an underlying fertility myth relating to
the founding of agriculture.

19. *Scede-lands*, the southern end of the Scandinavian peninsula (modern-
day Sweden) and its environs. This region is the Scandinavian heartland
and the setting of early Germanic heroic stories and other legends.

21. *in his father's bearm*, "bosom," "lap," but here used figuratively. To
consolidate his authority, young Beow must exhibit proper gift-giving to
build up a network of followers while still under his father's protection and
authority. The ways in which power is acquired and properly wielded by
leaders—as well as the ways power can be lost or squandered—is one of
the primary concerns of the poem.

25. *praiseworthy deeds* (*lof-dædum*), deeds worthy of *lof*. The ultimate
aim of all warriors, *lof* (praise) is the community's collective approval and
recognition, which ensures that the hero's name will live on after death.
One's public actions, not private or subjective state, are the defining factor
in the epic, which explains why so little attention is paid to the characters'
interior lives. *Lofgearnost*, "most eager for *lof*," is the very last word of the
poem, and sums up Beowulf's character.

27. *wær*, protection, keeping; a term ordinarily used for peace-pledges
between warring groups. Here it implies that Scyld, after his death, entered
into the security of God's protective power. Scyld is also said to remain
vigorous until the destined hour of his death. He is unlike other mortals.

the mære one by the mast. Many mathoms
were brought there, treasures from far away.
I have never heard of a ship more splendidly
prepared with battle-weapons and war-garments,
40   with blades and byrnies. On his bearm lay
a great many mathoms, which were to travel
far with him into the flood's keeping.
By no means did they furnish him with fewer gifts,
with people's treasures, than those had done
45   who sent him forth at the beginning,
as a child alone over the waves.
They set a golden ensign
high over his head, let the holm bear him off,

---

36. *the mære one by the mast. Many mathoms.* The body of the renowned
(*mære*) king Scyld is laid beside the ship's mast. *Mathoms* (OE *mathum, madme*)
are treasures or precious objects. The poet shows an evident fascination
with treasure and is blessed with a great stock of expressions for it.

40. The Danes lovingly pile treasures upon Scyld's lap (*bearm*) to accom-
pany him on his journey. The ship is also loaded with swords and coats
of chain mail (*blades and byrnies*), all of this being a tangible sign of Scyld's
power and heroic reputation. Although he arrived as a child in a ship with
nothing at all, Scyld now departs with incredible wealth.

43. *gifts.* OE *lāc,* "gift, offering," is a word with ritual implications, which
suggests that the treasure placed in the ship is not only intended to honor
Scyld, but is also an offering to the divinity responsible for sending Scyld
to them.

46. *a child alone over the waves.* A reference to Scyld Scefing's arrival
by water. Later writings mention both Scyld and Scef but attribute the
mysterious boat arrival to Scyld's father Scef, and it is unclear whether the
Beowulf poet himself revised the story (as Tolkien believed) or it underwent
a later development. Æthelweard's late-10th-c. *Chronicon* gives this account:
"This Scef [father of Scyld], surrounded by arms, was cast up in a boat onto
an island in the ocean which is called Scani, and he was a very young boy,
and unknown to the inhabitants of that country. Nonetheless, he was taken
up by them and they cared for him assiduously, as if he were one of their
own, and afterward they made him king. From his stock King Æthelwulf
[the father of Alfred the Great] traced his descent" (Klaeber 4: 292) To this
story William of Malmesbury (writing c. 1142) adds a further detail: "a sheaf
of grain stood at the head of the sleeping child, as a result of which he was
called Sceaf" (*idem*). In his imaginative retelling of the legend, "King Sheave,"
Tolkien picked up this detail and elaborated on it: the sleeping boy is washed
ashore carrying "a sheaf of corn . . . [but] men knew not what it was" (2014:
139); thus was agriculture introduced to the people. Norse sources also
describe Scyld and Scef (in their Norse name forms) as founders of heroic
families; in some of them Scyld is the son of Odin.

48. *the holm,* the sea. A word used only in poetry.

gave him to the sea. Their hearts were sorrowing,
50   their minds mournful. Men cannot say
for certain—neither hall-counselors
nor hæleths under the heavens—who received that freight.

FITT I. *The Scylding Dynasty & the Construction of the*
Great Hall Heorot

....

Then Beow of the Scyldings, the beloved people-king,
was in the burh for a long while,
55   famous among peoples—his father had passed elsewhere,
the aldor from the land—until to him in turn awoke
High Halfdane; as long as he lived he ruled
the glad Scyldings, gamol and battle-grim.

---

52. *who received that freight.* The image is of a shipment of cargo that is sent off for a delivery, but whose recipient remains unknown. These lines intimate that Scyld is sent back, on his own instructions, to the mysterious realm from which he came, but of which the Danes know nothing, not even the best and wisest among them. "Mystery surrounds him," Klaeber writes, "signalizing a being of supernatural, divine origin. He is sent by unknown powers on his high mission, and when his life work is done, he withdraws to the strange world whence he had come" (121–22). Tolkien echoes this sentiment: "He came out of the Unknown beyond the Great Sea, and returned into It: a miraculous intrusion into history" (2014: 151). Much as with the dying King Arthur's departure by boat in Malory's *Morte Darthur,* the ambiguity surrounding Scyld's passing is likely intentional.

Fitt 1 Synopsis. Scyld establishes the Danish Royal House of the Scyldings: he fathers Beow, who fathers Halfdane, who in turn becomes the father of Hrothgar. Because of his military success, Hrothgar amasses a large warband and next determines to build a hall greater than any before, which, once completed, he names Heorot. But the monster Grendel, a descendent of Cain, is angered by the revelry and songs of the hall, such as the court poet's song of Creation, and begins his attacks.

54. *burh,* stronghold (OE *burh, burg*; here the word is grammatically plural but with a singular meaning). A *burh* is a fortified dwelling, although it can also signify a fortified or walled town. *Burh* is the source of our Modern English *burg, burgh,* and *borough,* and probably of the *burrow* an animal digs out for protection and shelter. Castles will not appear in England until the 11th century, after the Norman Conquest has brought the Anglo-Saxon age to an end.

56. An *aldor* (also spelled *ealdor*) is a figure of authority, a king or war-leader, not necessarily an "elder" or a person of advanced age, since the term is applied to Beowulf while still young. ModE *alderman* derives from this word.

58. *gamol,* of advanced age, very old. In Old English poetry the word has mostly positive connotations: gamol warriors, swords, and the fabulous bird the Phoenix all come from an earlier age and have proven themselves indomitable.

To him four bearns, all told,
60   awoke into the world, to that leader of hosts:
Heorogar and Hrothgar and Halga the good;
I have heard that . . . was Onela's queen,
the Battle-Scylfing's embraced bed-companion.

Then battle-success was given to Hrothgar,
65   glory in war, so that his close kindred
eagerly obeyed him, until his young warband grew
to a mighty mago-dright. It came into his mind
that he would command men to make
a hall-building, a mead-ærn greater
70   than the sons of men had ever known,
and there within to share out everything
to young and old, such as God had given him,
all but the folkshare and the lives of men.

Then, as I have heard, the work was proclaimed far and wide
75   to many mægths throughout this middangeard,

---

62. *Onela's queen.* The manuscript appears to be defective here in both
meter and meaning. The missing portion likely included the name of Hrothgar's daughter, which some have suggested was Yrse (sometimes Latinized to
Ursula) on the basis of later Danish sources. Hrothgar's daughter is married
off to Onela, the "Battle-Scylfing" ("Scylfing" is another term for "Swede").

67. *mago-dright.* Hrothgar recapitulates the pattern of his forebears, prov-
ing himself in war and then consolidating his power by amassing followers,
a large *mago-dright*, an army (OE *driht*; *OED* s.v. *dright*) of young troops
(*mago*, son, kinsman, young man).

69. *mead-ærn.* A "mead-house," a banqueting hall. Once his control is
solidified, Hrothgar's first action is to build a hall as the seat and symbol of
Scylding power, as well as a place for distributing treasure and communal
celebration. Its importance for the poem would be hard to overstate: as John
Niles explains, the hall "serves as the radiant center of the hero's social world.
It is a semi-sacral place devoted to the humane rituals of gift-giving, of vows
over the mead-cup, of music and song and heightened speech" (Niles 77).
The location of Heorot also appears to have a religious significance, perhaps
as a cultic center. Tolkien speculates that the later battles fought at Heorot
between the Danes and the Heathobards (discussed later in the poem) were
in fact "a battle for the possession of a sanctuary" (2014: 323). The religious
significance might also play a part in Grendel's animosity toward Heorot.

73. *Folkshare* (OE *folc-scaru)* may be a reference to a public land held in
common and not controlled by the king; it is more likely, however, that
it refers to interfering with inherited properties, or even to the power to
determine royal succession.

75. *middangeard*, "middle realm," i.e., the world. The OE equivalent to
Midgard in Norse myth, this term reflects a common Germanic notion of

to adorn the dwelling place. In due time it came to pass,
swiftly with the men of old, that it was all made ready for him,
the greatest of hall-ærns. He assigned it the name "Heorot,"
he whose word had power far and wide.

80   He did not belie his bēot; he shared out bēags,
treasure at the symbel. The hall towered up,
high and horn-gabled. It awaited war-surges,
hateful flame—the time was not yet at hand
when sword-hate between son-and-father-in-law
85   would, after deadly strife, awaken.

Then the ellengæst suffered grievously
for a time, he who dwelled in darkness,
for each day he heard the drēam

---

a middle region in which humans dwell, separate from both the abode of
the gods and the underworld. Although the term was adapted to Christian
cosmology, where it is the world as situated between heaven and hell, the
earlier conception is one of an abode of human beings encircled by a vast
sea, and separated from the habitations of giants and of gods. Following
Tolkien, most translators render it "middle-earth," though *geard* in fact
means "inhabited enclosure" (from which we get *yard*).

    78. *Heorot,* the Old English word for "hart" or stag, was perhaps an
emblem of royal authority in early Germanic cultures, as suggested by
several archeological discoveries. An alternate explanation for the name is
that antlers were fixed to the hall's gables.

    80. *He did not belie his bēot; he shared out bēags.* Hrothgar fulfilled his sol-
emn vow (*bēot*) to complete the hall and to use it for the giving of treasure.
OE *bēagas* are ring-shaped treasures of various kinds, including neck-rings;
the word is distantly related to *bagel*.

    84. *sword-hate between son-and-father-in-law.* An allusion to the later
destruction of Heorot by fire in a conflict between Hrothgar and his future
son-in-law Ingeld, an event that occurs outside the action of *Beowulf.* In order
to create peace, Hrothgar will marry off his daughter Freawaru to Ingeld, son
of Froda, the king of the enemy Heathobards. As Beowulf predicts (2024–69),
this attempt at peacemaking will end in bloodshed. Although precise details
of the battle are no longer known to us, the poet clearly expected his audience to be familiar with this legendary battle, and the conflict is mentioned
in passing in another Old English poem called *Widsith,* which notes that
Hrothgar and his nephew Hrothulf defeated Ingeld, and "hewed apart the
force of the Heathobards at Heorot" (48–49). This *Beowulf* passage is significant for another reason as well: it includes an archaic kinship term, *athum-
sweoras* ("son-in-law [*athum*] and father-in-law [*sweor*]"), which the scribe,
because of his unfamiliarity with the obsolete compound, miscopied as *athum
swerian,* "to swear oaths." The word is evidence of the early date of *Beowulf.*

    86–88. *the ellengæst . . . heard the drēam.* The "bold spirit," "powerful demon,"
soon to be named as the monster Grendel, is tormented by the sounds of
the *drēam* (pronounced DRAY-ahm), the joyful revelry of the hall. In the

loud in the hall, where the harp's sound was,
90   the scop's clear song. He spoke, the one who could
recount the beginning of men from far back,
he said that the Almighty wrought the earth,
the bright shining plain which water encircles;
exulting, He set sun and moon,
95   the leams, as a light for land-dwellers,
and adorned the earth's surface
with limbs and leaves; He also created life
in every creature that quickens and wherves.

So the dright of men lived in drēam,
100   blessedly, until one began —
a fiend in hell — to carry out fyren.

---

poem this *drēam* represents the height of human communal joy, a kind of earthly bliss that occurs only within the semi-sacred space of the hall Heorot. (The same word is used in Old English literature for the rejoicing of the saints and angels in heaven.) Grendel seeks to destroy the communal bliss of Heorot in a parallel with the Genesis account of the serpent's destruction of the paradise of Eden.

90. *the scop's clear song.* The scop (pronounced *shope*), the court singer, recites the story of the creation of the world in a poetic paraphrase of Genesis 1. The harmonious order of the creation, described like the fashioning of an ornate artifact, echoes the building of the great hall Heorot, a place that likewise serves as an Edenic paradise.

95. *leams* (OE *leoma; OED* s.v. *leam*), lights, luminaries. The description corresponds to Genesis 1:16-17: "And God made the two luminaries (*dua magna luminaria*); the greater luminary to rule the day, and the lesser luminary to rule the night.... And God set them in the firmament of heaven to give light upon the earth."

98. *every creature that quickens and wherves,* i.e., all species of living things that move about (*cwice hwyrfath*). A paraphrase of Genesis 1:21: God "*creavit... omnem animam viventem atque motabilem,*" "created ... every living and moving creature."

101a. *a fiend in hell (feond on helle)*. How can Grendel be said to be a fiend in hell when he is also very much present on earth? Translators usually sidestep this difficulty by rendering the phrase "hellish foe," but what the text says is quite plain. The poet invests Grendel with a dual identity: he is as a creature of flesh and blood who is at the same time a creature of spiritual evil, a demonic being. In a world that is a battleground between divine and demonic forces, Grendel is not on the side of the angels. As Tolkien explains the phrase, Grendel and his ilk "carried hell ever with them in their hearts" (2014: 159).

101b. *fyren,* deeds of evil; crime, sin, wickedness, violence. The language of the poem makes no clear distinction between moral wrongs (sins) and legal offenses (crimes), but translators are forced to choose one or the other.

The grim gæst was called Grendel,
the famed mearcstapa who ruled the moors,
the fen and fastnesses; in the land of the fifel-cynn
105   that miserable man had dwelt for some time,
after the Creator condemned him
in Cain's cynn. He avenged that killing,
the eternal Drighten, because he slew Abel;
He took no joy in that feud, but He exiled him far—
110   the Metod, for his crime—away from mankind.
From him awoke all evil offspring,   *from Cain*
eotens and elves and orc-neas

---

102. *the grim gæst was called Grendel.* What kind of creature is Grendel? As one commentator has noted, "it is hard if not impossible to say exactly what he is—a troll, a giant, a misshapen human, a fiend from hell" (Cardew 189)—indeed he is called all these and more. His most common designation, however, is *gæst* (or *gast*), the source of ModE *ghost*, which can mean soul, spirit, angel, demon, or breath, as well as creature, and is not restricted to immaterial entities, as the very flesh-and-blood Grendel makes obvious. What can be firmly stated is that Grendel is a creature of supernatural evil, an adversary of God, magically protected from weapons, cannibalistic, and of immense size—it will require four men to carry his severed head. One of the most important clues to his identity comes from early records of English place-names that include the element *Grendel*, and which show a prevalence for watery, inaccessible regions, such as the *Grendlesmere* found in a charter from AD 931. These place names suggest Grendel was a fixture of native English folk belief, a monster thought to haunt the marshlands. Various etymological explanations have been suggested for the name Grendel ("to grind," "to bellow," "storm," etc.) but none has found widespread acceptance.

103. *mearcstapa.* A wanderer of the marches, a haunter of the borderlands. The phrase signals Grendel as the consummate outsider, an occupant of the dangerous peripheries of the human world. The hall Heorot, as the center of human community, is abhorrent to him. This outsider status has led many to interpret Grendel with a degree of sympathy, a view that would be incomprehensible to the poem's early medieval audience.

104. *the fifel-cynn*, the race of monstrous creatures. The lines that follow explain the origin of these monsters in their descent from the biblical Cain, who was cursed for murdering his brother Abel and exiled from human community. From Cain thus descends the monstrous race that remains at enmity with both humans and God, fighting against them in what scholars have labeled "the Great Feud."

107. *Cain's cynn.* A medieval tradition held that Cain was the ancestor of the giants and monstrous races, which provided an explanation for the origin of these creatures of evil. "In the medieval exegetical tradition, Cain's killing of Abel was regarded as the first act of human strife, from which all others ontologically arose" (Klaeber 4: 123).

112. *eotens and elves and orc-neas.* A partial list of the species of malevolent beings descended from Cain. Eotens (discussed in the note to line 421) are

and also the giants, who fought against God
for a long time. He paid them their reward for that.   *God*

FITT 2. *Grendel's Reign of Terror*

....

115   Then after night had come, he went to seek out

---

gigantic creatures, such as Grendel, who are entirely antagonistic to human
beings. The identity of elves (OE plural *ælfe, ylfe*) within early Germanic
societies is more ambivalent. Usually depicted as malevolent and unseen,
elves were thought to cause various maladies, as surviving Old English
charms against "elf-shot" and "elf-sickness" indicate. Old English medical
recipes also speak of *ælf-siden*, "elf-enchantment," believed to create fevers.
But the power of elves could also be benign; the word appears frequently in
Anglo-Saxon personal names such as Ælfred ("elf-counsel") and adjectives
like *ælf-scyne*, "elf-radiant, elf-beautiful." Regarding *orcneas* (singular *orcne?*),
little can be said with certainty since the word occurs only here. Tolkien has
analyzed it as a combination of *orc* (from Latin *orcus*, "hell," "death") and *ne*,
"dead body" (from proto-Germanic *nawi-s*), and hypothesized that it refers to
the undead who "inhabit tombs and mounds" and prey upon humans, which
Tolkien labeled "barrow-wights" in his own fiction (2014: 163). Possibly they
are the Old English equivalent to the *draugr*, the reanimated corpse, of Norse
legend. But piecing together the precise identity of these creatures is less
important than understanding their function as embodiments of distinct
kinds of fears. Eotens represent fears associated with the landscape—cliffs,
fens, pools—and the physical dangers these pose to humans, whereas elves
are suggestive of the unseen forces that work upon us internally, whether
physiological or psychological, which often seem outside our control and
thus attributable to a hidden, elvish influence. The orc-ne remains obscure,
but may reflect fears surrounding corpses and decomposition.

These creatures were very real to Anglo-Saxon people. Readers today,
steeped in fantasy novels, understand these supernatural creatures as literary fabrications, but this was not the perspective of the poem's earliest
audience; widespread belief in the existence of such beings is attested by
references to them in magical charms used to ward them off and place
names for where they were believed to lurk.

113. *the giants, who fought against God.* The term here for "giants," *gigantas*,
is borrowed directly from the Latin Vulgate (*gigantes*); unlike the monsters
of English folk belief discussed above, these are the biblical giants mentioned in Genesis who, according to postbiblical traditions, were destroyed
by God in the great Flood. Following other medieval authors, the *Beowulf*
poet takes what were originally separate conceptions (Cain, the giants of
Genesis, the great Flood, and the monstrous creatures of Germanic folklore)
and conflates them into a single explanatory narrative.

Fitt 2 Synopsis. Grendel begins a cycle of nighttime raids on Heorot,
slaughtering and devouring the Danish warriors until the remaining troops
desert the hall and great Heorot sits empty. For 12 years the ravages continue
while Hrothgar and his counselors remain powerless. In their desperation
the Danes turn to idol sacrifice, praying to the Devil for help. This, the poet
remarks, was their heathen custom, since they were ignorant of the true God;
the poet issues a stark warning to his audience about the torments of Hell.

> the high house, how the Ring-Danes
> had settled into it after beer-drinking.
> Inside he found a troop of æthelings
> sleeping after the symbel; they knew no sorrow,
> 120   the misery of men. The unhæl wight,
> grim and greedy, was ready at once,
> fierce and cruel, and seized from their rest
> thirty thanes; from there he went again,
> exulting in plunder, to fare home,
> 125   to seek his abode with his fill of slaughter.
>
> Then in the dawning before daybreak
> Grendel's war-craft was revealed to men.
> Then their weeping was lifted up after the feast,
> a mighty morning-sound. The mære theoden,
> 130   the ætheling, good of old, sat joyless;
> the great one tholed, suffered thane-sorrow,
> after they beheld the track of their hated foe,
> the accursed gæst. That strife was too strong,
> too loath and longsome. Nor was it a longer space of time,
> 135   but after one night he again carried out
> more murderous slaughter and did not mourn for it,

---

120. *unhæl wight*, creature of unholiness and ill-fortune (OE *wiht unhælo*). The *hæl-/hāl*-root belongs to the remarkably rich Germanic word cluster from which we get *hale, whole*, and the greeting *hail*, all ultimately descending from proto-Germanic **hailaz* (whole, complete, uninjured). In Old English this cluster encompasses notions of wholeness, healing, and health, as well as holiness, good fortune/omens, and even salvation. As Stephen Barney observes, "health, wholeness, and sanctity are synonymous in the Germanic languages" (68). Grendel, an agent of disintegration marked out as un-*hælo*, embodies the opposite of this set of values.

127. *war-craft* (OE *guth-cræft*). In Old English *cræft* can signify strength as well as skill, as in modern German *Kraft*, power.

130. *good of old* (OE *ǣr-gōd*, "ere-good"), a term of approbation appearing only in *Beowulf*. Besides Hrothgar, the adjective is applied to a trusted court advisor, the aged King Beowulf, and Beowulf's iron blade. It expresses the idea, prevalent in Old English poetry, that age enhances the worth of a person or object: such an entity has been tested, has accumulated a wealth of experience, and traces its origins in an earlier heroic era.

131. *tholed*, suffered, endured a time of trial. The verb continues in use in some northern English dialects.

136. *murderous slaughter* (OE *morth-bealu*). What makes Grendel's violence blameworthy when other heroic figures carry out killings and are praised for it? The term *morth-bealu* helps to answer this question. Anglo-Saxon

feuding and fyren—he was too fixed in them.
Then it was easy to find one who sought
his resting place elsewhere, farther away,
140   a bed among the outbuildings, after it was shown to him,
truly told with a clear token—
the hall-thane's hatred. He who escaped that fiend
kept himself farther away and more securely after that.

So he ruled and fought against right,   *Grendel*
145   one against all, until empty stood
the best of houses. It was a long while;
for a tide of twelve winters the friend of Scyldings   *Hrothgar*
endured affliction, every kind of woe,
great sorrows. So it became apparent
150   to the sons of men, unconcealed and
sadly known in songs, that for some time Grendel
strove with Hrothgar, waged hateful attacks,
fyren and feud for many half-years,
unceasing strife; he wanted no sibb

---

and Germanic law codes distinguish between licit and illicit killing, since
before the consolidation of state power with its means of law enforcement,
the kin-group had to be its own police force. Its members were responsible
for seeking redress for themselves, which included acts of retaliatory violence. Killing broadly understood (OE *cwellan*, to kill, the source of *quell*)
could be considered licit in a variety of circumstances, including revenge
and self-defense. Illicit killing, *morthor* (the source of our "murder"), on
the other hand, was distinguished by being premeditated and by being
carried out in secret rather than in public. Grendel's killings are secretive,
premeditated, and not intended to restore the social order, a point under-
scored by Grendel's refusal of any peaceful resolution through payment, the
customary means of ending cycles of blood feud. He thus stands outside
human systems of justice, incapable even of remorse, for he is "too fixed"
in his wicked ways. But the poet is not always consistent in his usage, and
occasionally uses *morthor* to simply mean "violent death."

138–42. *Then it was easy to find one . . . the hall-thane's hatred*. Hrothgar's
followers melt away, some of them withdrawing to the outlying buildings
for their sleeping quarters (if this is in fact the meaning of *buras*, the source
of *bower*, "private chamber"). In this way Grendel reverses Hrothgar's consolidation of power and empties his great hall. *Hall-thane* is a grimly ironic
reference to Grendel as a member of Hrothgar's hall-troop.

147. *tide*, a space of time (OE *tīd*) used for times and seasons ("Yuletide"),
as well as the Old English word for "hour." Only in the 14th century was
tide applied to the rising and ebbing of the sea.

154. *sibb*, kinship, friendship, peace (the source of *sibling*). Kinship is the
lens through which social relationships of all kinds are perceived.

155   with any of the men of the host of Danes,
       or to withdraw his deadly attacks, to settle with money;
       nor did any of the wise ones need expect
       bright compensation from the slayer's hands;
       but the aglæca, the terrible adversary, kept harrying them,
160   that dark death-shadow; he lay in wait and ambushed
       the young and old warriors; in endless night he held
       the misty moors; men do not know
       where hell-runes scrithe in their wanderings.

       So mankind's foe, the fearsome lone-walker,
165   continually carried out his many wicked deeds,
       harsh humiliations. He inhabited Heorot,
       the treasured-decked hall, in the dark nights
       (he was not permitted to approach the gift-seat,
       the mathom, on account of the Metod, nor did he know his
          myne).

---

158. *bright compensation from the slayer's hands*. A reference to the *wergild* ("man-price"), the money paid out to the family of the slain by the slayer in order to settle the conflict and thereby prevent further retaliatory killings. It would vary in amount depending on the social rank of the victim. Since Grendel stands apart from the human order with its customary means of reconciliation, there is no hope for an end to his ravages.

162–63. *men do not know / where hell-runes scrithe*, i.e., no one knows where occult creatures like Grendel go in their mysterious movements; they appear and then are gone again. To *scrithe* (OE *scrithan; OED* s.v. scrithe) is to move about in a continuous or gliding motion; demons, monsters, ships, and fish are all said to scrithe in Old English texts. OE *Hel-rune*, a rare and imperfectly understood word, probably means "one skilled in the mysteries of hell," and would encompass demons, diviners, sorcerers, and others possessing occult powers. *Rune* (OE *rūn*), a secret, mystery; secret knowledge or counsel (its original sense was probably "whispering"), from which we get the mysterious letters known as *runes*. The emphasis on mystery and the limits of human knowledge recurs throughout the poem, calling attention to the hidden reality which the human world only glimpses. Note how the poet switches from past to present tense to make this observation, indicating its universal nature.

169. *Myne* has a wide semantic range, signifying "mind, memory, thought, love, favor, desire, and purpose," among other notions, all stemming from the idea of holding something valuable in one's mind. The intended meaning of *myne* in this instance is uncertain, however, and lines 168–69 have long perplexed the most acute of critics. Why is Grendel prevented by God from approaching Hrothgar's throne and treasure, and what precisely is meant by the words *ne his myne wisse*? Many interpretations have been ventured: "Nor did he know His [God's] love/favor/purpose"; "nor did he understand its [the gift-seat's] purpose" (in OE *his* can refer to masculine nouns like *gifstol*,

170   For the friend of Scyldings that was great distress,
       heartbreaking grief. Many of the mighty ones
       often sat together in secret, they considered counsel,
       what might be best for the strong-hearted
       to do against these sudden terrors.
175   Sometimes at heargs — heathen shrines — they pledged
       worship to idols; with their words they implored
       the Slayer of Souls to provide them help
       against the people's distress. Such was their custom,
       the heathens' hope; in their hearts
180   they remembered Hell; the Metod they did not know,

"gift-seat"); or is it that Grendel doesn't feel any desire for the treasure ("nor
did he feel love for it")? However these lines are construed, they are best
understood as explaining why Grendel doesn't plunder the hall when he
haunts it at nighttime: the throne is supernaturally protected from Grendel,
and furthermore, the meaning of such things is alien to him. Despite his
ravages, Grendel only acts by permission of the divine will. The language
of the passage also hints at a sacred significance to the gift-seat and the
rituals that surround it, perhaps because for the poet it called to mind the
significance of the altar within Christian ceremony.

    175. *Heargs* were cultic sites, idol-shrines erected on hilltops that included
an altar and sacred images. They could be enclosed by a structure, as
specified by the second element of the term used here (*hærg-træf*, "hearg-
pavilion"). That such shrines once dotted the landscape of England and
Scandinavia is clear from the surviving place names that contain the word
"harrow" (in England) or *hörgr* (in Scandinavia).

    176. *worship to idols.* The literal sense of *wig-weorthung* is "the honoring
of idols," but combined with "pledged" it likely refers to the offering of sacrifices; the *Dictionary of Old English* renders the phrase, "to devote, dedicate
a sacrificial offering / sacrificial offerings" (*DOE* s.v., *ge-hatan*, 4.a.i.b.). Little
is known about pre-Christian Germanic religious ritual, but it evidently
included sacred images (*weoh, wig*; "idol") and human and animal sacrifice.
In his *Chronicle* (c. 1018), Thietmar of Merseburg describes massive mid-
winter sacrifices of men, horses, dogs, and fowls at the location of Lethra,
Denmark, the site attributed to Heorot.

    177. *the Slayer of souls* (OE *gastbana*), i.e., the Devil. Idol worship was
understood to be the worship of demonic powers.

    180b–88. A much-debated passage known as "the Christian Excursus,"
so called because for the space of these eight lines the poet appears to turn
from an epic poet into a fiery preacher, accusing the Danes of devil-worship
and warning of the eternal torments of Hell. The tone and topic of these
lines have raised a number of questions. Are the Danes being *condemned* for
their heathen idolatry, or being *excused* from it on account of their ignorance
of the true God? But how can they be ignorant of the true God when, just
one Fitt earlier, they listened in Heorot as the court poet sang of the creation
of the world by "the Almighty"? In one view, the "tragic paganism" thesis
advanced by Fred Robinson, the poet admires the pagan heroes of old but

the Judge of deeds, or know of Drighten God,
or even how to praise the Helm of heaven,
the Waldend of glory. Woe to him
who in terrible affliction must thrust his soul
185   into the fire's fæthm and expect no comfort,
no changing at all! Well it will be for him
who can seek the Drighten after his death-day,
and ask for refuge in the Father's fæthm!

FITT 3. *Beowulf's Journey to Daneland*

So Halfdane's kinsman continually seethed   *Hrothgar*
190   with the sorrows of the time; the wise hæleth could not
turn aside his woes — that strife was too strong,
too loath and longsome, which had come upon the people,
distress dire and nith-grim, the greatest of night-horrors.

---

understands them as tragically condemned to Hell. Others argue these lines are in flat contradiction to the rest of the poem (which depicts the Danes as pious monotheists, if not quite Christians) and claim the passage is therefore an interpolation, inserted at a later time by a different writer. In fact neither theory is necessary. What these lines are meant to convey is the Danes' dire straits and the desperate measures they take, having little else to fall back on. Examples of such backsliding can be found both in the Old Testament, where the Israelites repeatedly fall away into idol worship, and in Anglo-Saxon England, where newly converted kings like Rædwald would slip back into pagan practices in times of duress. While making clear that heathen practices are indeed very bad, the poet also explains that the Danes had only a dim knowledge of the Creator God and were completely lacking Christian revelation. To emphasize to his Anglo-Saxon audience that pagan sacrifices are by no means acceptable in the present day, the poet sternly warns his audience against these practices, reminding them of the pains of Hell. As for the eternal fate of the pagan Danes, the poet artfully leaves this question open-ended, though strongly suggesting elsewhere that at least some of the heroes of old (Scyld, Beowulf) enjoyed heavenly rewards after death.

185. *fæthm*, embrace. The two arms, when outstretched, measure approximately six feet, thus forming the unit of depth measurement that became known as the fathom, pronounced identically to the Old English word.

Fitt 3 Synopsis. While Hrothgar suffers, news of Grendel's attacks reaches Beowulf, a Geatish warrior known for his prodigious strength. To aid Hrothgar, he prepares a ship and leads a troop of 14 Geats across the sea to Daneland. Their arrival is observed by the Danish coast guard, who immediately rides closer to the shore to confront them. With his spear in hand, he calls out to the strangers, demanding that they identify themselves.

193. *nith-grim*, cruelly and violently hostile.

From his homeland Hygelac's thane,   *Beowulf*
195   a good man among the Geats, heard of Grendel's deeds.
He was the strongest of mankind in might
in that day of this life,
æthel and eacen. He ordered a good wave-traveler
readied for him, said he wished to seek
200   the war-king across the swan-road,   *Hrothgar*
the mære theoden, since he had need of men.
Wise men blamed him little
for that undertaking, though he was dear to them;
they urged the brave one on, examined the omens.

194–95. *Hygelac's thane / good among the Geats*, i.e., Beowulf, a Geat, dwells in what is now southern Sweden, across the sea from Heorot. He is nephew of the Geatish King Hygelac. The Geats were a north Germanic tribe, called Gautar in Old Norse, known as a seafaring people, who inhabited the lands directly to the south of the Swedes, their longstanding enemies. Over time the Geats were conquered and absorbed by the Swedes. The precise homeland of the Geats, their relationship to the Goths, and the historic fate of this people have all been matters of debate.

198. *æthel and eacen*, noble and of remarkable size and strength. The first term, *æthel*, marks Beowulf out as a man of the warrior class and possessing the qualities associated with that class—"excellent, glorious, noble." The second term, *eacen*, is more difficult to translate. Its root meaning is "augmented," "enlarged," "increased"; Tolkien maintains that this word indicates that Beowulf's "superhuman thirtyfold strength" is of supernatural origin, pointing out that in the poem *eacen* "in all instances may imply not merely size and strength, but an addition of power beyond the natural" (1940: xi).

201. *mære theoden*, renowned ruler. A term also used for God, *theoden* means the "chief of the *theod*," the people, tribe. The *-en* suffix indicates "leader of."

202. *Wise men blamed him little*, i.e., they didn't blame him at all, they applauded him. A typical instance of understatement by negation, a figure of speech known as *litotes*. It is a stylistic feature of Old English poetry that can be difficult to carry over in translation, but one deployed masterfully by the *Beowulf* poet. Just as "I'm not too happy about this" can pack more punch than "I'm really upset about this," this line achieves greater resonance though understatement than by a more direct statement such as "all the wise men in Geatland applauded Beowulf highly for his daring venture." Of this passage Tolkien remarks, it is "as though the poet . . . suddenly realized that shouting merely deafens and that at times it is more effective to lower the voice" (2014: 188).

204. *examined the omens*. The Geatish elders consult omens (*hæl*) to confirm that Beowulf's trip is divinely favored for success. Reliance on omens among the Germanic peoples is attested by Tacitus: "For omens and casting of lots they have the highest regard" (*Germania* 109). Tacitus claims that the flight of birds or the neighing of horses were scrutinized prior to any major undertaking, such as a battle (109–10).

205 From among the Geatish people the good man
   had chosen fighters, the boldest
   he could find. One of fifteen,   *Beowulf*
   he sought out the sea-wood, the man led the way,
   the sea-crafty one, to the land's edge.

210 A time went by; the vessel was on the waves,
   the boat beneath the cliff. The beorns eagerly
   stepped onto the prow. The streams swirled,
   sea against sand; the men bore
   into the ship's bearm bright trappings,

215 splendid battle-gear; the men shoved
   the well-joined wood out, the warriors on their desired
     journey.

   Then over the sea-waves it went, driven by wind,
   the foamy-necked vessel most like a fowl,
   until in due time on the second day

220 the curved prow had made such way
   that the seafarers saw land,
   shining sea-cliffs, steep headlands,
   broad sea-nesses. Then the sound was crossed,
   the eolet at an end. Up from there

225 the Weder people stepped swiftly onto the plain, *the Geats*
   they moored the sea-wood; they shook their mail-shirts,
   their war-garments. They thanked God

---

211. *beorns*, warriors, corresponding to Old Norse *bjǫrn*, "bear," which may have been the original meaning of *beorn*, although the OE word is never used for the animal (*OED* s.v. *berne*). This possible etymology is the inspiration for Tolkien's character Beorn, a were-bear in *The Hobbit*.

223. *sea-nesses*, rocky promontories that jut out into the sea (OE *sæ-næssas*).

224. *the eolet at an end.* Just what *eolet* means remains a mystery, since the word occurs only here. "Sea"? "Voyage"?

227. *They thanked God.* The characters are portrayed neither as polytheistic (as the historical Germanic peoples of the Migration Age were) nor as Christian (as the poet's own Anglo-Saxon culture was). Instead the poet opts for a middle path, depicting them as pious monotheists who pray to and acknowledge one God who guides all events and to whom human actions are accountable. Though the characters lack scriptural revelation, the theological basis for the poet's portrayal of them might be the concept of general revelation described by St. Paul in Romans 1:19–20: "For what can be known about God is plain to them because God has shown it to them. Ever since the creation of the world his invisible nature, namely, his eternal power and deity, has been clearly perceived in the things that

that the crossing of the ythes had been easy for them.
Then from the wall the Scyldings' weard,
230   he who had to guard the sea-cliffs,
saw bright shields borne over the gangway,
ready battle-gear. Alarm broke
within his mind's thoughts as to who these men were.
He went to the shore riding his horse,
235   Hrothgar's thane; with thrym he shook
the mighty wood in his hands, with methel-words he
        questioned them:

"What kind of weapon-bearers are you,
covered by coats of mail, who have come in this way,
leading your tall ship over the sea-road
240   here across the holm? I have for some time
sat stationed at the land's end, kept a sea-watch
so that in the land of Danes no enemies
should come ravaging with a ship-army.
Never have shield-bearers more openly
245   ventured to come here, nor did you know for certain
the leave-word of warriors,
the consent of our kinsmen. Never have I seen
a greater eorl on earth than the one among you,
the man in war-gear; that is no hall-thane
250   made worthy by weapons, unless his appearance belies him,
his peerless form. Now I must know

---

have been made." In Tolkien's interpretation, the characters in the poem
are "noble pagans of the past who had not heard the Gospel, knew of the
existence of Almighty God, recognized him as 'good' and the giver of all
good things; but were (by the Fall) still cut off from Him, so that in time
of woe they became filled with despair and doubt—that was the hour
when they were specially open to the snares of the Devil: they prayed to
idols and false gods for help" (2014: 170–71).

228. *ythes*, waves (OE *yth*).

236. *methel-words*, formal speech, language suitable to a formal assembly
or *methel*. The coast guard's challenge is curt but still courteous. This is
the first of the poem's many lengthy speeches.

244–51. The coast guard remarks that this troop has come to his land
boldly and openly, not stealthily as raiders would, even though they had
not been granted prior permission to do so. He singles out Beowulf for
his impressive appearance, suggesting, through litotes, that he is troop
leader—he is no hall-thane (servant, follower) = he must be your leader.

your lineage, your frum-cynn, lest from here
you travel farther as false spies
in the land of Danes. Now, dwellers from afar,
255   seafarers, hear my
onefold thought: haste is best
for cything where you have come from."

FITT 4. *The Exchange between Beowulf and the Coast Guard*

The eldest answered him,
the leader of the host unlocked his word-hoard:

260   "We are of the gumcynn of the Geatish people
and the hearth-companions of Hygelac.
My father was well known among the peoples,
the æthel leader called Ecgtheow;
he saw a great many winters before he went on his way,
265   aged, from the dwellings; he is well remembered
by every one of the wise throughout the wide earth.
We, with hearts loyal to your lord,
have come seeking the son of Halfdane,
the protector of the people. Be of good counsel to us.

---

256. *onefold* (*an-feald*), plain, straightforward. The coast-guard is saying in effect, Let's cut to the chase: tell me quickly where you come from.

257. *cything* (*cythan*), making known. The word survives in Scots as *kythe*.

Fitt 4 Synopsis. Beowulf explains to the coast guard that he and his men are Geats who have come to help Hrothgar against his monstrous enemy. After hearing his account, the coast guard decides to allow the Geats to travel in the land of the Danes and agrees to guide them to Heorot. After marching for a time, the men come within sight of the great hall, whose gold-plating glints in the sun. The coast guard then departs to return to his post.

259. *unlocked his word-hoard*. A poetic expression for "he began to speak," this is one of the most salient metaphors in Old English poetry. It construes language as a precious treasure that is hidden away within a person, and which can be shared in special circumstances. In this situation, Beowulf, confronted by the coast guard, opens his treasury of words to speak in an artful and diplomatic manner, deftly defusing any potential hostility.

260. *gumcynn*, tribe, race. Beowulf begins by introducing his ethnic group and then proceeds, in funnel-like fashion, to state his king, and last of all his father. He does not yet disclose his own name, which will only be revealed upon his arrival to Heorot. Delaying his self-identification builds suspense; it also demonstrates the primacy that group and kinship hold for one's individual identity.

270   We have a great errand to the famous
       lord of Danes; nor should there be anything hidden,
       as I think. You will know—if it is truly
       as we have heard told—
       that among the Scyldings some kind of ravager,
275   a mysterious evildoer in the dark nights,
       shows through terror strange violence,
       shame and slaughter. For this I can,
       with an open heart, advise Hrothgar with counsel,
       how he, frōd and good, can overcome his foe,
280   if a change is ever to come for him,
       relief once more from the evil of his afflictions,
       and his seething cares grow cooler;
       or else ever after he will endure a time of trouble,
       sore distress, so long as remains,
285   there on its high place, the best of houses."

       The weard matheled as he sat upon his horse,
       the fearless officer:

              "Between these two
       a sharp-witted shield-warrior must discern,

---

279. *frōd and good.* A rhyming pair in the original Old English, *frōd ond gōd*, neatly sums up Hrothgar's character. He is wise, aged, and of proven worth. *Frōd*, an important descriptor for rulers, is sometimes rendered by translators "old" and sometimes "wise." In fact, *frōd* signifies both "wise-and-old" and (therefore) "wise-because-old"—all of which carries a very different attitude toward aging than our own.

281. *his seething cares grow cooler.* For emotions of sorrow and suffering, Old English literature conventionally uses the image of a boiling pot. Anger, on the other hand, is described in terms of swelling (*ge-bolgen*, "swollen with rage"; cf. ModE *bag*).

286. *matheled* (OE *mathelian*), "gave a speech," "made a formal utterance." The high frequency of this verb, always at the start of a speech, indicates the prominent role speeches play in the poem (more than a third of *Beowulf* consists of speeches). The verb derives from the noun *methel*, an assembly; hence, *mathelian* is to give a speech suitable to the stately formality of such an occasion. Modern English has no equivalent, and translators usually render the verb as "spoke." But for the world depicted in the poem, the importance of speeches would be hard to overstate, and although less dynamic than the scenes of action, the speeches do a great deal of narrative work, forging alliances, diffusing tense situations, and conferring honor and recognition. Words, just as much as deeds, are where the action in *Beowulf* happens.

one who considers well: between words and deeds.
290 This I hear: that this is a host friendly
to the lord of Scyldings. Go forth bearing
your weapons and war-garments; I will guide the way.
I will also command my mago-thanes
to guard your ship against every enemy,
295 your newly tarred craft upon the sand,
to hold it with honor until it again bears
the beloved man over the sea-streams,
the curvy-necked wood to Wedermark,
to whichever of these doers-of-good is granted
300 to pass unscathed through the storm of battle."

Then they went to go. The ship remained still,
the wide-fæthmed vessel rested on its rope,
fast on its anchor; boar-figures shone
over cheek-guards, adorned with gold,
305 gleaming and fire-hardened; the fierce-minded war-masked
one
kept guard over life. The men hastened,

---

289. *between words and deeds* (OE *worda ond worca*). The coast guard is
stating a proverb: in the face of uncertainty, a man of wisdom will be able to
recognize the truth when he sees it, judging effectively between a person's
words and actions. The proverb applies to the present, high-stakes situation
in which he finds himself. Confronted with the arrival of what appears to be
a raiding party, the coast guard must judge quickly whether the incomers
are friends or foes. He decides to accept Beowulf's words and permits the
Geats to proceed to Heorot with their weapons. But a hint of apprehension
can be detected. He will escort them, and leave an armed guard with the
ship—acts of courtesy, but also caution.

293. *mago-thanes*, young troops.

302. *the wide-fæthmed ship*, the open-decked (literally, wide-embracing) ship.

303–4. *boar-figures shone over cheek-guards*. Here the narrative perspective
abruptly zooms in for a detailed close-up of the Geats' armor. That boar-
images adorned Germanic and Anglo-Saxon helmets has been confirmed by
archeology; the animal likely had a sacred or totemic function for warriors.
In the *Germania* (AD 98), Roman historian Tacitus comments on the use
of the boar-device among Germanic warriors, which provided the wearer
with "a sense of security even among his enemies."

305–6. *the fierce-minded war-masked one / kept guard over life*. A perplexing
passage. The scribe evidently miscopied *grummon*, an otherwise unknown
word, for *grim-mon* (probably "war-masked one," from *grima*, "war-mask,"
a helmet that covered the face). But it is unclear whether this passage is
describing the *helmet* that protects the men's lives, the *boar* depicted on

they marched together until they could see
the timbered hall, splendid and gleaming with gold.
Among the dwellers of earth that was the most famous
310   of halls under the heavens, in which the mighty one waited;
its light shone over many lands.
Then the battle-fierce man pointed out to them
the bright house of the bold, so that they might
go straight to it; one of the warriors   *the coast guard*
315   turned his horse, spoke after this word:

"It is time for me to go. May the Father Alwalda
hold you in his favor
safe in your journeys. I will go to the sea,
to keep watch against hostile bands."

FITT 5. *Beowulf Arrives at Heorot*

320   The street was stone-paved, the path guided
the men together. The war-shirt shone,
hard, hand-linked, the shining ring-iron
sang in the armor, when to the hall they first
came marching in their terrible armor.
325   Sea-weary, they set broad shields,

---

the helmets (which could offer talismanic protection), or the helmeted *coast guard* who escorts the men, providing them safe conduct. The editors of *Klaeber 4* argue persuasively for the third option. In their view, the entire passage "represents a collage of images of the scene as the group moves along: the ship left behind; the shining, boar-decorated armor of the Geats as they advance; the dutiful escort, ensuring that their passage is unopposed and orderly" (137).

311. *its light shone over many lands.* In literal terms, the gold plating that adorns Heorot, flashing dramatically in the sun, is visible from a great distance. Metaphorically, the hall's glory extends throughout the known world. To speak anachronistically, for the poet Heorot is "a city upon a hill."

316. *the Father Alwalda.* All-ruling one, God, from *walda*, ruler; cf. ModE to *wield*, to control [a weapon]. The depiction of God as both father and ruler melds biblical and Germanic conceptions of divine power.

Fitt 5 Synopsis. When Beowulf and his men reach Heorot, they are questioned by Wulfgar, a warrior who serves as herald to King Hrothgar. Beowulf explains that he and his men are thanes of the Geatish King Hygelac, and he reveals his name for the first time in the poem. He then asks to speak with Hrothgar. Wulfgar relays his request to Hrothgar, commenting favorably on the men's stately armor and Beowulf's impressive appearance.

wondrously strong shield-bosses, against the building wall;
then they sat upon the benches. Their byrnies rang,
the battle-armor of men; their spears stood
all together, the sea-men's war-gear,
330   the ash-wood gray from above; the iron-troop
was made worthy by its weapons. Then a proud hæleth there
asked after the warriors' æthelu:

"From where do you carry these plated shields,
gray sarks and grim-helms,
335   this host of war-shafts? I am Hrothgar's
herald and officer; I have not seen
so many foreigners braver in appearance.
I expect it is for pride, not on account of exile,
but for greatness of heart that you have sought Hrothgar."

340   Then the bold-spirited one answered him,
the proud man of the Weders spoke after this word,
hard under his helm:

"We are Hygelac's
table companions; Beowulf is my name.

---

326. *wondrously strong shield-bosses* (*rondas regnhearde*). The original sense of *regnhearde* may have been "having the strength of the gods," since OE *regn-* corresponds to Old Norse *regin*, "the gods" (Jack 47). *Rond* (also spelled *rand*) refers specifically to the shield boss—the round conical piece of metal affixed to the center of early medieval shields—although in poetry it is a synecdoche simply meaning "shield." Shields were the primary defensive weapon in early northern European warfare, available to common soldiers who could not afford such high-status items as chain-mail or swords. Anglo-Saxon shields were made of wood planking cut into a circular shape; the iron boss at the center was used to deflect blows.

332. *æthelu*, lineage, (noble) ancestry, as well as one's excellence of character—indeed, the two notions are inseparable in the poem. Identity in the world of *Beowulf*, as in many traditional societies, is defined by one's kinship ties and lineage. *Æthelu* derives from the same root as *ætheling*, "nobleman, member of the warrior class."

334. *sarks and grim-helms* (*syrcan ond grim-helmas*), mailshirts and masked helmets. *Syrce* has now disappeared from the English language except in Northern and Scots dialects, where *sark* refers to a long shirt.

343. *Beowulf is my name.* The hero Beowulf is not otherwise known in Germanic legend, which suggests he was a minor figure without historical basis, unlike many of the other figures in the poem. The poet likely took a minor folktale hero, known for his prodigious strength, and transformed him into the virtuous warrior of the poem. In effect the little-known

I wish to speak to Halfdane's son,
345   your mære theoden, of my errand,
       to your aldor, if he will grant us,
       good as he is, that we may greet him."

       Wulfgar matheled; he was a man of the Wendels;
       his mōd-sefa was known to many,
350   his war-prowess and wisdom:

                                            "About this I will ask
       the friend of Danes, the lord of Scyldings,
       the giver of rings, as you request,
       the mære theoden, concerning your sith,
       and make known to you at once the answer
355   the good one thinks to give me."

       Then he turned quickly to where Hrothgar sat,
       old and very gray amid his dright of eorls;
       the courageous one walked so that he stood before the
            shoulders
       of the lord of Danes; he knew the custom of the duguth.
360   Wulfgar matheled to his friend-drighten:

       "Here have arrived, having come from afar
       across the sea's expanse, people of the Geats;
       the warriors call their chief
       Beowulf. They are requesting,
365   my theoden, that they might be permitted
       to exchange words with you. Do not refuse them
       your answer, glædman Hrothgar;
       in their war-gear they appear worthy
       of the esteem of eorls. Strong indeed is their aldor,
370   he who has led the warriors here."

Beowulf was a blank canvas on which the poet could depict his theolog-
ical-heroic vision.

349. *mōd-sefa* is one's interior disposition or character; "mind, heart,
spirit, soul" are all passable translations. Wulfgar is the complete Germanic warrior package: he is of proven character, having demonstrated
this through his wisdom and his prowess in battle (OE *wig*).

353. *sith*, journey, venture, heroic undertaking.

359. *the duguth* is the proven troop, the host of veteran retainers. Wulfgar
knows how to bear himself both in battle and in courtly setting.

367. *glædman*, cheerful, kind, gracious.

FITT 6. *Beowulf Vows to Help Hrothgar*
....

Hrothgar matheled, the helm of Scyldings:

"I knew him when he was a boy;
his old father was called Ecgtheow,
to whom Hrethel of the Geats gave for his home
375   his only daughter; now his offspring
has come here, a hardy man, has sought a faithful friend.
Furthermore, seafarers have said—
those who for the Geats carried gift-sceatts
there in thanks—that he has
380   in his mund-grip the strength of thirty men,
the battle-brave man. Holy God
in his grace has sent him to us,

Fitt 6 Synopsis. Hrothgar answers that he knew Beowulf as a child, as well as Beowulf's father Ecgtheow, and bids Wulfgar admit the Geats into the hall. Wulfgar does so, asking them to leave their weapons outside. Beowulf then addresses Hrothgar: he tells him of his previous victories over monstrous foes and asks for permission to face Grendel, vowing to do so without weapons. He also asks Hrothgar to send his chainmail shirt back to the Geatish King Hrethel if he is killed by Grendel.

371b. *helm*, helmet, covering, protection; used figuratively for Hrothgar and other rulers, the image of a ruler as a protecting cover for his people says a great deal about early Germanic conceptions of warrior-kings who achieve and maintain authority through military dominance.

374. *gave for his home.* The phrase reflects exogamous marriage practices in which the bride leaves her family to live in the husband's household. The Geatish king Hrethel gave his (unnamed) daughter in marriage to his follower Ecgtheow, with Beowulf resulting from their union. Beowulf is thus nephew to the king and, as explained later, was fostered by Hrethel, a common Germanic practice.

378. *the Geats carried gift-sceatts.* A sceatt was a silver coin of varying value; according to the 7th-century Law of Æthelberht, for example, fifty such coins were the compensation to be paid out for *feaxfang*, "hair-pulling." In this passage the term probably indicates more broadly "treasure," "money," "tribute." Are the Danes paying tribute money to the Geats, or is some other scenario to be imagined? Some interpreters understand this line to mean the carrying of treasures *from* the Geats, who instead are paying tribute to the Danes.

380. *mund-grip*, hand-grip. *Mund* means "hand," but is also a metonym for strength, protection, guardianship, and thus a common element in Old English-derived names such as Edmund and Sigmund.

381–82. *Holy God in his grace* (OE *ar-stafum*) *has sent him.* Note the parallel with Scyld, whom God sent to deliver the Danish people from their distress in the opening lines of the poem. God is seen as working providentially through heroic leaders.

to the West-Danes, as I hope,
against Grendel's gryre. To the good man
385   I shall offer mathoms for his daring.
Now be in haste, call them to come in
to see this sibb-dright, this band of kinsmen, all assembled.
Tell them also with words that they are welcome
to the people of the Danes."

390   [To the people of the Weders] he offered a word within:

Wulfgar

"My victory-lord commanded me to tell you,
the aldor of East-Danes, that he knows your æthelu,
and that you, from across the surging seas,
hardy-minded, are welcome to him here.
395   Now you may go in your battle-gear,
under masked helmets to see Hrothgar;
leave here your battle-boards,
your wooden slaughter-shafts, to await the result of words."

Then the mighty one arose; about him were many warriors,
400   a powerful band of thanes. A few waited there,
they guarded the battle-gear as the hardy one bid them.
Together they hastened; the man guided them
under Heorot's roof; [the battle-brave one went,]
hard under his helm, until he stood upon the hearth.
405   Beowulf matheled; his byrnie shone,
the battle-net sewn with the smith's skill:

"Be hale, Hrothgar! I am Hygelac's
mæg and mago-thane; I have undertaken many
glorious deeds in my youth. The matter of Grendel
410   was made known to me, unhidden in my homeland.

---

384. *gryre:* terror, horror, violence, a thing that inspires dread; a term
often associated with Grendel.

390. *to people of the Weders* is a conjectural reconstruction. There appears
to be a half-line or more missing. The eye of the scribe copying the manuscript probably skipped from the word "people" (OE *leodum*) to the next,
a common scribal error. Another gap occurs in line 403 below, and the
half-line given in brackets, "[the battle-brave one went]" (*eode hildedeor*), is
likewise an educated guess.

408. *mæg and mago-thane:* kinsman and young troop-member. (The *g* in
mæg is pronounced like a *y*.)

Seafarers say that this hall,
the best of buildings, stands empty and useless
to all warriors after the evening light
is hidden beneath the vault of heaven.
415 Then my people instructed me,
the best men, wise cheorls, that I should seek you out, lord
    Hrothgar,
because they knew the power of my strength.
They themselves looked on when I came from battle
420 stained with my foes, when I had bound five,
destroyed a brood of eotens, and on the ythes slew
nicors by night, suffered dire distress,

---

416. *cheorls* (OE plural *ceorlas*) are freemen whose social status in Anglo-Saxon society would fall between that of an *eorl* (nobleman, man of the warrior class) and a *theow* (slave). But in *Beowulf* the term generally functions as a synonym for "man." The OE term has none of the negative associations of its Modern English descendant, the surly and contemptible *churl*.

420–23. *bound five*, that is, five monstrous creatures.

421. *Eotens* (OE plural *eotenas*; Middle English *ettin*) are monstrous creatures of great size and supernatural strength, usually translated as "giant," although the *Beowulf* poet distinguishes them from *gigantas*, "giants," in lines 111–14, and *eoten* can also be distinguished from *ent*, an ancient and extinct race of master builders also typically translated "giant." The eoten is related to the Jötunn of Norse mythology, who were the adversaries of the gods (both Jötunn and eoten derive from the same proto-Germanic word **ituno-z*). The chief characteristic of the eoten, along with its hostility to human beings, is its voracious appetite for them. The name likely derives from a word meaning "to eat, consume," suggesting that they were cannibalistic. Hints from later sources supports this notion; a 14th-century Wycliffite sermon, for example, criticizes the Catholic understanding of the Eucharist on the grounds that it would be cannibalistic for the worshiper to eat Christ's body like an "etene" ("No man is an etene to fede him thus bodili of Crist").

422. *nicors* (OE *nicor;* plural *niceras*), water-monsters, malevolent creatures inhabiting rivers, lakes, and the sea, where they prey upon humans. As with other monstrous creatures, we are not given a specific visual description of them, although later in the poem they are referred to as *sǣ-dracan*, "sea-dragons," and said to be of the *wyrm-cynn*, "the race of serpents" (ln. 1425–26). In lines 529–80, Beowulf will recount a battle with them at sea in which one such nicor dragged him to the sea bottom; later still, his men discover a number of them swimming in Grendel's Mere and there manage to kill one (ln. 1427). In later English folklore such creatures become associated with specific watery sites, variously known as nickers, nixes, nixies, or neckers. ("A supernatural being supposed to live in the sea or other waters; a water-demon, a kelpie"; *OED*, s.v. *necker.*) Cognates are found in most branches of Germanic, all of them descending from Proto-Germanic *nikwus*, from the Proto-Indo-European root meaning "to wash."

avenged the Weders' affliction—they asked for that woe!

I ground down angry foes; and now with Grendel,

425   alone with the aglæca—the terrible adversary—I shall hold
        a meeting,

a thing with the thyrs. I now

wish to ask of you, brego of the Bright-Danes,

shelter of the Scyldings, one favor

that you will not refuse me, protector of warriors,

430   freo-wine of the folk, now that I have come so far:

that alone with my band of eorls

and this hardy troop, I might cleanse Heorot.

I have also heard that this aglæca

in his recklessness does not care for weapons.

435   Therefore, so that Hygelac

---

426. *a thing with the thyrs.* The hero speaks ironically of having a *thing*—
a formal meeting or judicial assembly—with Grendel, here called a *thyrs*,
underscoring through grim humor that with infernal foes such as Grendel
the normal rules of human engagement do not apply. A *thyrs* is a massive human-like creature, often translated "giant" or "ogre"; the word is
sometimes used interchangeably with *eoten.* According to the *OED* (s.v.
thurse), "A giant of heathen mythology; in mediæval times, often, the devil,
a demon; later, a goblin or hobgoblin of rustic superstition." The place
names containing the word *thyrs* that dot the English landscape, such as
Thurspit and Thrusmyre, indicate a creature thought to inhabit marshy,
uncultivatable regions far from human society. "A thyrs must live in the fen,
alone in the land," declares one Old English proverb (*Maxims II*, 42–43).
This antisocial and fen-dwelling designation suits Grendel well.

427–30. *brego, shelter, freo-wine.* A remarkable string of ruler-epithets:
Hrothgar is styled *brego* (chief, prince), *eodor* (shelter) to his people, *hleo*
(cover, shelter), and *freo-wine* (noble friend). Together they provide a picture
of idealized kingship.

432. *cleanse Heorot.* The verb employed here is *fælsian,* to ritually cleanse,
purify, purge, a rare term with distinctly religious overtones that probably
hearkens back to pre-Christian ritual. The word occurs only ten times in
Old English literature, five of them in *Beowulf,* where it is used in each
case to describe the purging of monstrous foes from a specific site (the hall
Heorot and later Grendel's Mere). As has been noted by Nathan J. Ristuccia,
fælsian "refers not primarily to outward washing or cleansing"—there are
other, more common OE verbs performing that function—"but to internal
spiritual purification." *Fælsian,* then, "serves almost as a technical term for
the ritual purification of a holy place, complete with certain expected ritual
actions: the dramatic entrance of a cleansing figure, the purification of a
delineated space, and the eradication of some specific impurity" (7; 1–2).
Along with Beowulf, only Christ and St. Matthew are said to carry out the
sacral purification denoted by *fælsian,* a fact that heightens the spiritual
dimension of Beowulf's role.

my man-drighten may be glad of me in his heart,
I scorn that I should bear a sword or a broad shield,
a yellow rond to the battle; but with my grasp
I will grapple with the enemy and fight for life,
440   foe with foe. Then let him trust in
the Lord's judgment—the Drighten's dōm—whom death
    takes.

I expect that, if he can accomplish it, he wishes
to eat the people of the Geats in the war-hall
without fear, as he has often done
445   to the host of Hrethmen. You will have no need
to cover my head, for he will have me
stained with gore, if death carries me off.
He will bear away my bloody flesh, intending to taste it;
the lone-walker will eat without remorse,
450   leave markings in the moor-hops; no longer will you
need to trouble yourself with the sustenance of my body.
If battle carries me off, send to Hygelac
this best of battle-garments which protects my breast,
the finest of raiment; it is the heirloom of Hrethel,
455   Weland's work. Wyrd goes always as it must."

---

438. *rond*, a shield, shield-boss; also spelled *rand*.

441. *Drighten's dōm.* The loser, being dead, will have to face God's judgment in the afterlife. A less plausible interpretation is that the lines refer to a trial by combat, or *judicium Dei*, in which God decides the outcome of the contest, awarding the victory to the side of right.

445. *Hrethmen*, the Danes.

445–46. *no need / to cover my head.* There will be no need for the customary funeral rites if Beowulf loses the battle since his body will be devoured by Grendel.

450. *moor-hops. Hop* remains a rather obscure topographic term, probably indicating "an enclosed piece of ground in a marsh," hence, "a remote, secret place" in the marshland (Gelling 10). That marshlands were perceived as inaccessible, fearful landscapes, the abode of monsters, is reflected in English place names, including several that preserve the name Grendel.

455a. *Weland* is a master smith in Germanic legend. Splendid artifacts and weapons are conventionally attributed to him as "Weland's work."

455b. *Wyrd*, Fate, that which must come to pass. This word has attracted a great deal of scholarly attention. 19th-c. scholars were all but certain it was a pagan concept only lightly Christianized, but this view is not widely held today. The word has a range of meanings. Passages such as this one portray Wyrd as an almost active force, even one personified to some degree. But in other instances it is little more than a poetic expression

FITT 7. *Hrothgar Speaks of Grendel*

Hrothgar matheled, the helm of Scyldings:

"For former deeds, my friend Beowulf,
and for goodwill, you have sought us out.
With a slaying your father brought on the greatest of feuds;
460   he became the hand-slayer of Heatholaf
among the Wylfings; then the cynn of the Weders
could not keep him for terror of war.
From there he sought out the people of the South-Danes,
the Honor-Scyldings, across the rolling of the waves.
465   At that time I first ruled over the people of the Danes,
and in my youth held the wide realm,
the hoard-burh of hæleths—Heregar was dead then,
my elder kinsman no longer living,
Halfdane's bearn; he was better than I.
470   Afterwards I settled the feud with payment:
I sent to the Wylfings over the water's ridge
mathoms of old; he swore me oaths.   *Ecgtheow*
It is a sorrow in my heart to say

---

for a person's death. It can also refer to God's providential will as well as to
Classical conceptions of fate, fortune, and destiny (*wyrd* is used to translate
Fatum, Fortuna, and the *Parcae*, the Fates). At its weakest, the word means
no more than "what happens." Fate in some form was likely a feature of
pre-Christian Germanic belief: Old English has a remarkably rich store
of words for fate, and Tacitus comments on the practice of omens and
augury in his *Germania*. Ideas of fate in *Beowulf* may also be influenced
by Latin literature, especially Boethius's discussion of *fatum* in his *Consolation of Philosophy*, a text known in Anglo-Saxon England, perhaps by
the *Beowulf* poet.

   Fitt 7 Synopsis. Hrothgar speaks of Beowulf's father Ecgtheow, recounting
how he once came to Hrothgar seeking refuge from his foes following his
slaying of a Wylfing (Swedish) warrior, when his own Geatish people could
not shelter him for fear of reprisal. Hrothgar settled the feud by paying
out treasures to the Wylfings. Hrothgar then laments how Grendel's raids
have depleted his troop. He invites the Geats to partake of a feast.

   457. *For former deeds.* This rendering amounts to an educated guess,
since the manuscript at this point is clearly corrupt, and the original
meaning of this line is no longer certain. Probably what is meant is that
Hrothgar understands why Beowulf has come to his aid: it is because
of the help Hrothgar performed for his father Ecgtheow long ago (or
for Beowulf's proven fighting ability?), as well as because of Beowulf's
kindness, that Beowulf has traveled to Heorot to fight Grendel.

to any man what Grendel has done to me,
475   the humiliations in Heorot, with thoughts of hate,
the sudden attacks. My hall-troop,
my war-band, has waned; wyrd has swept them away
in Grendel's gryre. God can easily
put an end to the deeds of the mad ravager.

480   Very often warriors, having drunk beer, vowed
over their ale-cups that in the beer-hall they would await
Grendel's warfare with the terror of their sword-edges.
Then in the morning time this mead-hall,
this dright-hall, was stained with gore when day shone forth,
485   the bench-planks all besmeared with blood,
the hall with sword-gore; I had fewer faithful men than
    before,
less in my dear duguth, as death carried them off.
Sit now at the feast and unfasten your thoughts,
490   your glory of victory, for men, as your heart moves you."

Then a bench was cleared in the beer-hall
for the men of the Geats all together;
there the strong-hearted went to sit,
proud in their thryth. A thane did his duty,
495   he who bore in his hands the ornamented ale-cup,
poured shining sweet drink. At times the scop sang,
bright in Heorot. There was the drēam of hæleths,
no small duguth of Danes and Weders.

---

467. *hoard-burh*, "treasure-fortress," the stronghold housing the royal treasure.

480. *beer*. OE *beor* signifies a drink much stronger than the beer known today. With an alcohol content as high as 18 percent, it was a much more intoxicating and sweeter beverage, being made with honey and fruit, and akin to a strong cider. Ale (*ealu*), on the other hand, was a malted drink with a much lower alcohol content than either *beor* or *medu* (mead). Though distinct beverages, *beor*, *ealu*, and *medu* are not always kept distinct in Old English verse, as here where warriors appear to be drinking *beor* out of "ale-cups."

487. *duguth*, troop of experienced warriors, veteran retainers of a war leader (in a different context *duguth* can also mean "excellence," "virtue," "power"); often placed in contrast with *geoguth*, the band of young warriors, so that together "*duguþ and geoguþ*" sums up the larger body of troops.

494. *thryth*, strength, power. Its importance is made clear from the occurrence of this term in many Anglo-Saxon personal names.

FITT 8. *Beowulf's Swimming Contest with Breca*

....

Unferth matheled, Ecglaf's bearn,
500   he who sat at the feet of the lord of Scyldings,
he unbound his battle-rune—Beowulf's sith,
the bold seafarer's journey, was a great offense to him,
for he did not wish that any other man
on this middangeard should care more for glory
505   under the heavens than he himself:

"Are you the Beowulf who strove with Breca,
who contended by swimming on the wide sea,
where for pride you two tested the waters,
and for foolish boasting risked your lives
510   in the deep water? Nor could any man,
friend or foe, dissuade you two
from the sorrowful sith, when you rowed on the sea.
There you two enfolded the ocean streams in your arms,
measured out the mere-paths, wove it with your hands,
515   glided over the sea. The flood welled up with waves,
with winter's surgings. In the water's possession

Fitt 8 Synopsis. While the men sit at the feast, Unferth, a prominent member of Hrothgar's court, accosts Beowulf. He claims that Beowulf lost a swimming contest in his youth to his companion Breca and predicts that he will likewise be defeated by Grendel. Beowulf corrects him, explaining that Breca was unable to outswim him and that the two remained on the wintry sea together for five nights. There Beowulf was attacked by sea-monsters, one of which dragged him to down the ocean floor before Beowulf managed to kill it. Because of its unique and archaic language, scholars have surmised that the swimming contest passage derives from an older, pre-existing narrative poem adapted by the poet.

501. *unbound his battle-rune* (OE *onband beadurune*). Because *battle-rune* occurs only in this instance, its precise meaning is debated. Perhaps its sense is "he unloosed his secret hostility, disclosed his secret quarrel," or even "began his verbal assault." Tolkien translates it, more speculatively, as "a spell to bring forth strife he loosed" (2014: 27). In OE *run* (pronounced *roon*) refers to a thing which is secret, hidden, or mysterious, and thus can mean "counsel" as well as "a (secret) council"; it is also used for runic letters.

514. *mere-paths*, sea-paths.

515. *glided over the sea.* The word for "sea" here, *gar-secg*, is a puzzler. Although it obviously signifies "ocean," "sea" (it elsewhere translates Latin *oceanus*), the compound word literally means "spear-man." Exactly what a spear or a spear-man has to do with the ocean remains an unsolved riddle. An allusion to Triton or Poseidon? The question has never been convincingly answered.

you two toiled seven nights; in swimming he overcame you,
had the greater strength. Then in the morning time
the holm bore him away to the Heatho-Ræms;
520 from there he sought his homeland,
beloved by his people, the land of the Brondings,
the fair stronghold, where he had his folk,
his burh and bēags. His bēot with you
he, the son of Beanstan, in truth completely fulfilled.
525 Therefore I expect worse results for you—
though everywhere you have prevailed in the storm of battle,
in grim warfare—if for Grendel you dare
to wait nearby all the night long."

Beowulf matheled, bearn of Ecgtheow:

530 "Hwæt, you said a great many things, my friend Unferth,
having drunk beer, about Breca,
spoke concerning his sith. I reckon it the truth
that I had greater sea-strength,
might on the waves, than any other man.
535 We two agreed, being boys,
and vowed—both of us were then still
in our early youth—that out upon the sea
we would dare our lives; and so we did.

We had naked swords, when we rowed on the sea,
540 hard in our hands; against the whale-fish
we thought to defend ourselves. By no means could he
float far from me on the waves of the flood,
faster in the holm; nor would I go from him.
Then we two were together on the sea
545 a time of five nights, until the flood drove us apart,
the surging waters, coldest of weathers,
darkening night, and the north wind
wherved against us, battle-grim; the waves were rough,
the spirit of the sea-fishes was stirred up.

---

523. *his burh and bēags...bēot*, his fortress and (ring-shaped) treasures;
a *bēot* is a heroic vow, a promise to carry out a particular act of daring or
die in the attempt. Although often translated as "boast," *bēot* has none of
the negative connotations of that noun.
   548. *wherved against*, turned against (OE *ond-hweorfan*).

550   There, against hateful enemies, my mail-shirt,
       hard, hand-linked, performed help,
       the woven battle-garment lay on my breast,
       bedecked with gold; to the bottom
       a fierce assailant dragged me down, held me fast,
555   grim in its grip. Yet it was granted to me
       that I reached the aglæca with my sword-point,
       with my battle-bill; the storm of war carried off
       the mighty mere-beast through my hand."

FITT 9. *Beowulf's Bēot*
....

       "So again and again hateful ravagers
560   pressed me severely; I served them
       with my precious sword, as it was fitting.
       By no means did they have the joy of their fill,
       the evil-doers, so that they consumed me,
       sat around at feast near the sea-floor;
565   but in the morning, wounded with weapons
       they lay up among the wave-leavings,
       put to sleep by swords, so that never again
       on the high waterway could they hinder
       the passage of sea travelers. Light came from the east,
570   God's bright beacon; the seas grew still,

---

557. *battle-bill* (OE *hilde-bill*), battle-sword. Like *sweord, bill* denotes a broadsword—a double-bladed weapon used primarily for cutting rather than thrusting, and about a yard long on average. Although they feature prominently in *Beowulf,* swords in the Germanic period were comparatively rare (wooden spears being the ordinary weapon), and thus highly prized possessions. Social status was indicated by weaponry: swords belonged to the warrior elite, whereas spears were a marker of freeborn status, and thus the most common weapon found in male graves. Bows, on the other hand, were available even to slaves.

Fitt 9 Synopsis. Beowulf completes his account of the swimming contest, stating that he killed nine sea-monsters before eventually washing ashore in the land of the Finns (i.e., the Lapps). His account finished, he denounces Unferth for his cowardice, which has allowed Grendel's ravaging to go unchecked, and accuses Unferth of slaying his own brothers, an act for which he will be damned to hell. The feast then resumes. Queen Wealhtheow moves among the men bestowing cups of ale. Receiving the cup from her hands, Beowulf makes a *bēot,* a heroic vow to defeat Grendel or die. Pleased by his vow, Hrothgar departs for his sleeping quarters, entrusting the hall to Beowulf's protection.

so that I could see the sea-cliffs,
the windy walls. Wyrd often saves
the undoomed eorl when his courage avails him.
However, it so happened that with my sword I slew
575   nine nicors. Never have I heard
of a harder fight by night under heaven's vault
nor of a more miserable man on the ocean streams.
Yet I passed through the grasp of those foes with my life,
weary from the sith. Then the sea bore me off
580   to the land of Finns, the flood with its flow,
the surging waters. Not a whit about you
have I heard said concerning such armed strife,
blade-terrors. Breca has never yet
performed so daring a deed
585   —not either of you two—in the play of battle
with shining swords—not that I boast much of it—
though you became the slayer of your brothers,
of your head-kinsmen; for that in hell
you must suffer damnation, though your wit be good.
590   Truly I say to you, son of Ecglaf,
that Grendel never would have wrought so many horrors,
the awful aglæca, upon your aldor,
humiliations in Heorot, if your heart,
your spirit, was as battle-grim as you suppose.
595   But he has found that he need not much fear
a feud with the Victory-Scyldings,
a terrible sword-storm from your people;
he exacts his toll, shows no mercy
to any of the people of the Danes, but takes his pleasure,

572–73. *Wyrd often saves / the undoomed eorl when his courage avails him.*
Like "fortune favors the brave," this seemingly paradoxical proverb asserts
that courageous human efforts can play a part in the fated outcome of
a battle—unless the warrior is *fæge*, specially marked out for death (the
source of *fey*, "marked by an otherworldly air or by a foreboding of death").
Since a warrior cannot know his fate for certain, he should face every battle
boldly. A similar proverb appears in lines 2291–93, but with *wyrd* replaced
by *Waldend*, God. Thus *wyrd*, the controlling force of fate, can be understood as an alternate expression of God's power, possibly influenced by
Boethius's explanation of the interworking of fate and God's providence in
The Consolation of Philosophy.
    588. *head-kinsmen*, closest relatives (OE *heafodmæg*).

600   puts to sleep, dispatches, expects no struggle
       from the Gar-Danes. But of the Geats
       soon now I shall show him strength and courage
       in battle. Whoever can will go bravely
       to his mead once more, when the morning light
605   of another day shines upon the sons of men,
       the brightly clothed sun from the south."

       Then the giver of treasure, gray-haired and   *Hrothgar*
           battle-bold,
       was glad. He trusted in this help,
       the brego of the Bright-Danes; in Beowulf he heard,
610   the shepherd of the people, a steadfast intent.

       There was laughter of hæleths, joyous din resounded,
       words were winsome. Wealhtheow went forth,
       Hrothgar's queen, mindful of courtesies;
       gold-decorated, she greeted the men in the hall,
615   and then the noble woman gave the cup
       first to the ethel-weard of the East-Danes,
       bid him to be glad in the beer-drinking,
       beloved by his people; with pleasure he partook
       of feast and hall-cup, the victory-bold king.
620   Then the lady of the Helmings moved among   *Wealhtheow*
       every part of the duguth and youth,

603–4. *go bravely / to his mead.* Ever tactful, Beowulf avoids directly
accusing the Danes of being cowardly. But one can detect gentle irony in
moments such as this as Beowulf describes the Danish warriors as returning
"bravely" (OE *modig*, brave, proud, in high spirits) to their feasting once he
has destroyed their enemy for them.

609. *brego,* ruler, chief; a word used almost exclusively in poetry.

613. *mindful of courtesies.* Wealhtheow is mindful of *cynna,* of "what is
fitting" in relation to distinctions of social status. It is her role to recognize
the worth of warriors and members of the court, above all by the act of
bestowing the cup.

616. *ethel-weard.* i.e., Hrothgar, who as king acts as guardian (*weard*) of
the *ethel,* the native land. It is the lady of the house's prerogative to ceremonially bestow the cup first upon her husband and then upon individual
warriors in an act that confers honor and recognizes their worth. This
ceremonial role is described in an Old English proverb, which states that
at the mead-banquet of the troop, the woman of the house is first to greet
her husband and to "swiftly offer the first cup to her lord's hand" (*Maxims
I,* lines 86–90).

offered costly vessels, until the time came
that she, adorned with rings, excellent in mōd,
bore the mead-cup to Beowulf;
625   she greeted the man of the Geats, thanked God
with wisefast words that her wish had come to pass,
that she could trust in any eorl
for relief from wicked deeds. He received the cup
from Wealhtheow, the battle-fierce warrior,
630   and then he gydded, eager for battle.
Beowulf matheled, bearn of Ecgtheow:

"I resolved when I set out on the water,
sat in the sea-boat with my dright of men,
that I would wholly fulfill
635   the wish of your people, or fall in the slaughter,
fast in the enemy's grasp. I shall carry out
the ellen of eorls, the bold work of a warrior,
or await my end-day in this mead-hall."

---

623. *excellent in mōd.* A comment on Wealhtheow's character. She is
exemplary in every way: richly decked and well versed in court etiquette,
she is also outstanding in terms of internal disposition, her *mōd* (pronounced *mode*), which can be variously rendered "mind, heart, character,
spirit, pride."

623–24. *she . . . bore the mead-cup to Beowulf.* Wealhtheow's presentation
of the cup to Beowulf is a pivotal moment in the narrative; it is upon
receiving the cup that Beowulf ceremonially accepts his heroic role and
responds by uttering his *bēot,* a heroic vow that formally and publicly
binds him to a set course of action.

630. *he gydded,* uttered a speech. Ordinarily, *gyddian* means to recite, sing,
or chant (a *gydd* is a poem or song), but in this instance it is a poetic way
of saying, "Beowulf spoke in an elevated fashion." This verb emphasizes
the weightiness of what Beowulf is about to say: it is a *bēot,* or heroic vow,
to defeat Grendel or die.

633. A *dright* is the troop attached to a particular *drighten* (war-leader,
lord), in this case the band of Geats who followed Beowulf to Daneland.
(OE *driht, ge-dryht*; OED s.v. *dright.*)

637. At the heart of Beowulf's heroic vow is the promise to carry out *the
ellen of eorls* (OE *eorlic ellen*), an expression difficult to represent in Modern
English, and therefore followed in the text by an explanatory paraphrase
("the bold work of a warrior"). The wide-ranging translations of *eorlic ellen*
reveal just how challenging this phrase is to convey in a contemporary idiom:
"A deed of knightly valour" (Tolkien); "a deed of manly courage" (Liuzza);
"a heroic deed" (Chickering); "deeds befitting my birth" (Child); "a proud
deed" (Heaney). Although "courage," "valor," "heroic deed" are serviceable

These words pleased the woman well,
640   the gylp-speech of the Geat; she went, decked in gold,
the noble people's-queen, to sit beside her lord.

Then just as before, within the hall were
strong words spoken, the people in joy,
the sounds of a victorious folk, until all at once
645   the son of Halfdane wished to seek
his evening rest. He knew that for the aglæca
a battle had been arranged in the high hall
from the time they could see the sun's light
until night came darkening over all;
650   the shapes of shadow-helms came scrithing,
dark under the clouds. The troop all arose.
Then one man greeted the other,
Hrothgar to Beowulf, and bid him luck,
mastery of the wine-hall, and spoke this word:

655   "Never before, since I could raise hand and rand,
have I entrusted this mighty house of Danes
to any man, except to you now.
Have now and hold the best of houses,
be mindful of mærthu, make known your mighty courage,
660   keep watch against the enemy! There will be no lack of
what you wish
if you pass through that ellen-work with your life."

---

translations of *ellen*, the term amounts to something more aggressive and daring—not merely the absence of fear but a positive zeal for combat. *Ellen* is discussed further in the note to line 876.

640. *gylp-speech*, a vaunting speech. *Gylp*, pronounced "yilp," is the distant ancestor of ModE "yelp."

650. *the shapes of shadow-helms came scrithing*. A curious locution. The idea is apparently of creatures of darkness that come creeping (*scrithan*, to glide, stalk, wander) in the concealing shadows, but the language is construed so that the shadows themselves appear animate. Tolkien, for example, translates, "The shapes of mantling shadow came gliding." Tom Shippey observes, in reference to this passage and lines 705–7, that "'Shadow' in *Beowulf* is a power and it may be an active and even physical power," a notion that lies behind the invention of Tolkien's Ringwraiths (16–17).

659. *mærthu*, renown for glorious deeds.

661. *ellen-work*, work of daring and valor, courageous action (OE *ellenweorc*).

FITT 10. *The Geats Await Grendel's Attack*

....

Then Hrothgar went with his dright of hæleths,
the shelter of Scyldings from out of the hall;
the war-leader wished to seek out Wealhtheow,

665   the queen as his bed-companion. The King of Glory
had appointed a hall-guardian against Grendel,
as men later learned; he held a special task   *Beowulf*
for the aldor of Danes: he provided an eoten-guard.
Truly the man of the Geats readily trusted

670   in his courageous might, the Metod's favor,
when he took off his iron byrnie,
the helm from his head, gave his ornamented sword,
the best of iron, to an attending thane,
and bid him guard the battle-gear.

675   Then the good man spoke a few gylp-words,
Beowulf of the Geats, before he climbed into his bed:

"I consider myself no more lowly in battle-stature,
in deeds of war, than does Grendel himself;
therefore I will not put him to sleep with a sword,

680   deprive him of life, though well I could.

Fitt 10 Synopsis. After Hrothgar departs, Beowulf disarms and lies down; his men also bed down, expecting they will not survive the night. But God had woven for them a victorious destiny, so that they would overcome their foe. When Grendel arrives in the dark of night all are asleep except Beowulf, who, filled with fury, observes Grendel's approach.

665. *The King of Glory.* Does *kyningwuldor* here refer to God or Hrothgar? The word occurs only in this ambiguous instance. The immediate context points to Hrothgar, but the language suggests God is meant (the common *wuldor-cyning*, "King of Glory," is applied exclusively to God in Old English literature). Although abruptly introduced, the reference to the Deity is in keeping with the poet's repeated insistence on God's providential control of events, as stated in the lines following. It is possible, however, that the ambiguity is deliberate, making Hrothgar's kingship an echo of God's divine kingship.

668. *eoten-guard.* Beowulf has been assigned by God a special office (*sun-dornytte*)—that of "guardian against eotens"—a moment of dark humor.

669–70. *trusted in his courageous might, the Metod's favor.* It might seem odd that Beowulf trusts in his strength *and* in God's favor (OE *hyldo*, the grace, favor, or kindness shown by a human lord, or by God). But the poet and characters consistently take the view of "double determination," understanding God's purposes as enacted through human agency.

He knows nothing of the good things with which he might
   strike against me,
shatter my shield-boss, though he be bold
in nith-deeds; but in the night we shall both
forgo swords, if he dares to seek
685   war without weapons. And afterwards let wise God,
the holy Drighten, assign war-glory
to whichever hand seems fitting to him."

Then the battle-bold one lay down. The bolster received
the face of the eorl; and around him many
690   a swift sea-warrior sank to his hall-rest.
Not one of them thought that from there
he would ever again seek his beloved homeland,
his people or the noble burh where he was brought up,
for they had heard that far too many before them
695   had been carried off by deadly slaughter in that wine-hall,
people of the Danes. But the Drighten granted them,
people of the Weders, a woven destiny of war-victory,
comfort, and help, so that they would all overcome
their enemy through one man's strength,
700   by his own might. The truth is well known
that mighty God has ruled
over the race of men always.

                    In the dark night he came,
the shadow-walker scrithing. The shooters slept,   *Grendel*
those who had to guard that horned hall
705   —all but one. To men of old it was well known
that when the Metod did not wish it,

---

683. *nith-deeds*, hostile deeds, acts of violence (OE *nith-geweorca*).

701–2. *mighty God has ruled / over the race of men always.* In other words, the same God who now works through the saints and sacraments of the Church was active in the pre-Christian past, working through heroes of old such as Beowulf. The poet's theological project, evident here and elsewhere, is to build a bridge with the heroic pagan past, recuperating the heroic legends and enfolding them within a Christian vision, as opposed to the view of churchmen such as Alcuin who rejected the old legends for their heathenism.

705–6. *To men of old it was well known / that when the Metod did not wish it.* The poet once again interrupts the narration to interject a broader theological point. His purpose is twofold: First, to reiterate God's place

the scyn-scather could not drag them under the shadows;
but he, watching in anger against the enemy,   *Beowulf*
awaited, enraged, the outcome of battle.

FITT II. *Grendel Comes to Heorot*

710   Then from the moor, under the misty slopes,
Grendel came walking; he bore God's ire.
The mān-scather meant to ensnare
one of the race of men in the high hall.
Under the clouds he went to where he knew well
715   the wine-hall was, the gold-hall of men
gleaming with gold plating; it was not the first time
he had sought Hrothgar's home;
never before or after in the days of his life
did he find harder fortune, hardier hall-thanes.

720   He came then, the warrior journeying, to the hall,
deprived of drēam. The door gave way at once,

---

in the narrative as the *Metod*, ordainer of events, reminding his audience that creatures of evil such as Grendel, though adversaries of God, are in no way his equal, and that they operate only with his divine permission. Second—and more daringly—the poet declares that the pagan heroes of old were *aware* of this truth, despite their ignorance of Christian teachings. Precisely how the poet's pagan ancestors arrived at this knowledge of God is left unexplained (and their pagan religious practices are left all but unmentioned).

707. *scyn-scather* (OE *scyn-scatha*), demonic ravager, an opponent of supernatural evil. See more at *scinna*, "spectre," "demonic spirit" (line 939).

Fitt II Synopsis. In the dark of night Grendel approaches Heorot. Throwing open the door, he enters the hall and rejoices at the sight of the sleeping war-band, expecting a great feast. He snatches the nearest warrior and devours him while Beowulf watches. When Grendel reaches for his next victim he is surprised to find his hand suddenly seized. He attempts to flee but Beowulf's grip is too powerful; the two battle so fiercely that the hall is nearly destroyed. Then a wailing sound is heard—the Danes outside of Heorot hear it through the walls. It is Grendel howling in pain.

712. *mān-scather* (OE *mānscatha*), wicked ravager. *Scatha*, one who inflicts injury (ModE *scathe*; cf. *unscathed*), is here compounded with *mān*, crime, wickedness—not to be confused with the word "man."

720. *warrior.* Grendel is surprisingly styled a *rinc*, "warrior." Grendel, a monstrous enemy who lives outside of the human world, is incorporated linguistically into the poem's heroic warrior culture.

721. *deprived of drēam.* As bearer of God's wrath, Grendel is cut off from the joys of human communion, symbolized above all by the hall. He is an

fastened with fire-bands, when his hands touched it.
Then, bent on evil, swollen with rage, he swung open
the hall's mouth. Rathely after that
725   the fiend stepped onto the shining floor,
went with ire in his heart. From his eyes there came
an unlovely light, most like a flame.

He saw many warriors in the hall,
a sibb-dright all asleep together,
730   a host of young warriors. Then his heart laughed;
the terrible aglæca meant before day came
to sever the life from the body
of each one, for now the hope had come to him
for his fill of feasting. But it was no longer his fate
735   that he be permitted to partake any more of mankind
after that night. The mighty one,
Hygelac's mæg, watched how the mān-scather
would carry out his sudden attack.
Nor did the aglæca mean to delay,
740   but at the first chance quickly seized
a sleeping warrior, greedily slit him open,
bit into his bone-locks, drank blood from his veins,
swallowed up huge morsels; soon he had
completely devoured the lifeless man,
745   hands and feet. Forward he stepped, nearer—
with his hands he then grasped the strong-hearted
warrior at rest—he reached for him,
the fiend with his folm. At once he seized it

---

agent of disintegration, standing in contrast to the band of kinsmen all
asleep at peace together in Heorot.

724. *Rathely*, quickly, swiftly (OE *rathe*, *hrathe*; *OED* s.v. *rathely*).

713. *sibb-dright*, troop of kinsmen (*sibbe-gedriht*).

731. *Aglæca* probably means "awe-inspiring adversary," "terrifying opponent," but its precise meaning and etymology are disputed. The word is
most often used in poetry to refer to monstrous or demonic foes, but it is
once used for both Beowulf and Sigemund the dragon-slayer, respectively.

742. *bone-locks* are muscles, "bone-enclosures" (*ban-loca*).

746ff. The ambiguous pronouns in this passage make it difficult to discern who is doing what. Probably Grendel reaches down to the floor where
Beowulf rests, and his arm is seized by Beowulf, who leans upon his own
arm while sitting up, and clenches Grendel's fingers in his grip.

748. *folm*, the hand or palm of the hand.

with hostile purpose and sat up against his arm.
750 Instantly the shepherd of sins found
that never on this middangeard, on the regions of earth,
had he met with a mightier hand-grip
in another man. In his mind he grew
fearful in spirit; not for that could he escape any sooner.
755 His heart was eager to get away, he wished to flee into
   darkness,
to seek the swarm of devils; his plight there was not
like any he had met before in the days of his life.

Then the good one, Hygelac's mæg, remembered   *Beowulf*
his evening-speech; he stood upright
760 and grasped him fast. Fingers cracked;
the eoten was striving to escape, the eorl stepped closer.
The mære one meant to turn wherever
he could get further away, to flee from there
into the fen-hops; he knew that the power of his fingers
765 was in the grasp of his grim foe. That was a grievous journey
that the harm-scather took to Heorot.

The dright-hall resounded; for all the Danes,
for fortress-dwellers, for all the bold warriors,
it was an ale-serving for eorls. Both were enraged,
770 the fierce house-guardians. The hall thundered—
it was a great wonder then that the wine-hall
withstood those battle-beasts, that the fair building
did not fall to the ground; but so firmly was it made fast
775 inside and out with iron bands,
cunningly smithed. From the floor there

---

762. *mære one*, the renowned one. Another surprising designation for
Grendel, since *mære* is an epithet for illustrious rulers and warriors. Trans-
lators "fix" this appellation by rendering it "notorious" or "infamous," but
Grendel's renown is what makes him a worthy opponent for Beowulf.

766. *harm-scather*, harmful ravager (OE *hearm-scatha*).

769. *ale-serving* (*ealu-scerwen*) is an obscure term that occurs only here,
where it apparently means "terror" or "panic." But how this panic relates
to the dispensing of ale has not been convincingly explained. An instance
of sardonic humor? A figurative reference to the cup of death? Or did the
scribe mistake *ealu* for *alu*, "luck," a word found inscribed with runes on
various objects, so that the compound signifies "the taking away of good
luck"? Tolkien renders it "a ghastly fear."

were wrenched many mead-benches, as I have heard,
adorned with gold, where the grim foes fought.
The wise ones of the Scyldings had thought
that no man could ever by any means
780   break it down, splendid and bone-adorned,
sunder it with skill—unless the fæthm of fire
should swallow it in flame. A sound rose up,
often renewed; upon the North-Danes
there came a terrible fear, in each of them
785   who heard the wailing from the wall,
God's adversary singing a gryre-lay,
a victoryless song, the captive of hell
bewailing his wound. He held him fast,   *Beowulf*
he who was strongest of men in might
790   in that day of this life.

FITT 12. *Beowulf's Victory over Grendel*
....

Not for anything would the shelter of eorls
let the murderous guest go alive;
he did not consider the days of his life
of use to any man. There many of Beowulf's
795   eorls drew out their swords, ancient heirlooms,

---

780. *bone-adorned*. The meaning of this phrase is uncertain. A reference
to antlers adorning the hall? Or walrus-tusk ornamentation?

786. *gryre-lay* (*gryre-leoth*), a terror-song. An ironic description of Grendel's
howling as a kind of singing.

Fitt 12 Synopsis. While Beowulf holds firmly to Grendel's arm, refusing to
let him escape, his men draw out their swords and strike at him. But their
blades are useless; Grendel is protected from weapons by a spell. Then
Grendel's shoulder is ripped away; he flees without his arm to die in his
home in the marshlands. Victorious, Beowulf hangs the severed arm from
the roof of Heorot as an unmistakable sign of Grendel's defeat.

791. *shelter of eorls*. Beowulf is termed the *hleo*, "refuge," "shelter," "protector," of his men. *Hleo* survives to this day in certain contexts, such as "the
lee of the island," the side sheltered from the wind. This and other epithets
for leaders, such as *helm*, project an image of authority as a protective covering for one's people—a far cry from the later idea of the sovereign who
is served by his subjects.

795. *ancient heirlooms* (*ealde lafe*). As Mitchell and Robinson explain, "old
swords . . . were valued more than new since the durability of a blade could
be known only if it had stood the test of heavy use in the past" (74). The
same might be said of warriors.

wished to defend their lord's life,
their mære theoden's, if they might.
They did not know, the brave-minded warriors,
when they took up the fight,
800 and thought to hew at him from every side,
to seek his soul, that no war-sword,
not the best of iron on earth,
could touch the syn-scather, the wicked ravager,
for he had sworn away victory-weapons,
805 every sword's edge. His severing from life
on that day of this life
was to be wretched, and the ellor-gæst
would journey far into the power of fiends.

Then he found, he who before had wrought
810 so much trouble of mind upon mankind,
wicked deeds—he was at feud with God—
that his body-garment would do him no good,
but the courageous kinsman of Hygelac
had him by the hand; each was hateful
815 to the other while living. The loathsome aglæca
suffered bodily pain. On his shoulder
a gaping wound was seen; sinews sprang open,

---

804. *sworn away.* Grendel has rendered weapons useless by a curse or magic spell in the view of most commentators. But this interpretation is contested, since the verb *forswerian* usually refers to perjury, swearing falsely, and in the later medieval period comes to mean "renounce." The translation *sworn away* is a compromise intended to preserve the ambiguity.

807. *ellor-gæst.* Alien spirit, otherworldly creature. The first element, *ellor,* "elsewhere," appears only in poetry in references to distant places and the supernatural realm beyond this world. At his death, for example, Scyld is said to have "departed elsewhere" (*ellor hwearf, 55*). The poet leaves no doubt regarding Grendel's final destination: after death he must travel into the domain of demons (*on feonda geweald*).

811. *he was at feud with God.* A parenthetical explanation for Grendel's attacks. The monster ravages the Danes not for any offense they have done to him but because he is in a state of declared hostility with God. Within the collective logic of feud, an attack against one is an offense against all; Grendel is therefore taking out his hatred of God by making war on the race of men.

812. *body-garment (lic-hama).* This is a literal translation of a metaphorical expression meaning "body," but the compound betrays an underlying view of the body as the covering or enclosure of the soul. By itself *hama* can refer to a cloak, or even the skin of a snake.

bone-locks burst. To Beowulf
war-glory was granted. From there Grendel
820   had to flee, life-sick, under the fen-slopes,
to seek his joyless abode; he knew the more surely
that his life's end was reached,
the number of his days. For all the Danes
their wish had come to pass after deadly onslaught;
825   the one who had come from far away,
wise and strong-hearted, had then cleansed Hrothgar's hall,
saved it from nith. He rejoiced in his night's work,   *Beowulf*
his glorious deeds. To the East-Danes
the man of the Geats had fulfilled his gylp, his proud vow;
830   he had also remedied all grief,
the evil sorrows they had earlier endured,
and the dire distress they had to thole—
no little trouble! It was a clear sign
when the fierce warrior placed the hand,
835   arm, and shoulder—there all together was
Grendel's grasp—under the vaulted roof.

FITT 13. *The Tales of Sigemund and Heremod*

Then in the morning, as I have heard,
around the gift-hall were many warriors;
folk-chiefs traveled from near and far
840   over the wide ways to gaze upon the wonder,
the tracks of the hated foe; nor did his parting from life

---

827. *saved it from nith.* The verb *nerian* (to save, redeem, deliver) under-
scores Beowulf's role as a savior figure. Like Christ, who in Old English
literature is titled the *Nergend* (Savior), Beowulf delivers the people from
demonic oppression. *Nith* is an all-purpose word for hostility: it is violence
done out of ill-will. In Norse the *nith-stang*, "nithing pole," was a wooden
pole with a decapitated horse's head affixed to the end, used to publicly
shame and curse one's enemies.

833. *a clear sign.* Grendel's arm is a trophy of victory; it also provides
indisputable proof that he has defeated Grendel and put his ravages to an
end. Other victory tokens in the poem include the giant sword hilt and the
dragon's hoard. Beowulf can offer no such token of his victory over Breca
in the swimming contest he narrates earlier, which makes it possible for
Unferth to question his claim.

Fitt 13 Synopsis. In the morning people from all around gather at Heorot to
see Grendel's severed arm and his gigantic blood-stained footprints. Some

seem sad to any of the men
who looked upon the footprints of the inglorious one,
how he, weary-hearted on his way from there,   *Grendel*
845   overcome in battle, bore his life-tracks
into the mere of nicors, doomed and put to flight.

There the water boiled with blood;
the terrible swirl of waves, all mingled
with hot gore, surged with the blood of battle.
850   He hid away, doomed to die, drēamless,
when in the fen-refuge he laid down his life,
his heathen soul; there hell received him.

From there the old gesithas turned back again,
many young ones as well, on their joyful journey
855   from the mere, high-spirited men riding horses,
beorns on shining steeds. Beowulf's glory
was there proclaimed; many often said
that, south or north between the seas,

---

of the men mount horses and follow the bloody trail to Grendel's Mere, a pool inhabited by water monsters located in the fenlands. There Grendel had plunged into the water to die, and the men now find the pool swirling with his blood. They then return home rejoicing, racing their horses and praising Beowulf's deeds. As they ride, one of Hrothgar's thanes, a poet versed in the legends of old, recites the story of Beowulf, and then recounts the tales of two legendary figures, Sigemund the dragon-slayer and the wicked King Heremod. As the men return to Heorot, Hrothgar and Wealhtheow also arrive there from their sleeping quarters.

845–46. *bore his life-tracks / into the mere of nicors*. The mortally stricken Grendel dragged himself to his swampy home, leaving a trail of his life-blood behind him.

850. *He hid away*. This translation is an educated guess. If *deog*, a verb that occurs only here, is related to *deogol* (secret, hidden), then it presumably means "to hide away, conceal (oneself)." An alternate explanation is that *deog* is a scribal error for *dēaf*, "he dove (into the mere)." In either case, Grendel plunges into his watery abode to die.

852. *hell*. Related to OE *helan*, "to conceal," OE *hell* therefore "means the hidden world, the underworld, Hades, the Realm of the Dead" (Tolkien 2014: 167). The notion of an underworld called in OE *hell* (*halja* in Gothic) pre-dated the coming of Christianity but was adopted into Christian use.

853. *gesithas* are followers and companions of the king, members of his *comitatus;* literally, *ge-* ("with") + *sith*, "journey," that is, one who accompanies on military expedition.

858. *between the seas*. The North and Baltic Seas; the idiom assumes the vantage point of Denmark and its environs, but over time it develops into a stock expression meaning "from sea to sea," "everywhere."

over the spacious earth, there was no
860   better shield-bearer under the sky's expanse,
none more worthy of a kingdom.
Yet they found no fault at all with their friend-drighten,
glad Hrothgar, for he was a good king.

At times the battle-brave men
865   let their fallow horses gallop, go racing
where the paths seemed fair to them,
known to be best. At times the king's thane,
a gylp-laden man, mindful of gydds,
one who remembered a great many of the old stories,
870   a vast number, found other words
bound truly together. The man began again
to recite Beowulf's sith with skill,
to fluently perform a ready tale,
varying his words. He recounted everything

864–916. *The Sigemund and Heremod episodes.* The story of Beowulf is
interwoven with numerous inset stories or digressions, and it is not always
apparent what narrative purpose they serve. Nineteenth-century scholars
saw the episodes as evidence that *Beowulf* had been stitched together
out of earlier heroic tales or "lays," while more textually minded readers
have argued that episodes such as these are interpolations, inserted by
later scribes. Both views are not without merit. *Beowulf* obviously draws
upon earlier heroic legends (although few believe today that the *Beowulf*
poet merely stitched together pre-existing tales), and it is also true that
passages such as lines 864–916 could be removed without disturbing the
main narrative one jot. But the dissection approach has fallen from favor
because it overlooks the artful "interlace" technique of the poem (as John
Leyerle has termed it) and imposes foreign textual-literary standards on
a poem derived from oral tradition. While not always directly related to
the main storyline, the inset stories provide echoes and parallels to it,
and invariably deepen the narrative.

865. *fallow* (OE *fealu*) has come to mean a reddish yellow or pale brown,
but at this stage *fealu* might signify "pale" or "glossy-pale." Our understanding of Old English color terms is complicated by the fact that they
often denote reflective surface as much as hue.

868. *a gylp-laden man, mindful of gydds.* The unnamed poet on horse-
back is full of proud words (*gylp*, vow, boast) and knowledgeable of *gydds*,
poetic or artful utterances. Old English has no single word for "poem," and
poetry was predominantly experienced as oral performance; even a written
text like *Beowulf* was typically read aloud. Hence *gydd*, the closest term
to "poem," can refer to any artful speech act, including songs, eloquent
speeches, and proverbs.

875   that he had heard said about Sigemund's
       ellen-deeds, of many things unknown —
       the Wælsing's strife, his distant journeys,
       which the sons of men did not fully know,
       his feuds and fyrens — except for Fitela with him,
880   when of such things he wished to speak,
       the eam to his nephew, as they were always
       companions at need in every struggle —
       a great many of the eoten-cynn they had felled
       with their swords. For Sigemund there sprang up
885   no little dōm after his death-day
       after he, hardy in war, killed the wyrm,
       the keeper of the hoard; under the hoary stone
       he alone, the ætheling's bearn, had ventured

---

875. *Sigemund.* Beowulf's triumph over Grendel places him in the illustrious company of the legendary monster-slayer Sigemund. A much fuller version of the Sigemund story is known from the late 13th-century Old Norse *Saga of the Volsungs*, although there are noteworthy differences between the two versions. In the Old Norse saga, Sigmund (as he is there called) is the son of Volsung (OE *Wæls*), the grandson of the god Odin. The saga spans several generations of the divinely descended yet doomed Volsungs, encompassing intra-family violence, incest, werewolves, and unexpected appearances of the gray-hooded, one-eyed Odin. In this later account, however, it is not Sigmund but his son Sigurd who is the dragon-slayer.

876. *ellen-deeds* are feats of heroic daring. No term better characterizes the heroic ethos of Beowulf than *ellen*, a word that occurs a total of 34 times. It is precisely their *ellen* that sets heroes like Sigemund apart from ordinary fighters. The word is usually translated as "courage" or "valor," but these are only approximate, since *ellen* derives from the (reconstructed) Proto-Germanic *aljanq*, "zeal," "strength," "power." Tolkien describes *ellen* as "the strength and heat of spirit driving a man to vigorous action" and "the competitive, combative spirit of proud individuals" (2014: 257). More than a mere mastery of fear, *ellen* amounts to a zeal for battle and an almost reckless disregard for one's own life. When Sigemund takes on the dragon alone, for example, he is said to win the treasure through his *ellen* (893), and Beowulf exhibits the same quality in his willingness to battle Grendel and the dragon. The term is expressive of the distinctive mentality of heroic figures in northern European literature that Tolkien labeled the northern "theory of courage," a "creed of unyielding will." In the myth of Ragnarök, for example, the gods themselves will choose to fight a battle they know is doomed. It is not outcome but *ellen* that matters most.

881. *eam to nephew*, maternal uncle and nephew. Sigemund is in fact Fitela's uncle *and* his father, as a result of an incestuous union. Either the *Beowulf* poet is being discreet here or the incest motif is a later plot development.

that daring deed; nor was Fitela with him.
890   Still it was granted that his sword pierced
       the wrætlic wyrm, so that it stood fixed in the wall,
       the lordly iron; the dragon died by the murder.
       The aglæca had brought about by his ellen
       that he could enjoy the ring-hoard
895   at his wish. He loaded his sea-boat,
       carried into the ship's bearm bright treasures,
       Wæls' offspring; the hot wyrm melted away.

       He was the most widely famed of exiles
       among the peoples, the protector of warriors,
900   on account of his ellen-deeds — for that he had flourished —
       after Heremod's war-prowess waned,
       his strength and ellen. Among the Jutes he was   *Heremod*
       betrayed into the power of his foes,
       swiftly dispatched. Surging sorrows
905   crippled him too long; to his own people,
       to all his æthelings, he had become a mortal grief.
       Many of the wise ones also often lamented

---

891. *wrætlic*, mysterious, intricate in appearance. Wondrously wrought objects, strange creatures, and riddle-like objects are all designated by this adjective, which is used only in poetry.

897. *the hot wyrm melted away*. In OE *meltan* can mean "burn up": the dragon is consumed by its own inner fire.

901. *Heremod*. King Heremod had ruled the Danes prior to the coming of Scyld Scefing. In fact, his disastrous rule and subsequent demise resulted in the Danes' distressing leaderless condition depicted at the opening of *Beowulf*, a situation remedied by the coming of Scyld and the Scylding dynasty he founded. Yet before his decline Heremod had been an exemplary figure, famous for his strength and courage. Despite his initial promise, we learn here and later (in lines 1709–23) that Heremod proved unjust and miserly as a king, killing his own men and refusing to give out treasure. In the end he is betrayed and slain among the Jutes, a rival tribe occupying the Danish peninsula. Although many details about him are now obscure, Heremod is clearly presented by the poet in contrast to Beowulf.

902–3. *Among the Jutes he was / betrayed into the power of his foes*. An ambiguous sentence. The phrase *mid eotenum* can mean either "among the Jutes," a Germanic tribe, or "among the eotens," gigantic creatures such as Grendel. *Feonda*, translated here as "of his foes," can also mean "of fiends, demons." Most interpreters favor the translation given above, but both *eoten* and *fiend* fit the moralizing tone of the passage, especially since we are told in line 915 that "wickedness (*fyren*) entered" Heremod, and eotens would connect Heremod to the eoten-fighting figures of Sigemund and Beowulf.

in those earlier times the strong-hearted one's course,
those who had trusted in him as a remedy for evils,
910 that their prince's son would prosper,
receive the noble rank of his father, rule over the people,
the hoard and stronghold, the kingdom of hæleths,
the homeland of Scyldings. There he,   *Beowulf*
Hygelac's kinsman, became dearer to his friends,
915 to all mankind; him, wickedness entered.   *Heremod*

At times competing on horses
they measured out the fallow street. By then morning light
was advanced and hastening on; many warriors went,
stout-hearted, to the high hall
920 to see the strange wonder; the king himself,
the guardian of ring-hoards, also came striding
with a great host from the bride chamber, glory-firm,
known for excellence; and with him his queen
measured out the mead-path with a company of maidens.

FITT 14. *Hrothgar Praises Beowulf*
....

925 Hrothgar matheled—he walked to the hall,
stood upon the stapol, saw the steep roof
gleaming with gold, and Grendel's hand:

---

917. *they measured out.* That is, "they traversed." *Metan,* "to measure," is
a poetic idiom for "to pass over," "to measure by one's paces."

Fitt 14 Synopsis. Hrothgar gazes up at Grendel's severed arm as it hangs
from the roof of Heorot and makes a speech. He gives thanks to God and
declares his great joy at Grendel's defeat after he had given up all hope. Beowulf is praised for his deeds and Hrothgar adopts him as his son, promising
him gifts. Beowulf graciously reaffirms his good intentions and expresses
regret that Hrothgar can look only upon Grendel's arm rather than his entire
corpse. But he explains it was not God's will for him to destroy Grendel in
the hall; though Grendel fled Heorot he cannot flee his coming death, and
he must face God's judgment after dying. As the men look up at Grendel's
arm suspended from the roof, Unferth, who before had belittled Beowulf,
is shamed into silence.

926. *Stapol* ordinarily refers to a supporting structure such as a pillar, but
that makes little sense in this context; here it is best understood as a raised
platform in front the hall's entrance, "a stone block in the form of a pedestal
of some kind" (Klaeber 4: 173) that served a ceremonial function. Such structures were also associated with pagan shrines, some of which were connected
with great halls, and clearly had a cultic purpose. It is while standing upon
the stapol that Hrothgar adopts Beowulf and declares their "new sibb."

"For this sight let thanks be given at once
to the Alwalda. Much have I endured from my enemy,
930   many griefs from Grendel. God may always work
wonder upon wonder, the Shepherd of glory!
It was not long ago that I thought
never in my life to see
relief from woes when, stained with blood,
935   the best of houses stood sword-gory,
a far-reaching woe for each of my counselors
who did not expect they would ever
defend the people's stronghold from enemies,
from scuccas and scinnas—demonic spirits. Now a warrior
940   has, through the Drighten's might, done the deed
that that none of us in our cleverness
could contrive. Hwæt, this can she say—
whichever woman brought forth this son
among the race of men, if she is still living—

---

936. *counselors* (OE *witena*, wise ones, counselors). In Anglo-Saxon England this group of the *witena* developed into a formal body known as the *witan*, the king's advisory council, the meeting of which was known as a *witenagemot*. The authority of the witan was considerable: "An early principle seems to have been that the *witan* had to approve and elect a new king. The corollary of this was that they might also deselect a king who was deemed unsatisfactory" (*Blackwell* 124).

939. *scuccas and scinnas* (OE *scuccum ond scinnum*) are creatures of evil who, as spirits, are not subject to the laws of nature. Against such spectral foes Hrothgar's counselors are powerless, a situation that leads to the idol sacrifices mentioned in lines 171–83. *Scucca* (probably from the root *skuh-*, "to terrify") is a term used in Christian writings for demons and, in the singular, for Satan himself. It is also clear from place names that such creatures were also believed to haunt the land, particularly barrows ("Shucklow"), hills, water-courses, and pits ("Schokepit") (Whitelock 73). Belief in such creatures lasted well beyond the medieval period: a demonic hound known as the Black Shuck was said to haunt the countryside of East Anglia, reported as "a black shaggy dog, with fiery eyes and of immense size" (OED, s.v. *shuck*). *Scinna*, on the other hand, refers to the insubstantial, spectral quality of such spiritual beings, and is defined as "specter," "phantom," "magical image," "evil spirit," deriving from the root *scin-*, "shine," "appear." A person haunted by such spirits was said to be *scinn-seoc*, "specter-sick," while magic and sorcery were labeled *scinn-cræft*. Certain places were likewise associated with such spirits; the word appears in place names such as Skinburness (from OE scinnaburh, "specter hill").

942. *Hwæt* is an interjection of exclamation and affirmation: "Indeed!," "Yes," "Listen now!" It is the first word of *Beowulf* and several other Old English poems.

945   that God, the Metod of old, was gracious to her
       in her child-bearing! Beowulf,
       best of men, as a son I will now
       love you in my heart; hold well from now on
       our new sibb; you will not lack
950   any joy in the world that I hold in my power.
       Very often I have allotted a reward for less,
       hoard-honors to a lowlier warrior,
       one weaker in fighting. You yourself have
       done such deeds that your dōm will live
955   forever and always. May the Alwalda
       reward you with good, as he has even now done."

       Beowulf matheled, bearn of Ecgtheow:

       "With much goodwill we carried out that ellen-work,
       that fight, ventured boldly against
960   the strength of one unknown. I would have wished
       rather that you could have seen him,
       the fiend himself in his trappings, fall-weary.
       I had thought to quickly bind him
       on his death-bed with a hard grasp,
965   so that for my handgrip he must
       lie struggling for life, had not his body escaped.
       I could not, when the Metod did not wish,
       hinder his going, however eagerly I held to him,
       my life's enemy; he was too powerful,
970   the fiend in his foot-flight. Yet to save his life
       he left his hand behind to guard his track,
       his arm and shoulder. Yet not by that

947–8. *as a son I will now / love you in my heart.* Hrothgar's adoption of
Beowulf probably does not constitute a legally binding one, which would
make Beowulf his heir. Instead Hrothgar declares he will cherish Beowulf
as a son "in my heart," indicating a close emotional bond accompanied by a
set of mutual obligations. Yet this "new sibb" between them is real enough
to alarm Queen Wealhtheow, who in lines 1175ff will feel the need to remind
Hrothgar to leave the kingdom to their sons.

    962. *fiend himself.* Beowulf means, "I wish you could see Grendel's corpse
rather than just his arm."

    967. *when the Metod did not wish.* Beowulf perceives every event as divinely
ordained by the Metod, the one who *metes* out, or distributes, outcomes,
rewards, and punishments.

did the wretched man buy himself any relief;
the loathsome foe will live no longer for that,
975 beset by sins, for a wound
has seized him fast in its nith-grip,
its deadly bonds; there he must await,
the man guilty of crime, the Great Judgment,
how the shining Metod will pass sentence on him."

980 Then the man, Ecglaf's son, was more silent   *Unferth*
in his boasting speech of battle-deeds,
after the æthelings, through the eorl's strength,
gazed over the high roof upon the hand,
the fiend's fingers; at the front each was,
985 all the nail-places, most like steel,
the heathen's hand-spurs, the warrior's
awful spike. Everyone said
that no harder thing would hurt him,
no iron, good of old, would harm
990 the aglæca's bloody battle-hand.

FITT 15. *Celebration and Gift-Giving in Heorot*

Then swiftly it was ordered that Heorot
be adorned within by hands. There were many
men and women who made ready the wine-hall,
the guest-house. Gleaming with gold,
995 woven hangings shone along the walls, many wondrous sights
for any man who will gaze upon such things.

---

976. *nith-grip*, hostile grasp.

978. *the Great Judgment* (OE *miclan domes*). An unmistakable reference to the Christian doctrine of the Last Judgment. Though scholars
have attempted to erect a division between the Christian narrator and
the pagan characters, such a division is untenable, as it is the character
Beowulf who speaks these words. The poet imbues the characters with
Christian attitudes and ideas, while combining these qualities with traditional heroic values.

989. *no iron...would harm*. By a magic spell Grendel has been made
impervious to weapons.

Fitt 15 Synopsis. The damaged hall is quickly repaired and a great celebration ensues. Hrothgar and his nephew Hrothulf joyfully share in the
drinking cup, and a friendly mood prevails. Then Hrothgar bestows on
Beowulf four precious gifts: a sword, banner, helmet, and a mail-shirt; this is
followed by a further gift of eight horses along with Hrothgar's own saddle.

That bright house was badly broken,
all of it held fast within by iron bands,
its hinges split apart; the roof alone survived
1000 wholly unscathed, when that aglæca,
stained with fyren-deeds, turned in flight,
despairing of life. That is not easy   *i.e., death*
to flee, try it who will!
But forced by necessity, one must seek out
1005 the place prepared for soul-bearers,
for earth-dwellers, for the children of men,
where the body, lying fast on its bed of death,
sleeps after the symbel.
      Then it was due time
that to the hall came Halfdane's son;
1010 the king himself wished to partake in the symbel.
Never have I heard of a people in a greater host
that bore themselves better around their treasure-giver.
They sat then, possessing glory, upon the benches,
they rejoiced in their fill; their kinsmen,
1015 Hrothgar and Hrothulf,
shared courteously in many a mead-cup,
strong-hearted in the high hall. Heorot within
was filled with friends. At that time facen-staves,

1002. *That is not easy.* No one, the poet soberly observes, can escape death, try as one might. The inevitability of death and the transience of all things are recurring themes in Old English poetry.

1008. *sleeps after the symbel.* The poignant image of life as a drinking-banquet (*symbel*), joyous yet brief, occurs elsewhere, most famously in Bede's allegory of the sparrow from his *Ecclesiastical History of the English People* (c. 731). In it the pagan priest Coifi advises King Edwin to accept the new Christian religion: "The present life of man upon earth, O King, seems to me in comparison with that time which is unknown to us like the swift flight of a sparrow through the mead-hall where you sit at supper in winter, with your ealdormen and thanes, while the fire blazes in the midst and the hall is warmed, but the wintry storms of rain or snow are raging abroad. The sparrow, flying in at one door and immediately out at another, whilst he is within, is safe from the wintry tempest, but after a short space of fair weather, he immediately vanishes out of your sight, passing from winter to winter again. So this life of man appears for a little while, but of what is to follow or what went before we know nothing at all."

1018. *facen-staves* (OE *facen-stafas*, "deceit-staves"). A moment of fore-shadowing (again in 1164), like the reference to the future burning of Heorot in lines 82–85. The poet and the original audience alike know

acts of treachery, were not practiced at all by the
People-Scyldings.

1020   Then to Beowulf he gave Halfdane's sword,   *Hrothgar*
a golden standard of victory as a reward,
an ornamented battle-banner, helm, and byrnie.
Many saw the famous mathom-sword
brought before the warrior. Beowulf drank
1025   of the cup in the hall; of those costly gifts
he had no need to be ashamed before warriors.
I have not heard of many men
giving four mathoms in a more friendly manner,
adorned with gold, to another on the ale-bench.
1030   Around the roof of the helmet a ridge on the outside,
wound about with wire, kept guard over the head,
so that the remnants of files, shower-hardened,
would not severely harm him when that shield-warrior
must go against his enemies.
1035   Then the protector of eorls ordered eight horses
with gilded bridles led onto the floor,
in under the enclosures. On one of them was
a saddle decorated with skill, ennobled with treasure;
that was the war-seat of the high king,
1040   when Halfdane's son would engage in
the swordplay — never had his widely-known war-prowess
failed at the front when the slain fell.

---

that the harmony between Hrothgar and his nephew Hrothulf will not
last, undone by a future act of treachery. But that act is now obscure.
Since later tradition has Hrothulf ruling the Danes after Hrothgar, it is
possible that Hrothulf will seize the throne upon Hrothgar's death instead
of allowing it to pass to Hrothgar's son Hrethric. The poem *Widsith*, in
the only other surviving reference to Heorot, remarks that Hrothgar and
Hrothulf "held the longest sibb [peace, kinship] together" (45–49), and
together fought off Ingeld and the Heathobards at Heorot — again hinting
by "longest" that this peace came to an unfortunate end.

   1030–32. The narrative perspective zooms in for a detailed look at the
helmet. The ridge (OE *walu*, wale, ridge; cf. *gunwale*), inlaid with gold
filigree, runs along the top of the crown from front to back, where it
served to deflect blows from swords, here poetically termed "the remnants
of files," which are called "shower-hard" because the swords proved hard
in the rain of blows (or were "hardened" in the storm of battle by being
dipped in the enemy's blood?). A ridged helmet of this description has
been recovered from the Sutton Hoo archeological site.

And then the protector of the Ingwine
  granted Beowulf possession of both
1045 the horses and weapons; he bid him use them well.
  So the mære theoden, the hoard-guardian of hæleths,
  repaid him manfully for the storms of battle
  with horses and mathoms, such that no man could ever
      fault them,
  he who will speak the truth in accord with right.

FITT 16. *The Singer Recites the Story of Finnsburg*

1050 Then further the lord gave to each of the eorls   *Hrothgar*
  who had undertaken the sea-voyage with Beowulf
  a mathom on the mead-bench,
  an heirloom, and ordered
  compensation paid with gold for the one Grendel
1055 had wickedly killed—as he would have done to more
  if wise God and the man's courage
  had not prevented that fate. The Metod ruled
  over all mankind, as he does still.

1043. *the Ingwine*, "the friends of Ing," are the Danes. Ing was a god widely worshiped among the Germanic tribes inhabiting the North Sea coastlands (now Denmark and the Netherlands), called after him the Ingaeovones ("worshippers of Ing"), of which *Ingwine* is likely a corrupted form. Tacitus identified them as one of three tribal groups descended from the three sons of Mannus, son of the god Tuisto, progenitor of all the Germanic peoples. The name Ing was also given to one of the runic symbols; the Old English *Rune Poem* (lines 67–70) describes Ing in cryptic fashion, in a way reminiscent of Scyld Scefing: "Ing was first seen by men among the East-Danes, / Until afterwards he went away again / across the waves, his wagon running after him; / thus warriors named the hero." Fulk, Bjork, and Niles speculate that "from Jutland and Zealand the cult of Ing spread to the other Danish lands, to Skane, and then to Sweden and perhaps Anglo-Saxon England" (Klaeber 4: lviii). A Swedish royal dynasty, the Ynglings (perhaps equivalent to the Scylfings of *Beowulf*), was also said to descend from Ing. Later Norse traditions claim Odin fathered both Ing and Scyld, who then founded the Swedish and Danish royal families, respectively.

Fitt 16 Synopsis. After giving gifts to Beowulf, Hrothgar bestows a treasure on each of Beowulf's men and orders money paid for the Geatish warrior killed by Grendel, a compensation system known as wergild. Then Healgamen, Hrothgar's *scop*, or court singer, recites a tale, which scholars have labeled "the Finnsburh Episode," about a bloody conflict between the Danes and the Frisians.

1057–58. *The Metod ruled / over all mankind, as he does still.* A reminder of the universality of God's providential control over each person's fate. God,

Therefore everywhere understanding is best,

1060 forethought of mind; he must abide much

that is loved and loathed, whoever long here

would enjoy this world in these days of trouble.

There in the presence of Halfdane's battle-leader,

song was joined with music,

1065 the joy-wood touched, a gydd often recited,

when from the mead-bench

Healgamen, Hrothgar's scop, was to speak

of the sons of Finn. When the sudden attack befell them,

the hæleths of the Half-Danes, Hnæf of the Scyldings

1070 was to fall in the Frisian slaughter.

---

the poet insists, was not absent from the lives of the heroes of old. This
comment is part of the poet's repeated efforts to bridge the (pagan) heroic
past with the poet's own Christian culture.

1059–60. *understanding is best, forethought of mind.* This proverb asserts
that humans have some degree of agency and control over their lives, even
if they cannot perceive the divine design of events and must endure the
ups and downs of mortal life. While we lack final control, we nevertheless
have tools at our disposal to help us mitigate the difficulties of life: we can
exercise our understanding (*andgit*) and prepare ourselves for the future
by careful deliberation (*forethanc*). The larger point the poet is making is
this: "God—who has restrained the malevolent monster—reigns over all;
therefore it is best (not to struggle against his providence, but) to accept
one's lot with understanding; and to always be prepared for its course;...
in our lives we experience much of both good and evil" (Klaeber 1911–12: 5).

1065. *joy-wood* (*gomen-wudu*) is a kenning for harp, the wood that causes
joy. Here the scop Healgamen ("Hall-joy") strokes the harp strings to begin
reciting the tale of Finnsburh.

1070. *the Frisian slaughter.* The specific events of the Finnsburg Story
remain fuzzy, and, as with other inset stories, the poet speaks allusively,
clearly expecting his audience to be already familiar with the tale. But thanks
to another surviving Old English text that, though fragmentary, describes
the same events, a plausible reconstruction of the storyline is as follows:
Hildeburh, a Danish princess, has been married off to the Frisian King Finn
in order to end hostilities between the Danes and Frisians (a woman given
in marriage to a hostile tribe in this way is known as a "peace-weaver").
Decades pass, and when Hildeburh's brother Hnæf comes to Friesland
(modern-day Holland) to visit her with a troop of 60 Danes, Hildeburh
now has grown sons. During his visit, Hnæf and his men are attacked while
inside Finn's hall by a combined force of Frisians and Jutes (a people who
inhabited the top of the Danish peninsula). For five days the Danes fight
to defend the hall, until at last Hnæf falls in battle, along with many of
Finn's men—including Finn and Hildeburh's grown sons. Hengest, who has
assumed leadership of the Danes, then makes peace with the Frisians and
Jutes, and the two agree to share a hall (or perhaps share two different halls

Truly Hildeburh had no need to praise
the good faith of the Jutes; guiltless, she was
bereft of loved ones in the shield-play,
of her sons and brothers; they fell to their fate,
1075 wounded by the spear. That was a sorrowful lady!
Not without cause did Hoc's daughter
mourn the Metod's decree after morning came,
when under the shining sky she could see
the baleful killing of her kinsmen, where once she had possessed
1080 the greatest worldly joy. War carried off
all of Finn's thanes except a few only,
so that in that meeting-place he could by no means
fight his war with Hengest to its finish,
or with warfare drive out the survivors of that woe,
1085 the theoden's thane; but they offered them terms,
that they would completely clear another floor for them,
a hall and a high seat, so that they might have
control of half with the sons of the Jutes,
and that at the giving of treasure Folcwalda's son   *Finn*
1090 would honor the Danes each day,
present Hengest's host with rings,
just as much with precious treasure
of plated gold as he would gladden
the cynn of the Frisians in the beer-hall.
1095 Then on the two sides they pledged
a firm wær of peace. Finn to Hengest

---

near one another). Funeral ceremonies ensue, in which the bodies of Hildeburh's grown sons are burned beside her brother Hnæf. Hengest remains
in Friesland through the winter, his thoughts ever on revenge. When one
of his men places a sword on his lap, and two of the Danes begin to openly
speak out against the Frisians, hostilities are renewed. Finn is slain, his hall
is looted, and Hildeburh is taken back to her people. The story likely has
some historical basis, and the legend appears to have been widely known
both in England and throughout northwestern Europe, since the names of
the characters appear in several genealogical lists. Why the tale held such
significance for early medieval people is unclear; some speculate that the
Hengest mentioned in the poem is the same Hengest who, according to
legend, founded the first Anglo-Saxon kingdom in England.

1077. *the Metod's decree* (OE *metod-sceaft*), that is, the time specially
appointed for one's death.

1086. *the other floor for them*. OE *flet* can mean "floor" or "hall." It is unclear
whether both sides are occupying portions of one hall or two different halls.

declared with oaths, boldly and without dispute,
that by the judgment of the counselors he would hold
the survivors of that woe in honor; that no man there
1100 would break the wær with words or deeds,
or ever make mention through cunning malice
that they, lordless, followed the slayer of their ring-giver,
since the necessity was forced upon them.
Then if, with daring speech, any of the Frisians
1105 should continue to call to mind the murderous hostility,
then the edge of the sword would settle it.

A pyre was prepared and icge gold
brought up from the hoard; from the Host-Scyldings
the best of their warriors was ready on the bæl.   *Hnæf*
1110 Upon the pyre it was easy to see
a blood-stained sark, gilded swine,
iron-hard eofor, many an ætheling
destroyed by wounds — more than a few fell in that slaughter!

Then Hildeburh ordered that beside Hnæf's pyre
1115 her own sons be given over to the flame,
their bone-vessels burned, and placed upon the bæl
at the shoulder of their eam. The lady mourned,
lamented with gydds. War-smoke rose,
wound up to the clouds, the greatest of wæl-fires

1097. *without dispute.* OE *unflitme* is an otherwise unrecorded word;
"without dispute" is simply one educated guess among many.

1107. *icge gold.* The meaning of *icge* is unknown.

1109. *bæl,* funeral pyre. These pre-Christian funeral practices reflect a
belief that the spirit is released from the body upon cremation.

1111–12. *blood-stained sark, gilded swine, / iron-hard eofor.* The slain warriors are burned in their armor. A sark (OE *syrce*) is a chain-mail shirt. *Swine*
and *eofor* (boar) both refer to boar-crested helmets. "Boar" often functions
as a poetic shorthand for "helmet." The boar was thought to offer talismanic
protection to its wearer.

1117. *eam,* maternal uncle. Though Frisians, Hildeburh's sons are burned
at the side of their Danish uncle, a poignant image of her loss and conflicted
loyalties.

1118. *War-smoke rose.* The word in the manuscript is *guth-rinc,* "war-man,"
"warrior," but this is most likely a scribal error for *guth-rec,* "war-smoke."
Some have defended "warrior," however, arguing that the warrior's soul is
released by the cremation fire and thus ascends into the air with the smoke.

1119. *wæl-fires,* slaughter-fires, used to burn the slain. The Norse word
Valkyrie ("chooser of the slain") begins with the Old Norse equivalent of *wæl.*

1120 roared before the barrow; heads melted,
wound-gashes, the hateful bites of the body, burst
when blood spurted out. The fire,
greediest of gæsts, swallowed up all there whom war had
    carried off
from both peoples. Their glory had passed away.

FITT 17. *The Finnsburg Story Concludes*

1125 Then the warriors went to seek their dwellings,
bereft of friends, to see Friesland,
their homes and the high burh. Hengest still
remained with Finn that slaughter-stained winter;
he eagerly remembered his homeland,
1130 though on the sea he might not drive
his ring-prowed ship—the sea surged with storms,
strove with wind; winter locked the waves
in icy bonds, until another year came
into men's dwellings, as it does still,
1135 the gloriously bright weather that always
observes its proper seasons. Then winter was gone,
the bearm of earth fair, the exile eager to go,
the guest from the dwellings. He thought more about
revenge for wrongs than the sea journey,
1140 whether he might bring about a grievous meeting,

Fitt 17 Synopsis. The poet continues the tale of Finnsburh: Hengest, the leader of the Danes, remains in Friesland through the winter. When spring arrives and the sea ice melts, he and his men attack and kill Finn, plunder his hall, and sail with Hildeburh back to Daneland. The song ends, and Wealhtheow approaches King Hrothgar, who sits beside his nephew Hrothulf, offering him the cup. She urges him to be generous to the Geats, but sounds a note of concern over Hrothgar's "adoption" of Beowulf. She reminds him to leave the kingdom to his sons and kin, and voices trust that Hrothulf will protect their sons should Hrothgar die before him. Wealhtheow is implying that Hrothulf will not seize power for himself—which suggests that this is exactly what Hrothulf does, although these later events of the story are no longer known.

1129. "Eagerly" is one conjectured meaning of *unhlitme*, a word that occurs only here.

1130. *he might not drive.* Although the word "not" is missing from the manuscript, the line makes little sense without it, and has been added here. It was likely omitted by the scribe while copying the text.

that with iron he might remember the sons of Jutes.
So he did not refuse the world's custom
when Hunlafing placed Battle-leam,
the best of blades, in his bearm—
1145 its edges were known among the Jutes.
That cruel sword-bale also befell Finn in turn,
the bold-hearted man, in his own home,
after Guthlaf and Oslaf spoke of the grim attack,
their sorrow after the sea-journey,
1150 laid blame for their share of woes; the restless heart
could not be held back in the breast. Then the hall was
    reddened
with the lives of foes, Finn slain also,
the king amid his troop, and the queen taken.
Scylding warriors carried to their ships
1155 all the household goods of that earth-king,
whatever they could find at Finn's home
of jewels and wrought gems. On their sea journey
they carried the noblewoman to the Danes,
led her back to her people.

                                        The song was sung,
1160 the gleeman's gydd. Gladness arose once more,
bench-sounds brightened; cup-bearers gave out
wine from wondrous vessels. Then Wealhtheow came forth,
walking under her golden circlet, to where the two good men,
nephew and paternal uncle, were sitting; there was still sibb
    between them,
1165 each was true to the other. There too Unferth the thyle
sat at the feet of the lord of Scyldings; each of them trusted
    his spirit,

1142. *the world's custom* is probably the universal imperative for vengeance.

1160. *gleeman* (*gleo-mann*), "entertainer," "musician," refers to the scop Healgamen.

1164. *there was still sibb between them.* This comment hints at a future conflict between Hrothgar and Hrothulf.

1165. *thyle.* Unferth holds the position of *thyle* in Hrothgar's court, a term which seems to mean "spokesman" or "orator," although some have suggested "jester," "entertainer."

1166. *trusted his spirit* (*ferhth*) is a play on Unferth's name. Unferth's characterization is complex; where other characters are marked out as

that he had great courage, though to his kin he had not
    been
kind in the play of swords. Then the lady of the Scyldings
    spoke:

"Take this cup, my noble lord,
1170 giver of treasure. Be glad,
    gold-friend of men, and to the Geats speak
    with mild words, as a man should do.
    Be gracious to the Geats, mindful of gifts,
    which you now have from near and far.
1175 Someone has said to me you wish
    to have this warrior as a son. Heorot is cleansed,
    the bright bēag-hall; enjoy while you can
    your many rewards, and leave to your kinsmen
    the people and kingdom when you must go forth
1180 to see the Metod's decree. I know my
    gracious Hrothulf, that he will hold the youths
    in honor, if you, the friend of Scyldings,
    should leave this world before him;
    I expect that he will repay our sons
1185 with good if he remembers everything—
    what favors we two did before
    for his joy and honor, when he was a child."

Then she turned to the bench where her boys were,
Hrethric and Hrothmund, and the sons of hæleths,
1190 the youthful warriors all together; there the good man sat,
Beowulf of the Geats, beside the two brothers.

---

either good or evil, Unferth is more ambiguous. He has treacherously killed his own kindred, for which Beowulf declares he will be damned, and he boisterously accosts Beowulf upon the hero's arrival. Yet he seems to hold an important court position and to be admired for his abilities, and it is likely that he played some special role in legend that is no longer known to us.

1180. *to see the Metod's decree.* In other words, when Hrothgar dies (OE *metod-sceaft*).

1186. *what favors we two did before.* Left fatherless at the age of eight, Hrothulf was raised by his uncle Hrothgar, according to later Norse saga accounts. It may be that he usurps the throne at Hrothgar's death. In Norse texts Hrothulf is a much more famous king than Hrothgar.

FITT 18. *Wealhtheow Gives Beowulf a Magnificent*
Neck-Ring

The cup was carried to him and friendship   *Beowulf*
offered with words, and wound gold
bestowed with good will, two armlets,
1195 a garment and rings, the greatest neck-bēag
that I have heard of on earth.
Never under the heavens have I heard of a better
hoard-treasure of hæleths since Hama carried off
the necklace of the Brosings to the bright stronghold,
1200 the jewel and precious cup. He fled the treacherous strife
of Eormenric; he chose eternal counsel.

Fitt 18 Synopsis. Wealhtheow carries the cup to Beowulf and bestows on
him rich gifts of clothing and ornaments. The most remarkable of these is a
neck-ring so magnificent that it recalls the legendary necklace of the Brosings.
Beowulf's neck-ring, the poet explains, will later be worn by King Hygelac
on his disastrous raid into Frisia, where he will be killed and the neck-ring
plundered by the Franks and Frisians. Wealhtheow then gives a speech praising Beowulf and entreating him to treat her sons with kindness. After the
feast ends the men clear away the benches and spread their bedding upon the
floor. They sleep with their weapons beside them to be ever ready for battle.

1195. A *neck-bēag* is a circular neck ornament, such as the Migration
Age golden collar from Färjestaden (Öland), now housed in the Swedish
History Museum.

1199. *the necklace of the Brosings.* In Old Norse legend this was a necklace
fashioned by dwarfs for the goddess Freyja and later stolen by Loki. In the
version of the story alluded to by the *Beowulf* poet, the necklace is apparently
stolen from the King Eormanric of the Goths by Hama, who flees with it
to a stronghold. A version of the story is told in the Old Norse *Thidreksaga*
(c. 1250), in which the warrior Hama (ON Heimir) escapes from the enmity
of King Eormanric (ON Erminrikr) and later enters a monastery (perhaps
the "bright stronghold" mentioned in *Beowulf*, line 1199), carrying with
him weapons and treasure, although no mention is made of the famous
necklace. Little is now known about Hama as he figured in early Germanic
legend. In the OE poem *Widsith* he is mentioned as a companion of Widia
(or Vidigoia), with whom he battled the Huns.

1201a. *Eormenric* was the historical 4th-c. ruler of the Ostrogoths who
battled the invading Huns; in heroic legend, however, he became "the
type for the ferocious, covetous, and treacherous tyrant," renowned for his
fabulous wealth and his excessive cruelty (Klaeber 4: 193).

1201b. *he chose eternal counsel* (*ecne ræd*) likely means that Hama traded
temporal wealth (his treasure) for eternal rewards, especially if the "bright
stronghold" refers to his entering a monastery and converting to Christianity, as this figure does in later Norse saga. The phrase could also imply
Hama died. OE *ræd* means "counsel" as well as "help," "benefit," "gain."

This ring Hygelac of the Geats had,
Swerting's nephew, on his last sith,
when he defended treasure beneath his banner,
1205 protected spoils of slaughter. Wyrd carried him off
when for his pride he sought trouble,
feud with the Frisians. He wore that treasure,
the eorclan-stones, over the cup of the waves,
the powerful lord; he fell beneath his shield.
1210 The king's life then passed into the power of the Franks,
his breast-garments together with the bēag.
Less worthy warriors plundered the slain
after that war-shearing; men of the Geats
occupied the place of corpses.

His neck received the ring.

1215 Wealhtheow matheled; she spoke before the host:

"Enjoy this bēag, beloved Beowulf,
young warrior, with hæl, and make use of this garment,

Hama's choice of eternal gain over temporal treasure sets up a contrast with Hygelac, who loses the neck-ring and his life while on a raid carried out "for pride" (*wlenco*, line 1206). Later in the poem (line 1760) Hrothgar will use the same phrase, warning Beowulf against pride and greed and exhorting him to "choose what is better, eternal gains" (*ecne rædas*), since glory and riches soon pass away.

1207. *feud with the Frisians.* Hygelac's doomed raiding expedition in Frisia c. 525 is one of the few datable events in the poem, recorded in Gregory of Tour's (d. 594) *History of the Franks.* Gregory relates that Hygelac had loaded his ships with plunder and was finishing operations on shore when he was attacked and killed by the Franks, who then recovered all their plundered goods. His legend spread throughout the Germanic world. The *Liber Monstrorum* (c. 650–750) also speaks of his death, as well of his immense stature, claiming that his massive skeleton could still be seen lying on an island in the Rhine.

1208. *eorclan-stones,* precious stones, the neck-ring being inlaid with jewels. *Eorclan-* (also spelled *eorcnan-stan, eorcna-stan*), the inspiration for Tolkien's Arkenstone in *The Hobbit*, ultimately derives from a Proto-Germanic word, *erknaz,* "pure," "holy," "genuine," "precious," which denoted a sacral significance (for example, the equivalent Gothic word *airknis* means "good," "holy"). In Old English homiletic literature *eorcnan-stan* is used figuratively to describe Christ and the Virgin Mary.

1214a. *occupied the place of corpses.* That is, the bodies of the Geats covered the battlefield.

1214b. *His neck received the ring.* "The hall received the sound [of applause]," is another possible rendering of this half-line.

1217. The word *hæl* encompasses a range of divinely bestowed blessings: good fortune, wellbeing, health, and even, in Christian use, salvation.

the people's treasure, and prosper well;
make yourself known by your might, and to these boys
1220 be kind with your counsels. For that I will remember your
        reward.
You have brought it about that far and wide
men will esteem you forever,
just as widely as the sea, home of winds, surrounds
the cliff walls. Be blessed, ætheling,
1225 for as long as you live! I wish you well
of your precious treasures. To my sons
be just in deeds, as you hold joy.
Here every eorl is true to the other,
mild of heart, loyal to his lord;
1230 the thanes are as one, the theod fully prepared;
the men of this dright, having drunk, do as I ask."

She went then to her seat. It was the finest of symbels;
the men drank wine. Wyrd they did not know,
grim fate ordained of old, as it came to pass
1235 for many of the eorls after evening came,
and Hrothgar had departed to his own dwelling,
the powerful one to his rest. Countless warriors
inhabited the hall, just as they had often done before.

They cleared the floor of benches; it was overspread
1240 with beds and bolsters. A certain one of the beer-drinkers,
ready and fated to die, lay down to his floor-rest.
By their heads they set their battle-shields,
their bright wooden boards; there on the bench
above each ætheling it was easy to see
1245 his battle-steep helm, ringed byrnie,
his mighty wooden spear. It was their custom
to be always ready for battle,

1223–24. *the sea . . . surrounds / the cliff walls.* The image is one of a world encircled on all sides by water similar to Old Norse conceptions of Midgard.

1230. *Theod,* nation, tribe, people-group, or here, a troop of warriors. The theod is led by the theoden, the tribal leader. The Modern German word for "German," *Deutsch,* derives from the same etymological root.

1233. *The men drank wine.* Much rarer than beer and ale, wine was enjoyed only on special occasions. The drinking of wine exemplifies how this banquet was "the best of symbels."

both at home and amid the host, and at any time
whatever that their man-lord
had need of them; that was a good troop.

FITT 19. *The Attack of Grendel's Mother*

Then they sank to sleep. One paid sorely
for that evening's rest, as had often happened to them
when Grendel inhabited the gold-hall,
did what was unright, until his end came,
1255 death after sins. It came to be seen,
widely known to men, that an avenger
still lived after that enemy, for a long time
after the grievous strife: Grendel's mother,
a woman, an aglæc-wife, remembered her misery,
1260 [s]he who had to dwell in dreadful waters,
cold streams, after Cain became
a sword-slayer of his only brother,
his paternal kinsman; he then departed, outlawed,
marked by murder to flee the joys of men,
1265 he inhabited the wastes. From him awoke many
of the gæsts fated of old; one of these was Grendel,

Fitt 19 Synopsis. The men fall asleep in Heorot, unaware that another monstrous creature—Grendel's mother—is still alive and is coming to seek revenge for her son. She enters Heorot and snatches a sleeping warrior—later identified as Hrothgar's faithful counselor Æschere—and flees with him, along with Grendel's severed arm, back to her home in the fens. Heartbroken by the news, Hrothgar quickly summons Beowulf, who had been lodged with his troop of Geats elsewhere, and was unaware of the attack.

1259. *aglæc-wife*, fierce female adversary. Old English *wif* has the more general meaning "woman," along with "wife," "female spouse."

1260. *[s]he.* Puzzlingly, Grendel's mother is occasionally designated with male pronouns and demonstratives, here as well as in lines 1392, 1394, and 1497. Either the poet lost sight of the grammatical antecedent or he shifted to masculine pronouns perhaps because he considered her "first and foremost as a deadly warrior, a category that is customarily gendered male" (Klaeber 4: 197). She is also called a "sinful man" in line 1379, unless this is a stray reference to Grendel.

1264. *The gæsts fated of old* (OE *geo-sceaft-gasta*) are the cursed progeny of Cain, such as the elves, eotens, orc-neas, and giants mentioned at the beginning of the poem (lines 106–14). Like that earlier passage, the lines here are intended to explain the origin and nature of the Grendelkin's malevolence. They oppose humans because, in the "Great Feud," they side with the diabolic forces against the divine order. The question of the monsters'

the hateful battle-wearg, who at Heorot found
watchful man awaiting battle.
There the aglæca laid hold of him,   *Grendel*
1270 yet he remembered his mighty strength,   *Beowulf*
the bounteous gift that God had given him,
and he trusted in the Anwalda's favor to him,
his solace and support; by this he overcame the enemy,
laid low the hell-gæst. He then departed humiliated, *Grendel*
1275 deprived of drēam, to seek his death-place,
mankind's foe. And his mother,
greedy and grim-minded, still wished to go upon
a sorrowful sith, to avenge her son's death.

She came then to Heorot, where the Ring-Danes
1280 slept throughout the hall. Immediately there came about
a reversal for eorls, after she entered within,
Grendel's mother. Her gryre was less
by just so much as a maiden's strength,
a woman's war-terror, is compared with an armed man's,
1285 when the bound blade, forged by hammers,
the sword stained with battle-sweat, strong in edges,
cuts through the boar upon a helm.
Then in the hall the hard edge was drawn,
the sword over the seats, many a broad shield
1290 raised firmly in hand; none remembered his helm,

---

free will and individual responsibility is never addressed, probably because
the poet perceives this wider conflict in group rather than individual terms,
in accord with the logic of feud. By this same rationale, Beowulf fights on
the side of God.

1267. *battle-wearg* (*heoru-wearh*), "fierce outcast" or perhaps "savage
wolf"; in Tolkien's expansive translation of the term, "outlawed by hate as
is the deadly wolf" (2014: 49). In OE *wearg/wearh* is an outlawed person,
a criminal, or malignant non-human creature; it may also have had the
sense "wolf," since this meaning is found in the Norse cognate, *vargr*, which
together with OE word is the basis for Tolkien's *warg*.

1272. *Anwalda*. Ruler, one possessing power. The word is used for God
as well as human rulers.

1282. *her gryre was less*. The lines are stating that, just as a woman inspires
less fear than a man, the terror of Grendel's mother's attack was less than her
son's, probably on account of her smaller size, as indicated in lines 1350–53.

1286. *battle-sweat*, blood. OE *swat* can mean blood as well as perspiration,
so *battle-* has been added for clarification. Blood was thought to temper
sword blades, imbuing the metal with enhanced strength.

his broad byrnie, when terror seized them.
She was in haste, wished to depart from there,
to save her life, now that she was discovered.
Quickly she seized one of the æthelings
1295 firm in her grasp, when she departed for the fen.
To Hrothgar he was the most beloved of hæleths
with status of gesith between the seas,
a powerful shield-warrior, whom she destroyed at rest,
a glorious beorn. Beowulf was not there,
1300 but had been assigned another lodging
after the treasure-giving to the renowned Geat.

Outcry arose in Heorot; she had carried off
the widely known hand, covered in gore. Care was renewed,
came again to the dwellings. It was not a good exchange,
1305 that on both sides they had to pay
with the lives of friends.
                                   Then the frōd king,
the hoary warrior, was troubled at heart
once he knew his dearest one was dead,
his aldor-thane no longer living.
1310 Quickly Beowulf was fetched to his bedchamber,
the victory-blessed man. At daybreak
together with his eorls he went, the æthel champion
himself with his gesithas to where the wise one awaited
whether the Alwalda, the All-Ruling one, should ever wish
1315 to bring about a change for him after the woeful tidings.

Then the war-distinguished man walked across the floor
with his hand-troop—the hall-wood resounded—
so that he addressed the wise one with words,
the lord of the Ingwine, asked if for him
1320 the night was agreeable according to his desires.

1297. *status of gesith*, that is, with the rank of troop member. The slain
warrior Æschere is the most beloved member of Hrothgar's troop, or *comitatus*, the body of warriors attached, by personal bonds of loyalty, to a
chieftain or king.

1309. *aldor-thane*, chief thane.

1314. *Alwalda*. The wording in the manuscript is actually *alf walda*, "elf
ruler," but the scribe probably added the *f* by mistake, since "elf ruler" would
be out of place, and inconsistent with the other divine titles. All editions of
the poem emend it to *Alwalda*.

FITT 20. *Hrothgar Tells of Grendel's Mere*

Hrothgar matheled, the helm of Scyldings:

"Do not ask after my happiness! Sorrow is renewed
for the people of the Danes. Æschere is dead,
Yrmenlaf's elder brother,
1325 my run-wita and my ræd-bora—advisor and counselor,
my shoulder-companion when in war
we defended our heads, when foot-troops clashed,
struck eofors. So should an eorl be,
a good-of-old ætheling, just as Æschere was.
1330 His hand-slayer in Heorot was
a wandering wæl-gæst; I do not know where
the horrid one went, proud with her carcass, on the return
        journey,
emboldened by the feast. She avenged the feud
in which last night you killed Grendel,
1335 fiercely, with hard grasps,
because for too long he had diminished and destroyed
my people. He fell in battle,
his life forfeit, and now another has come,
a mighty mān-scather, one who would avenge her kin,
1340 and has carried far her revenge—
as it may seem to many a thane
who weeps in his spirit for his treasure-giver,
a harsh sorrow of heart; now the hand lies low
that had availed you every joy.

1345 I have heard my people, land-dwellers,
hall-counselors, say
that they have seen two such

Fitt 20 Synopsis. This fitt consists entirely of Hrothgar's speech to Beowulf.
After lamenting the loss of his beloved thane and counselor Æschere, Hrothgar
tells Beowulf what he knows about the attacker who has avenged Grendel's
death. Stories have reached him of two monstrous creatures lurking in the
wastelands, one of them male, the other female. They dwell in a desolate and
forbidding land, in a pool that burbles and swirls, and whose depths none
knows. At times strange fire can be seen in the water, and it is avoided by
wholesome creatures. Hrothgar tells Beowulf to seek out the attacker there,
if he dares, and promises to reward him with treasure if he returns victorious.

    1331. *wæl-gæst,* slaughter-spirit, creature of deadly evil; probably with a
pun on *gyst,* "murderous guest."

mighty march-stalkers inhabiting the moors,
ellor-gæsts. One of them was,

1350   as far as they could clearly tell,
a woman's likeness; the other wretched shape
walked the tracks of exile in the form of a man,
except he was larger than any other man.
In days of old, earth-dwellers

1355   named him Grendel; they knew of no father,
whether any mysterious creatures were begotten before him.
They inhabit a hidden land,
wolf-slopes, windy nesses,
a fearful passage through the fen, where a mountain stream

1360   passes down beneath the darkness of the cliffs,
the flood under the earth. It is not far from here
in measure of miles that the mere stands;
over it hang hoar-frosted groves,
fast-rooted woods overshadow the water.

1365   There each night a fearful wonder can be seen —
fire in the flood. There lives none so frōd

1348–49. *march-stalkers .../ ellor-gæsts.* The Grendelkin are labeled *mearc-stapas* — wanderers of the borderlands, in that they roam the edges of human society, as literal outsiders. They do so because they are *ellor-gæstas,* alien spirits, creatures of elsewhere.

1259ff. *a mountain stream / passes down beneath the darkness of the cliffs, / the flood under the earth.* The description seems to be that of "a pool surrounded by cliffs and overhung with trees, a stream descending into it" (Klaeber 182), and with the water flowing down beneath the earth. "Mere" usually means "pool"; because in poetry it can refer as well as to the sea, some have argued that Grendel's Mere is a fjord or inlet of the sea, but this is less likely.

1363. *hoar-frosted groves.* The description of Grendel's Mere closely parallels early medieval depictions of hell. Just as Grendel has a doubled identity, as a creature of flesh and blood as well as a being of metaphysical evil, Grendel's Mere is a physical place while also a representation of hell. This description shares remarkably similar language and imagery to the hell mouth depicted in the *Vision of St. Paul* as it is retold in an Old English homily (*Blickling Homily 17*). In this apocryphal vision of hell, St. Paul sees in the far north a place where all the waters go down, and where a hoary stone stands beside frosty trees and dark mists; there black waters flow beneath the cliffs. The souls of the damned are clinging to the branches of the trees, and as they fall, the nicors below seize hold of them. The detail of frost-covered trees in line 1363, hardly suitable to the context, suggests that this passage has been borrowed. The description of Grendel's Mere may also owe something to portrayal of Lake Avernus in the *Aeneid.*

1366. *fire in the flood.* The mysterious fire seen in the water marks the Mere out as a place of supernatural evil, associated with hell.

among the sons of men that knows its bottom.
Even if a heath-stepper, a hart pressed hard by hounds,
strong in horns, should seek the holt-wood,
1370 driven far in flight, it will sooner give its life,
its spirit on the shore, than it will enter it
to save its head. It is not a pleasant place.
From there churning waves rise up,
dark to the clouds, when wind stirs up
1375 hateful storms, so that the air stifles,
the heavens weep. Now the remedy depends
once more on you alone. You do not yet know that country,
the fearful place where you can find
that sinful man. Seek it if you dare.
1380 For this feud I will reward you with wealth,
treasures of old, as I did earlier
with wound gold, if you should come away."

FITT 21. *The Journey to the Mere*

Beowulf matheled, bearn of Ecgtheow:

"Do not grieve, wise guma. It is better for every man
1385 that he avenge his friend rather than greatly mourn.
Each of us must await the end
of life in this world; let him who can
win dōm before death: that for a warrior is best
after he is no longer living.

1368ff. *heath-stepper, a hart pressed hard by hounds*. Grendel's Mere is a place
of such evil that a stag chased by hounds will die rather than leap into its
foul waters to escape its pursuers. The word "save" (*beorgan*) in line 1372,
missing from the manuscript, has been added for the sake of sense and meter.
  Fitt 21 Synopsis. Beowulf consoles Hrothgar and promises to avenge
Æschere by killing Grendel's mother. Then they both travel with a troop of
warriors through a forbidding landscape until they reach Grendel's Mere, a
pool inhabited by water monsters. A Geatish bowman shoots one of them
and it is dragged ashore, where the men examine it. Beowulf then arms
himself for combat, accepting from Unferth a famous sword called Hrunting.
  1384a. *guma*, man. A word widespread in Old English poetry, it will
fade out by the 15th century, and today it remains only in *bridegroom* (OE
brydeguma, EModE *bridegome*, "man of the bride").
  1384b–89. *It is better for every man / that he avenge his friend . . . that for
a warrior is best / after he is no longer living*. This is the most famous passage in all of *Beowulf*, and for good reason, since it stirringly encapsulates

1390   Arise, guardian of the kingdom, let us quickly go
         examine the track of Grendel's kin.
         This I vow to you: [s]he will not hide away under helm,
         nor in earth's fæthm, nor in mountain forest,
         nor at the bottom of the sea, go where [s]he will!
1395   This day have patience
         in all of your woe, as I expect of you."

         Then the gamol one leapt up, thanked God,   *Hrothgar*
         the mighty Drighten, for what the man had said.
         A horse was then bridled for Hrothgar,
1400   a steed with wound mane. The wise fengel
         rode richly arrayed; the band of shield-bearers
         marched on foot. Along the forest paths
         the tracks were widely visible,
         where she had gone over the ground,
1405   made her way across the murky moor
         bearing along, soul-bereft, the best of mago-thanes,
         who with Hrothgar had defended their home.

         Then the son of æthelings traversed   *Hrothgar*
         steep stone hliths, narrow tracks,

---

the heroic code. But it is all too often quoted as evidence of a submerged
paganism lurking beneath a layer of superficial Christianity, since these
lines appear to reject an afterlife and promote violent revenge. The most
widely-read translation, by Seamus Heaney, creates exactly this impres-
sion by adding words not found in the Old English, transforming these
lines into an outright denial of heavenly rewards: "Let whoever can / win
glory before death. When a warrior is gone, / that will be his best and *only*
bulwark." But the passage is making no such claim, nor is it promoting
indiscriminate violence. Beowulf is simply stating a truism: taking action
to right wrongs is better than sitting passively complaining about them. It
is important to remember that, in the tribal society of the early Germanic
world depicted in the poem, "the feud was not regarded as an expression
of personal grudge or an outlet for uncontrolled violence, but rather an
obligation owed to society, as a means of maintaining law and order" (D.
H. Green 63–64). Since the Grendelkin are unwilling to settle the feud
through wergild, the system of compensation through money payment,
force is the only means of seeking justice and restoring order.

   1391, 1394. *[s]he.* The pronouns for Grendel's mother are grammatically
masculine.

   1400. *fengel,* prince, ruler. A word found only in *Beowulf,* where it occurs
four times.

   1406. *mago-thanes,* warriors, young thanes (*mago/magu,* son, young man).

   1409. *hliths,* slopes, cliffs.

1410   straitened footpaths—an unknown way—
        sheer nesses, a great many nicor-dwellings;
        he went ahead with a certain few
        men of wisdom to examine the land,
        until suddenly he found mountain trees
1415   leaning over hoary stone,
        a joyless wood; water stood below,
        turbid and bloody. For all the Danes,
        friends of the Scyldings, for many a thane,
        it was painful for their hearts to endure,
1420   a grief to each of the eorls when on the holm-cliff
        they came upon the head of Æschere.
        The flood boiled with blood—the folk stared—
        with hot gore. The horn sang out time and again,
        a ready war-song. The foot-troop all sat.
1425   In the water they saw many of the wyrm-cynn,
        strange sea-dracas exploring the water,
        nicors, too, lying on the ness slopes,
        such as those that in the morning time often attend
        a sorrowful journey on the sail-road,
1430   wyrms and wild beasts. Away they fell,
        bitter and enraged; they heard the sound,
        the war-horn singing. With an arrow from his bow
        a man of the Geats sundered a certain one from life,
        from its wave-struggle, so that in its vitals there stood
1435   a hard battle-dart; in the holm it was
        slower at swimming for that, when death carried it away.
        Speedily it was beset hard on the waves
        with cruelly barbed boar-pikes,
        violently assailed and dragged onto the ness,

   1421. *the head of Æschere.* The poet delays revealing the source of the
Danes' distress for three lines, building suspense. When the reader finally
encounters Æschere's severed head at the end of the sentence, the shock it
creates mirrors that of the Danes.
   1425–57. *wyrm-cynn, / strange sea-dracas ... nicors.* Sea-serpents and sea-
monsters. *Wyrm-cynn* and *sea-draca* refer to the same creature—a serpentine sea beast. A different kind of monster, nicors are creatures of evil that
inhabit the water and are especially malevolent toward humans. Their
shape—whether human or animal-like—is unclear.
   1429. *sail-road* is a kenning for "sea." The notion is that these sea monsters
often prey on passing ships.

1440 the wondrous wave-roamer; the men gazed upon
   the grisly guest.
         Beowulf readied himself
   with warriors' armor, he worried not at all for his life;
   his war-byrnie, woven by hand,
   broad and cunningly wrought, was to try the water;
1445 it knew how to defend his bone-house,
   so that the battle's grip could not harm his breast,
   the foe's evil grasp scathe his life;
   but the white helm protected his head,
   which was to mingle with the mere-bottom,
1450 seek the surging water, made worthy by treasure,
   encircled with lordly bands, just as in ancient days
   the weapon-smith wrought it, wondrously formed it,
   set it about with swine-shapes, so that afterward
   no brand or battle-blade could bite it.
1455 By no means was it the least of aids to his strength
   that Hrothgar's thyle then lent him in his need: *Unferth*
   the name of that hafted blade was Hrunting—
   it was preeminent among treasures of old;
   the edge was iron, gleaming with poison-twigs,
1460 hardened with the blood of battle; never had it failed in war
   for any who had wound his hands around it,

1441. *grisly guest.* OE *gyst/gist*, stranger, visitor, guest. The idea underlying the word *gyst* is of an unfamiliar person, an outsider, whether threatening or welcome. It derives from Proto-Indo-European *ghosti-*, "someone with whom one has reciprocal duties of hospitality. In practical terms it refers to strangers in general, as well as to both *guests* and *hosts* (both words are descended from it)" (Watkins 31).

1445. *It knew how to defend his bone-house.* Armor and weapons are frequently personified, depicted as though they had a power and agency of their own; indeed, swords are commonly given names. Such practices reflect the central place of weapons in early European society, and the centrality of warrior identity. *Bone-house* (*ban-cofa*) is a poetic phrase meaning "body."

1454. *brand* (also spelled *brond*): sword, sword-blade. The word can also mean "flame."

1457. *hafted blade* (*hæftmece*), hilted sword (*hæft*, haft, handle, or hilt).

1459. *gleaming with poison-twigs* (*attortanum fah*): "An obscure phrase which has been variously explained as perhaps referring to the patterning on a sword-blade, or to the acids used in its fashioning, or, perhaps figuratively, to the injurious effect of the ornamented sword, as sure as poison" (*Dictionary of Old English*).

who had dared to go upon gryre-siths, fearful journeys
into the dwelling place of foes; it was not the first time
that it must carry out a work of courage.

1465 Truly, the son of Ecglaf did not remember,   *Unferth*
crafty in strength, what he had spoken before,
drunk with wine, when he lent that weapon
to the better sword-warrior; he himself did not dare
to risk his life beneath the tumult of waves,

1470 to perform drightship; there he lost dōm,
renown for courage. For the other it was not so,
after he had readied himself for battle.

FITT 22. *Beowulf's Fight with Grendel's Mother*

Beowulf matheled, bearn of Ecgtheow:

"Consider now, renowned kinsman of Halfdane,
1475 wise fengel, now that I am ready for the sith,
gold-friend of men, what we two spoke of before,
that if ever in your service I should
lose my life, you would always be
in the place of a father for me when I have gone forth.

1480 Be a mund-bora—protector—to my young thanes,
my close companions, if battle takes me;
also, beloved Hrothgar, send to Hygelac
the treasures which you have given me.
Then the lord of Geats may perceive from the gold,

1485 the son of Hrethel will see, when he looks upon
that treasure,

1470. *perform drightship* (*dryhtscipe*), carry out heroic action, perform a
lordly or courageous deed.

Fitt 22 Synopsis. After some parting words to Hrothgar, Beowulf dives
into the mere. Some time passes; as soon as he reaches the bottom he
is spied by Grendel's mother, who quickly seizes him and carries him off
to her lair while water-monsters assail him from every side. When they
reach her lair, a hall-like cavern that is protected from the water, Beowulf
strikes her with the sword Hrunting but it fails to injure her. He tosses
the sword away and instead uses his strength to hurl Grendel's mother
to the ground. When she springs back up, snatching at him, he stumbles
and she holds him down while drawing out a long knife. She strikes him
with the blade but his mailshirt protects him. With God's help, Beowulf
once more rises to his feet.

that I found a ring-giver, one good in the virtues of a man,
that I enjoyed these while I could.
And let Unferth have the old heirloom,
the widely known man have my wrætlic wave-sword,
1490   hard of edge; for myself with Hrunting
I shall win dōm, or death will take me."

After these words the man of the Weder-Geats
hastened boldly, he would not wait
for any answer; the surging water received
1495   the warrior. Then it was a day's while
before he could perceive the bottom.
Soon she who had inhabited the flood's expanse   *Grendel's*
for one hundred half-years, bloodthirsty,   *mother*
grim and greedy, discovered that some man
1500   from above was exploring the æl-wights' abode.
She grasped at him then, seized the warrior
in her terrible grip; yet not for that did she harm
the sound body: the ring-mail outside surrounded him,
so that she could not pierce the war-garment,
1505   the linked limb-shirt with her loathsome fingers.

When she reached the bottom, the brim-wolf
carried the ring-thengel to her abode,
so that he could not, no matter how courageous,
wield his weapons, for such a multitude of wonders

1486. *one good in the virtues of a man.* OE *gum-cyst,* "manly excellence," carries the sense of one outstanding in the qualities of men, above all generosity.

1491. *I shall win dōm, or death will take me.* It is noteworthy that although Beowulf enters boldly into each monster fight, he never boasts that he will win. Instead he vows to achieve glory (*dōm gewyrce*) or die in the attempt, entrusting the ultimate outcome to God. The courage, not the outcome, is what matters most, since the outcome is ultimately outside of his control.

1495. *a day's while.* The phrase *hwil dæges* likely means "a good part of the day"—in other words, the mere is so deep that it takes hours to reach the bottom. But some argue these words signify instead "a brief space of time," which might explain how Beowulf does not run out of breath. More likely, however, the mythical dimension of the monster fight has overshadowed concerns for realistic description: Beowulf must descend into an underworld-like realm to face primordial enemies.

1500. *æl-wights' abode* (OE *æl-wiht*), the dwelling of alien creatures, monsters.

1510   assailed him in the sea, many a sea-beast
       broke upon his battle-shirt with war-tusks,
       afflicted the aglæca. Then the eorl perceived
       that he was in some kind of hostile hall,
       where the water could not harm him at all,
1515   nor, on account of the roofed hall, could it reach him,
       the flood's sudden grasp; he saw firelight,
       a brilliant leam brightly shining.
       Then the good one saw the wearg of the deep,
       the mighty mere-wife; he gave a great thrust
1520   with his battle-blade — his hand did not withhold the blow,
       so that the ringed sword sang out upon her head
       a greedy war-song. Then the guest found   *Beowulf*
       that the battle-leam would not bite,
       harm her life, but its edge failed
1525   the theoden in his need; it had endured many
       hand-meetings before, often sheared through a helm,
       a fæge man's war-garment; that was the first time
       for the dear treasure that its dōm failed.

       Once again he was resolute, not slow of courage,
1530   the kinsman of Hygelac mindful of mærth:
       he threw away the wound-sword, bound with wrætt,
       the angry warrior, so it lay upon the earth,
       stiff and steel-edged; he trusted his strength,
       the might of his hand-grip: so should a man do
1535   when in war he intends to gain
       lasting lof, enduring praise; he cares nothing for his life.
       The man of the Gūth-Geats then seized Grendel's mother
       by the shoulder — by no means did he mourn that feud.

1513. *hostile hall* (OE *nith-sele*). As soon as Beowulf reaches the bottom of the mere, he is seized by Grendel's mother and dragged through an underwater entrance into an above-water cavern where she dwells, in which a fire is burning. *Beowulf* draws from a folktale type, shared by other surviving stories such as the Old Norse Grettis saga (c. 1300), in which a hero dives through water to reach a hidden cave and there defeats a troll. In the Grettis saga the troll's cave is located behind a waterfall.

1518. *the wearg of the deep*. Grendel's mother is an outcast, an accursed dweller of deep waters.

1537–38. *seized Grendel's mother / by the shoulder*. It is possible that in the original text the hero seizes her by the *feaxe*, hair, rather than by the *eaxle*,

Then, swollen with rage, the battle-hardy man flung
1540   his life's enemy so that she fell to the floor.
     She quickly repaid him in turn
     with her grim grip and grasped at him;
     then, weary-hearted, the strongest of warriors stumbled,
     so that he, the foot-warrior, fell.
1545   She then set upon the hall-guest, and drew out her seax,
     broad and brūn-edged; she wished to avenge her bearn,
     her only offspring. On his shoulder lay
     the woven breast-net; that defended his life,
     withstood entry against point and edge.
1550   The son of Ecgtheow would have then perished
     beneath the vast ground, the champion of Geats,
     had not his battle-byrnie offered help,
     his hard war-net, and holy God
     wielded war-victory; the wise Drighten,
1555   the Rædend of the heavens, rightly decided it,
     easily, once he stood up again.

FITT 23. *Beowulf's Victory*

Then he saw among the war-gear a victory-blessed blade,

---

shoulder, and that the scribe made a copying error. While less heroic, hair-pulling might make more logistical sense in this context, and would also alliterate with the other OE words in this line. Anglo-Saxon law assigned a punishment for the insult of *feaxfeng*, hair-pulling.

1545. *seax*. A multipurpose, single-edged knife, typically about 12 inches in length. Strapped to the waist, the seax could be used for everyday tasks as well as in warfare. The tribal name Saxon derives from this word. In his fight with the dragon, Beowulf will use his seax when his sword shatters.

1546. *brūn-edged*. Like many Old English color terms, *brūn* can refer to reflectivity as well as to hue, so that here it likely means "burnished" rather than "dark brown."

1555. *Rædend*, the Ruler. Just as with his triumph over Grendel, the hero's victory is attributed, through double determination, to both natural and supernatural causes: Beowulf is saved both by his mail-shirt and by God.

Fitt 23 Synopsis. Beowulf spies a giant sword and uses it to kill Grendel's mother, decapitating her. A light suddenly shines forth, seemingly from the sword, and in the bright light he is able to explore the underwater hall. He finds Grendel's corpse and beheads it. Meanwhile, the Danes and Geats waiting above for Beowulf see the water turn bloody and believe Beowulf has been killed; the Danes depart while Beowulf's men continue to wait for him, but without hope. Down below, the blade of the gigantic sword

an ancient eotenish sword, strong in edges,
the glory of warriors; it was the finest of weapons,
1560 except it was larger than any other man
could bear into the play of battle,
good and well-adorned, the work of giants.
He seized the fetel-hilt, the fighter of the Scyldings;   *Beowulf*
fierce and battle-grim, he drew the ringed sword.
1565 Despairing of life, he angrily struck
so that it gripped hard against her neck,
broke the bone-rings; the blade went all the way through
the doomed flesh-covering; she fell to the floor.
The sword was bloody; the man rejoiced in his work.

1570 A leam shone, light glowed within,
just as heaven's candle shines brightly
from the sky. He looked around the hall;
then he went along the wall, raised the weapon
hard by the hilt, Hygelac's thane,
1575 angry and resolute—its edge was not useless
to the warrior, for he wished to quickly
repay Grendel for the many storms of battle
he had wrought upon the West-Danes,
much more often than on one occasion,

---

melts away as a result of Grendel's poisonous blood, leaving only the hilt.
Carrying the hilt and Grendel's head, Beowulf swims back up through the
mere and greets his men; together they march back to Heorot, bearing
Grendel's head in triumph.

1558. *ancient eotenish sword*. When his blade proves useless against
Grendel's mother—who like Grendel is magically protected from ordinary
weapons—Beowulf seizes a weapon from her own dwelling. A massive,
eotenish sword (made by or used by eotens), is said to be the work of giants
(*giganta geweorc*) and, later in the text, the work of ents and of "wonder-
smiths." Rather than aiming at precision, the narrator is emphasizing the
sword's mythical origins, massive size, and magical properties.

1563. *fetel-hilt*, perhaps a ringed or linked hilt. The precise meaning of
fetel is uncertain. Rings were affixed to the early medieval sword hilts for
both practical and ornamental purposes. Several Anglo-Saxon swords with
this design have been recovered by archaeologists.

1570. *a leam shone*. At the death of Grendel's mother a light immediately
shines forth, apparently from the sword blade. Whatever its source, the
sudden light flooding the cave is a physical manifestation of the cleansing
of evil, like the heavenly light that appears in hagiography following the
saint's struggle against demons.

1580 when he slew Hrothgar's hearth-companions
in their slumber, devoured while they slept
fifteen men of the Danish folk,
and carried off as many others—
a loathsome plunder. He paid him back for that,
1585 the fierce champion, when he saw
Grendel lying at rest, battle-weary,
lifeless, as the fight at Heorot
had injured him earlier. The corpse sprang wide apart,
when after death it suffered a blow,
1590 a hard sword-stroke—and he cut off his head.

Soon the wise cheorls,
those who were watching the water with Hrothgar,
saw that the surging waves were all mingled,
the brim stained with blood. Gray-haired,
1595 gamol, together they spoke about the good man,
that they did not expect the ætheling again,
that he would come, exulting in victory, to seek
their mære theoden; many agreed then in thinking
that the brim-wolf had destroyed him.
1600 Then came the ninth hour of the day. The brave Scyldings
abandoned the cliff. The gold-friend of men
set out from there for home. The visitors sat,   *the Geats*
sick at heart, and stared into the mere;
they wished, but did not expect, that they would
1605 see their beloved lord himself.

Then the sword,
the war-blade, began to dwindle into battle-icicles
on account of the war-blood—it was a wondrous thing,

1599. *brim-wolf*, the wolf of the sea (OE *brim*), that is, Grendel's mother.
    1600. *The ninth hour* is 3 pm. As Howell Chickering notes, "This is an almost unavoidable echo. It is the same hour that Christ, abandoned by all but a faithful few, died on the Cross (see Luke 23:44–46). This detail and others have led critics to see a parallel between this episode and Christ's death, the Harrowing of Hell, and the Resurrection" (338). The poet clearly saw theological resonances in the traditional materials he used, and sensitively drew them out, adding details such as this. In the subsequent lines, Beowulf's men will wait, like the disconsolate disciples after Christ's death, "sick at heart," wishing but not expecting "that they would see / their beloved lord himself" (1604–5).

that it melted away just like ice
when the Father loosens the bonds of frost,
1610 unwinds the water's fetters, he who wields power
over times and seasons; he is the true Metod.

The man of the Weder-Geats took no more treasures
from that dwelling place, though he saw many there,
only the head together with the hilt,
1615 shining with jewels; the sword had melted,
the patterned blade had burned away—so hot was the
blood,
so venomous the ellor-gæst who had died within.
Soon he was swimming; he who in strife had endured
the fall of enemies in war dove up through the water.
1620 The surging waves were completely cleansed,
the vast regions, after the ellor-gæst
relinquished the days of her life and this loaned world.

Then the helm of seafarers came to land,
the strong-hearted one swimming; he rejoiced in his
sea-plunder,
1625 the mighty burden he had with him.
They went to meet him then, thanked God,
the powerful band of thanes rejoiced in their theoden,
that they were able to see him safe and sound again.
Then from the vigorous man helm and byrnie
1630 were quickly loosed. The lake grew still,
the water under the wolcens, stained with slaughter-gore.
They went forth from there by footpaths
with glad hearts, they measured out the earth-way,
the familiar road. Bold as kings, the men

1611. *he is the true Metod.* It is God, not evil forces (or pagan deities), who
controls the created order and the elemental forces of the world. Though
unseen, God's power is evident through its effects—including the defeat
of Grendel and his mother.

1517. *ellor-gæst,* alien spirit.

1620. *the surging waves were completely cleansed.* Each monster fight is
also an exorcism: the hall Heorot, Grendel's Mere, and later the dragon's
barrow are each purged of evil as a result of the hero's victory. Here, the
turbulent surface of the Mere will grow calm as a physical sign of its spiritual cleansing.

1631. *wolcens* (OE *wolcen,* cloud); in the plural, clouds, sky, "welkin."

1635 bore the head from the holm-cliff—
with difficulty for each pair
of the great-hearted men. It took four
to carry Grendel's head to the gold-hall
with great pains upon a slaughter-stake,
1640 until at last to the hall they came
walking, fourteen bold, warlike
Geats. Their lord, their great-hearted
man-drighten, walked in their midst across the mead-plain.

Then in came the aldor of thanes,   *Beowulf*
1645 daring in deeds, exalted in dōm,
the battle-brave hæleth, to greet Hrothgar.
Grendel's head was carried by the hair
into the hall where men were drinking,
terrible to the warriors and the woman with them,
1650 a wondrous sight. The men stared.

FITT 24. *The Giant Hilt*
···

Beowulf matheled, bearn of Ecgtheow:

"Hwæt, this sea-plunder, son of Halfdane,
man of the Scyldings, we have gladly brought you
as a token of glory, which you look upon here.
1655 Scarcely did I survive it with my life
by warfare under the water, ventured the deed
with difficulty. The battle would have
ended at once if God had not shielded me.
With Hrunting I could do nothing
1660 in the fight, though the weapon is good;
but the Waldend of men granted me
that I should see a beautiful sword hanging on the wall,
ancient and immense — often he has guided

Fitt 24 Synopsis. Beowulf presents the head and hilt to Hrothgar, and
Hrothgar, gazing upon the remarkable hilt, inscribed with runes and the
story of the Great Flood, gives a long speech, conventionally known as
"Hrothgar's Sermon." He warns Beowulf against pride and covetousness
and contrasts him with Heremod, a malicious king.

1663. *ancient and immense.* The massive sword is termed an *eald-sweord
eacen*. More than merely "large in size," *eacen* signifies "endowed with

the friendless man—so that I drew the weapon.
1665 In that strife, when the chance came, I struck down
the guardians of the house. Then the battle-bill,
the braid-patterned blade, burned away as the blood
    sprang out,
the hottest sweat of battle. From there I carried away
the hilt from my foes, I avenged their fyren-deeds,
1670 the deadly slaughter of Danes, as was fitting.
Now I promise you that in Heorot you may
sleep without sorrow among your troop of men,
and every thane of your people,
the duguth and youth; for them you need not dread,
1675 lord of Scyldings, any mortal harm to your men
from that quarter, as you did before."

Then the golden hilt was given into the hand
of the hoary battle-leader, the aged warrior.
The ancient work of ents, it passed into the possession
1680 of the lord of Danes after the fall of demons,
a work of wonder-smiths; and when the cruel-hearted man,
God's adversary, gave up this world,
guilty of murder, and his mother too,
it passed into the power of the best
1685 of world-kings between the seas,
of those who shared out sceatts on Sceden-isle.

Hrothgar matheled; he gazed upon the hilt,

---

an added power" and possessing a "supernormal power" (Tolkien 2014:
306, 302).
    1669. *fyren-deeds*, wicked or criminal deeds.
    1679. *ancient work of ents*. Unlike the troll-like eotens such as Grendel
who exist within the world of the poem, the ents are a vanished giant race
of master builders. To them is attributed anything ancient, impressively
constructed, or intricately devised, whether it be ancient ruins or enormous swords. Unlike the eotens and the biblical gigantas, the ents are
not portrayed as creatures of evil. Occasionally the poet does blur these
various giant creatures together, however, since part of his aim is to graft
Germanic legend onto the Biblical narrative.
    1686. *sceatts on Sceden-isle*. The sense is, "of all kings who give out treasure
(*sceattas*, silver coins) in the central region of Scandinavia."
    1687. *he gazed upon the hilt*. The following eleven lines describing the
hilt have inspired a small mountain of scholarship. Exactly what the hilt

the old heirloom. On it was engraved the origin
of the ancient strife, when the flood slew
1690   the race of giants, the rushing sea—
they fared terribly. That was a people alien
to the eternal Drighten; he gave them their final reward for
    that,
the Waldend, through the surging water.
On the sword-guard of shining gold
1695   it was also rightly marked out with rune-staves,
set down and said, for whom the sword
had first been made, the finest of irons,
with its wreathed-hilt and wyrm-patterning. Then the wise
son of Halfdane spoke; all fell silent:

---

portrays, the role of writing and literacy it implies, the Patristic and Biblical lore involved, as well as the thematic role this scene plays within the poem as a whole—all of these remain topics of considerable debate. What is apparent is that the hilt is an emblem of the continual rebellion of created beings against their Creator. Thus while gazing upon the hilt Hrothgar will deliver his so-called sermon, warning Beowulf against pride and overreach.

1688–89. *On it was engraved the origin / of the ancient strife.* It is not clear whether this phrasing refers to the Flood itself or an earlier event, such as the fall of angels, that eventually resulted in the Great Deluge. (It is also debated whether OE *writen* means "carved [pictorially]" or "written [in letters]," since *writan* originally meant "to cut.") In any case, the poet's focus is on the origins of evil and the primordial antagonism to God—in Cain and the biblical *gigantes* mentioned in Genesis and in extrabiblical literature. The poem is connecting this earlier rebellion and the divine retribution to the battles with Grendel and his mother. The battles with the Grendelkin are thus a continuation of the "Great Feud" with God that began long ago. Tolkien goes so far as to speculate that there was once a Germanic flood myth that was later merged with the biblical story (2014: 305).

1695. *rune-staves.* Beside the depiction of the Great Flood, the hilt also states the name of the owner. Such inscribed weapons have in fact been discovered, such as the Thames Scramasax, giving the owner's name in runic letters. The runic alphabet or "Futhorc" is distantly related to the Roman alphabet; it was in use in the Germanic-speaking world as early as 100 BC, but was employed only for short inscriptions that could be cut into wood, bone, metal, and later stone.

1698. *wyrm-patterning (wyrm-fah).* Either a reference to the serpent shapes that adorn many early medieval artifacts, or an allusion to the serpentine patterning of the sword blade that resulted from "pattern-welding"—heating a bundle of iron rods together and pounding them into a single blade in order to improve its strength.

1700   "Lā, this may he say, he who practices truth and right
       among his people, who remembers everything from far back,
       an old ethel-weard — that this eorl was
       born the better man! Your renown is raised up
       throughout the wide ways, my friend Beowulf,
1705 over every people. You hold all of it with patience,
       strength with wisdom of heart. To you I shall
       fulfill my friendship, as we spoke at first. You shall
       prove a long-lasting comfort to your people,
       a help to hæleths.

Not so proved Heremod

1700–84. *Hrothgar's "Sermon."* This long sermon-like speech stands at the midpoint of the poem and serves as its moral and philosophical center. Yet these 84 lines are considerably more homiletic in tone and style than the rest of the poem, and the "sermon" does nothing to further the plot — in fact, the entire speech could be deleted without any loss to the storyline. For these reasons, some scholars have regarded some or all of Hrothgar's sermon as an interpolation by a later writer. While the interpolation theory has fewer adherents today, it is true that this passage sounds less like Hrothgar speaking than a Christian homilist (Tolkien noted that "it is too 'Christian' in coloring" to sound convincingly like a Germanic king [2014: 308]). Nevertheless the sermon contributes ideas and themes that deepen the heroic narrative, and the poem would be much diminished without it. It allows for a philosophical and moral assessment of the heroic tradition itself, as represented by the young Beowulf who, fresh from his victory over the Grendelkin, is at the height of his heroic prowess. The message of the sermon is that heroic action and kingship must serve the greater good. When powerful men like Heremod become self-seeking, this leads to violence, avarice, and isolation, with communal dissolution the ultimate result. When power is oriented outward, however, toward the wider community, it serves as a force for stability and peace.

The Sermon consists of four main sections: (1) praise for Beowulf's accomplishments and character (1700–9); (2) the negative example of King Heremod, whose cruelty and greed serve as a warning for Beowulf (1709–24); (3) reflections and moral teachings (1724–68); (4) the application of these themes to Hrothgar's own life (1769–84).

1700. *Lā.* An interjection signaling the start of Hrothgar's speech. "Indeed," "lo!"

1705–6. *patience, / strength with wisdom of heart.* Hrothgar begins the speech by praising Beowulf for his well-earned renown, strength, and wisdom, all of which will redound to the benefit of his people. In R. E. Kaske's influential interpretation, the pairing of wisdom with strength (*sapientia et fortitudo*) is the primary theme of the poem, and "the poet used this old ideal as an area of synthesis between Christianity and Germanic paganism" (273).

1709–24. *The negative example of Heremod.* As the poet discusses earlier (lines 901–15), it was the disastrous rule of King Heremod that resulted in the desperate plight of the Danish people, and thus he is the opposite of "a

1710 to the sons of Ecgwela, to the Honor-Scyldings;
he grew not to their delight but to their destruction,
and to the deadly slaughter of the people of the Danes.
Swollen with rage, he cut down his table-companions,
his shoulder-fellows, until he passed alone,
1715 the mære theoden, from the joys of men.
Though mighty God raised him up in power,
in the joys of strength, established him
above all men, yet in his spirit
the breast-hoard grew bloodthirsty; no bēags did he give
1720 to the Danes for dōm; he endured drēamless,
so that he suffered pain for that strife,
long-lasting leod-bale. Learn from this,
understand gumcyst, manly virtue. This gydd
I have spoken, wise in winters, for your sake.

It is a wonder to say
1725 how to mankind mighty God
in his vast spirit shares out wisdom,
land, and eorlship; he has power over all.
At times he allows the mind of a man
of mære cynn to turn to his desire,
1730 gives him earthly joy in his ethel,
a stronghold of men to hold.
He thus makes portions of the world his to rule,
a vast realm, so that he himself
in his unwisdom cannot imagine its end.
1735 He dwells in plenty; nothing hinders him at all,

---

long-lasting comfort to your people," as Beowulf is predicted to be. Like the young Beowulf, Heremod showed early promise, but "wickedness entered him" (915) and he became a type of the miserly, vengeful king. His calamitous demise results in *leod-bale* (*leodbealo*), lasting harm to his people, the Danes.

1721. *he suffered pain for that strife, / long lasting leod-bale.* That is, "he suffered the eternal pains of hell," according to Klaeber's interpretation.

1724. *It is a wonder to say.* The third section of the "sermon" moves from the specific example of Heremod to a more general lesson, illustrating how a situation such as Heremod's comes about. It begins with a reflection on the mystery of God's distribution of His gifts among human beings, a recurrent theme in Old English poetry. God is depicted as a treasure-giving ruler, dispensing gifts of wisdom, rank, and land. The passage warns against the danger of forgetting that power wielded by rulers is a gift bestowed by God.

1730. *ethel,* home, native land.

not illness or age, neither do evil sorrows
darken his spirit, nor does strife, sword-hate
appear anywhere, but all the world
wends to his will; he does not know the worse."

FITT 25. *Hrothgar Concludes His Speech*
....

1740   "And then within him a portion of pride
grows and spreads, while the guardian slumbers,
the soul's shepherd; the sleep is too deep,
bound with cares, the slayer very close at hand,
who wickedly shoots from his bow.

1745   Then under the helm he is struck in the heart
with a bitter arrow—he cannot protect himself—
with the crooked, mysterious biddings of the accursed spirit;
what he has long held seems to him too little,
he grows greedy, grim-minded, gives no

1750   plated bēags in pride; he forgets his future destiny,
and disregards his share of honors,
that which God, the Waldend of glory, has given him.
In the end it happens in turn
that his fleeting flesh-covering fails,

1739. *wends to his will.* Bends or turns to his desire—in other words,
everything goes his way (OE *wendan*, to turn).

Fitt 25 Synopsis. Hrothgar's "Sermon" continues. He warns Beowulf
against covetousness and reminds him of the transitory nature of this
life. Beowulf and the Geats prepare to depart.

1740. *pride.* Old English has a more expansive vocabulary for pride than
Modern English, and the connotations are more varied. The term used
here, *oferhygd*, can mean "arrogance," as it does in this context, and also
in line 1760, where Hrothgar warns Beowulf against this vice. The fall of
the angels from heaven is said, in another OE poem, to result from *oferhygd*. But the word can occasionally be used in a positive sense, as "high
spirits," "honorable pride."

1741–42. *the guardian . . . / the soul's shepherd* is the man's conscience,
which has grown dull and thus "slumbers," making him vulnerable to the
Devil's attacks.

1743. *the slayer.* The Devil, who shoots fiery darts of envy.

1754. *fleeting flesh-covering* (*lǽne lic-hama*). The discourse now shifts to
the mutability of life on earth, where all things are transitory (*lǽne*) and
final stability is found only in eternity (*ece rǽdas*, eternal gains). This transience theme is a prominent one in Old English poetry, most memorably
expressed in the *The Wanderer*, an elegiac poem that meditates on personal
loss and social dislocation. *Beowulf*, however, is a heroic narrative, not a

1755 death-fated, it falls; another takes possession,
     one who gives out mathoms ungrudgingly,
     the eorl's ancient treasure, heeds no terror.

     Guard against that deadly affliction, beloved Beowulf,
     best of men, and choose what is better:
1760 eternal gains. Give no heed to pride,
     renowned fighter. Now is the flowering of your might
     only for a while. Soon it will be
     that sickness or sword-edge deprives you of strength,
     or the fire's grip, or the flood's surge,
1765 or the sword's grasp, or the spear's flight,
     or terrible old age, or the eyes' brightness
     will fail and darken; all at once it will be
     that death will overpower you, dright-guma.
     Just so for a hundred half-years I ruled the Ring-Danes
1770 under the skies, and by warfare protected them
     from many mægths throughout this middangeard,
     with ash and edge, so that I counted no one
     under the sky's expanse my enemy.

---

lament poem, and it is striking that this passage occurs in the context of Beowulf's triumphs, not at a moment of loss. The effect of its placement, then, is to inquire into the meaning of heroic achievement, viewing feats such as Beowulf's *sub specie aeternitatis*, and in this way revealing the limitation of heroic action and all human works. In Tolkien's words, the poem is "rehandling in a new perspective an ancient theme: that man, each man and all men, and all their works shall die," for "all glory... ends in night." This is not to say that Beowulf's victories are futile—as God's agent he has redeemed Heorot from the forces of evil—but rather that since all human achievement will come to an end, it cannot be an end in itself, but only a means to a greater end. All human *dōm*, glory, is finally subject to God's *dōm*, his judgment and eternal decree.

1762–68. The discourse now moves through a litany of the likely ways that Beowulf's life will come to an end: whether it be through war, disaster, disease, or simply old age, death is inevitable. Remembering this truth will help the hero to guard against pride and to generously give out goods.

1768. *dright-guma* (*dryht-guma*), warrior, a man of the dright, or war-band.

1769–81. For the final section of the sermon, Hrothgar draws a lesson from his own life: one's situation can abruptly shift through a reversal of fortune (*edwenden*, "turning-about," 1774). Earthly power is limited, subject to forces beyond human control, and one should be spiritually and psychologically prepared for abrupt changes. This passage may show the influence of Boethius's *Consolation of Philosophy*.

1772. *with ash and edge*, by means of ash(-spear) and (sword-)edge.

Hwæt, a reversal came to me in my own homeland,
1775 grief after gladness, when Grendel,
      the old adversary, became my invader.
      For that incursion I continually bore
      great anguish of mind. Thanks be to the Metod for this,
      the eternal Drighten, that in my life I have lived to see it
1780 so that, after the old strife, I stare with my eyes
      upon his battle-bloodied head.
      Go now to your seat, enjoy the feast-joys,
      war-honored one; between us a great many
      mathoms shall be shared when morning comes."

1785 The Geat was glad-hearted; he went forth at once
      to seek out his seat, as the wise one bid him.
      Then it was again as before for the ellen-bold men;
      for those seated along the floor a feast was finely prepared
      for this new occasion. Night's helm deepened,
1790 grew dark over the dright of men. The duguth all arose;
      the gray-haired one wished to seek his bed,   *Hrothgar*
      the aged Scylding. The Geat desired immeasurably,
      the bold shield-warrior, to rest.
      Weary from his sith, having come from afar,
1795 he was quickly led along by a hall-thane,
      who out of courtesy attended to all
      the thane's needs, such as in those days
      seafaring warriors should have.

      Then the great-hearted one rested. The hall stood high,
1800 vaulted and gleaming with gold; the guest slept within,
      until the black raven, blithe-hearted,
      announced heaven's joy. Then came the bright [light],
      hurrying [over the shadows]; the scathers hastened,
      the æthelings were eager to return
1805 to their people. The bold-spirited visitor wished
      to seek his ship far from there.
      Then the hardy man bid Hrunting be brought
      to the son of Ecglaf, bid him take his sword,

1802–3. *the bright [light], / hurrying [over the shadows].* The scribe copying
the manuscript appears to have omitted a half-line; the text in brackets is
a plausible conjecture based on the sense and alliteration of the passage.

the lovely iron. He told him thanks for that loan,
1810 said he reckoned the battle-friend good,
strong in war, in no way with his words did he fault
the sword's edge; that was a noble-minded man.
And then, eager to depart, the warriors
were ready in their war-gear; he went,
1815 the ætheling honored by Danes, to the high-seat where the
other was.
The battle-bold hæleth greeted Hrothgar.

FITT 26. *Beowulf Prepares to Depart*
....

Beowulf matheled, bearn of Ecgtheow:

"Now we seafarers, come from afar,
wish to say that we are setting out
1820 to seek Hygelac. Here we were hosted rightly,
just as we might wish. You treated us well.
If then on earth I might obtain
any more of your heart's love
than I have already done, drighten of men,
1825 with my battle-deeds, I will be ready at once.
If from across the flood's expanse I hear
that neighboring peoples threaten you with terror,
as at times enemies have done to you,
I will bring a thousand thanes,
1830 hæleths as a help. I know of Hygelac,
the drighten of Geats, though he is young,
the shepherd of the people, that he will support me
with words and deeds, that I might honor you well,
and bring to your aid a gar-holt, a forest of spears,
1835 the support of might, where you have need of men.
Then if to the halls of the Geats Hrethric,

Fitt 26 Synopsis. Beowulf takes his leave of Hrothgar, promising future help and renewed friendship between the Danes and Geats. Hrothgar praises Beowulf for his courage, wisdom, and diplomacy. He gives Beowulf further treasures and tearfully embraces him.

1832. *the shepherd of the people.* Epithets for rulers tend to depict them in terms of service to their people: as shelter, refuge, protector, and, here, shepherd (OE *hyrde,* keeper, herdsman).

1836. *Hrethric.* In an act of tactful diplomacy, Beowulf invites Hrothgar's

the theoden's bearn, determines to go,
he may find many friends there. Far countries
are better sought by one who is himself worthy."

1840   Hrothgar matheled to him in answer:

"The wise Drighten sent those words
into your heart; I have never heard
a man so young in age arrange matters more wisely.
You are strong in might and frōd of mind,
1845   wise with words. I think it likely
if it happens that the spear takes
Hrethel's offspring, sword-grim battle,
illness or iron your aldor,
the shepherd of your people, and you have your life,
1850   that the Sea-Geats would have no better
king to choose,
a hoard-weard of hæleths, if you wish to rule
the realm of your kinsmen. Your mōd-sefa
pleases me better the longer known, beloved Beowulf.
1855   You have brought it about that between these peoples,
men of the Geats and Gar-Danes,
there shall be shared sibb, and strife shall rest,
the hateful enmities which they endured before;
as long as I rule this wide realm

---

eldest son Hrethric (the likely successor to the Danish throne) to visit the
Geatish court, in order to further strengthen the newly restored alliance
between Danes and Geats.

1843. *arrange matters.* The verb *thingian* means to make arrangements
or settlements, or, as here, to conduct diplomacy. It derives from the noun
thing, a formal meeting or judicial assembly where such actions would
take place.

1844–45. *You are strong in might and frōd of mind, / wise with words.* As
strong, wise, and fluent in speech, Beowulf is an ideal figure. Friedrich
Klaeber sees in this portrait an image of the righteous pagan: "the old
Danish king praises Beowulf as being perfect in every respect—thought,
word, and deed—from a Christian perspective, with some adaptation to
the heroic ideal, of course" (35).

1857–58. *there shall be shared sibb, and strife shall rest, / the hateful enmi-
ties which they endured before.* The nature of this earlier conflict between
Geats and Danes is never explained. A hint can be gleaned from Saxo
Grammaticus's remark that the son of Skiold (Scyld) conquered the Götar
(Geats). Perhaps the Geats were once tributaries to the Danes but had
broken this arrangement.

1860 mathoms shall be shared, many a man
      shall greet the other with goods across the gannet's bath;
      over the sea the ringed ship shall bring
      gift-offerings and tokens of love. I know these peoples
      are made fast, toward both foes and friends,
1865 blameless in every way in the manner of old."

      Then within the hall, Halfdane's son, the refuge of eorls,
      gave him twelve further treasures,
      he bid him seek out his own people
      in safety with those gifts, and to return swiftly again.
1870 Then the king, good in ancestry,
      the theoden of Scyldings, kissed the best of thanes
      and took him by the neck; tears fell from him,
      the gray-haired one. Old and exceedingly frōd,
      he had two expectations, but one was stronger than the
          other:
1875 that they would not see each other again,
      the brave-hearted ones in methel. So beloved was the man
          to him
      that he could not hold back the breast-surges,
      but in his heart, fast in the bonds of thought,
      hidden longing for the dear man
1880 burned in his blood. From him Beowulf,
      the gold-proud battle-warrior, walked across the grassy
          ground,
      exulting in treasure. The sea-goer awaited
      its lord and owner, rode at anchor.
      Then along the way Hrothgar's gift was
1885 often praised; that was a peerless king,
      blameless in all things, until old age took from him
      the joys of strength, that which has often injured many.

    1861. *gannet's bath*. A kenning for the sea, the place where the gannet, a large white seabird, swims.

    1872. *tears fell from him*. Hrothgar's overpowering emotions at Beowulf's departure may strike readers as puzzling; it helps to understand them as a father's final goodbye to his (adopted) son. For the poet, Hrothgar also represents an image of heroic strength reduced by old age; in this the king stands in contrast to Beowulf, now at the height of his powers, who marches off to a long heroic career while the king remains passively behind — a poignant illustration of the transience theme of Hrothgar's sermon.

FITT 27. *The Geats Sail Home*

The men of great courage then came to the flood,
the young band bearing ring-nets,
1890 linked limb-shirts. The land-weard spied   *the coast guard*
the eorls' return, as he had before.
He did not greet the guests with insults
from the hlith's cape, but he rode toward them,
1895 he said that the raiders in shining raiment went to their
           ship
welcome to the people of the Weders.
Then on the sand the sea-vaulted ship
was loaded with battle-garments, the ring-prowed vessel
with mares and mathoms; the mast stood high
over Hrothgar's hoard-treasures.
1900 To the boat-weard he gave a sword   *Beowulf*
bound with gold, so that afterwards
he was worthier on the mead-bench for that mathom,
the old heirloom. The ship went forth
stirring up the deep water, it left the land of Danes.

1905 By the mast was then a certain sea-garment,
a sail, made fast by rope; the sea-wood resounded;
by no means did the wind hinder the wave-floater
from its voyage over the ythes; the sea-goer went forth,
it floated, foamy-necked, over the wave,
1910 the bound prow across the brim-streams
until they could make out the Geats' cliffs,
the well-known nesses; the ship surged up,
driven by wind, it stood on the land.

Fitt 27 Synopsis. The Geats return to their boat, and a precious sword
is given to the coast guard they had encountered previously. They cross
the sea and are met by the Geatish harbor-guard, and then make their way
to King Hygelac's great hall. The poet praises the generosity of Hygelac's
young wife Hygd; he contrasts Hygd with the cruel queen Modthryth.

1900. *To the boat-weard he gave a sword*. The many passages devoted
to gift-giving reveal the importance of this practice. More than a kind
of payment for services rendered, gifts are a means of establishing social
bonds; the gift is a tangible sign of the relationship. They are also a crucial
means of establishing peace. To put the matter more starkly: gifts are
exchanged so that violence won't have to be.

At the sea the hythe-weard was ready at once,   *the harbor-guard*
1915 he who for a long while at the shore
had eagerly watched from afar for the beloved men.
He moored the wide-fæthmed ship in the sand,
fast with anchor-bands lest the force of the waves
should drive away the winsome wood.

1920 He then bid the athelings' treasure borne up,   *Beowulf*
their war-gear and plated gold. From there it was not far
    for them
to seek their treasure-giver,
Hygelac Hrethling, where he dwells at home,
he himself with his gesithas near the sea-wall.
1925 The building was splendid, the king lordly and brave,
high in his hall, Hygd very young,
wise, well-accomplished, though few winters
had she passed within the walled stronghold,
Hæreth's daughter; yet she was not miserly
1930 or grudging with gifts to the people of the Geats,
with mathom-treasures.

                    Modthryth carried out
terrible crimes, the excellent people's queen.
No bold one of her own company,

1923. *where he dwells at home.* The narration shifts abruptly to present tense, either for metrical reasons or to heighten the immediacy of the narrative.

1926. *Hygd* is Hrothgar's young wife. Her name means "thought." (Women's names are frequently formed from abstract nouns.) Despite her youth, Hygd is presented as an exemplary queen; she is wise and, most importantly, generous with gifts. She stands in contrast with Queen Modthryth.

1931–62. *The Modthryth digression.* Though a difficult and highly debated passage, the Modthryth episode is clearly intended to create a contrast with the portrait of good Queen Hygd. Unlike the wise and treasure-giving Geatish queen, Modthryth is cruel and vengeful, but later has a change of heart after she is married to King Offa of the Angles. Perhaps the story is a "taming of the shrew" tale, although the episode is too cryptic and allusive for us to be sure. Even the name of the queen is uncertain, since Germanic names are formed from common nouns and proper names are not capitalized by scribes. Is it Modthryth (possibly meaning "arrogance"), Thryth ("strength"), or perhaps Fremu ("benefit")? Several medieval Latin texts tell of a King Offa married to a cruel queen with a name resembling "Thryth," though the significance of this resemblance has recently been called into question.

except her great lord, dared venture
1935   to look upon her with his eyes by day,
but she could count him ordained for deadly bonds,
twisted by hand; swiftly afterward,
after the hand-grasp, a blade was appointed,
so that the patterned sword must settle it,
1940   make known the baleful killing. Such is not a queenly custom
for a woman to perform, though she be peerless,
that a peace-weaver should deprive
a beloved man of life for a feigned injury.
Yet Hemming's mæg put a stop to that:
1945   ale-drinkers said further,
that she wrought fewer wrongs upon the people,
evil afflictions, after she was first
given, decked in gold, to the young champion,
excellent in ancestries, when she sought the journey
1950   over the fallow flood at her father's instruction,
to Offa's hall. Afterwards there
on the throne, renowned for goodness,
she used well the life fate allotted while she lived,
held a high love toward the ruler of hæleths,
1955   the best of all mankind, as I have heard,
between the two seas
of the eormen-cynn. Therefore Offa,

1934. *her great lord* (*sin-frea*). A reference to her father, rather than her husband.

1940. *Such is not a queenly custom.* The story of a beautiful but haughty princess who condemns to death any man who looks upon her face is a recurrent folktale motif.

1942. *peace-weaver* (*freothu-webbe*). The term is usually read as "peace-bride," a woman married to another tribal group in order to end a conflict.

1944. *Hemming's mæg* (kinsman) is Offa, who becomes the husband of Modthryth.

1951. *Offa* was a legendary king of the Angles (occupying what is now northern Germany), whose reign is usually placed in the 4th century; his exploits are celebrated by Saxo Grammaticus, in the Old English poem *Widsith*, and in several other medieval texts. The ruling dynasty in Mercia, in Anglo-Saxon England, claimed descent from his line, and an 8th-century king (Offa II) was named after the legendary king. It was common in earlier scholarship to claim that *Beowulf*, or the Modthryth episode, was written to flatter Offa II, but there is little evidence for this.

1957. *the eormen-cynn*, "the immense race," is the human race, which is spread throughout the vast earth.

the spear-bold man, in gifts and in battles
was honored far and wide, ruled with wisdom
1960 his own homeland; from him awoke Eomer
as a help to hæleths, Hemming's mæg,
nephew of Garmund, skilled in violence.

FITT 28. *Beowulf Greets King Hygelac*

Then the hardy man went with his hand-troop
along the sand, treading the sea-plain,
1965 the wide warths. The world's candle shone,
the sun eager from the south. They undertook the journey,
went boldly to where they heard the refuge of eorls,
the slayer of Ongentheow, was inside the stronghold,
the good young war-king,
1970 sharing out rings. To Hygelac
Beowulf's journey was quickly made known,
that there in the outer enclosure the refuge of warriors,
of shield-companions, had come walking, alive,
unharmed to the hall from the play of battle.
1975 Quickly, as the mighty one commanded,
the floor inside was cleared for the foot-guests.
Then he himself sat with the one who had survived that strife,
mæg with mæg, after the man-drighten
had greeted the faithful man with ceremonious speech,
1980 with meagol words. With mead-cups
Hæreth's daughter passed throughout   *Hygd*
    the hall-building,
cared lovingly for the people. She bore cups of drink
to the hands of hæleths. Hygelac began

Fitt 28 Synopsis. King Hygelac greets Beowulf warmly and inquires about his expedition. Beowulf tells of his victories and speaks of Hrothgar's daughter Freawaru; she is betrothed to Ingeld, son of Froda, the ruler of the Danes' enemies, the Heathobards, in an attempt to create peace between the two warring peoples.

1965. *warths* (OE *waroth*), shores, beaches.

1980. *meagol*, firm, earnest, strong, hearty. Hygelac's concerns are heart-felt; his questions are not a mere show of courtesy, but represent his deep concern for his nephew.

1983. *hæleths.* The word in the manuscript is actually *hæthnum*, "heathens," but passing cups "into the hands of heathens" makes little sense in the context and is surely an error for *hælethum*.

to question his companion with fair words
1985 in the high hall, his curiosity broke him,
as to what the siths of the Sea-Geats had been:

"How did your journey befall you, beloved Beowulf,
after you resolved suddenly
to seek strife far away across the salt water,
1990 battle at Heorot? And for Hrothgar,
the mære theoden, have you at all remedied
his widely known woe? For you
I seethed with cares of heart, surging sorrows, distrusted
    the sith
of my beloved man. Long I entreated
1995 you not to go near the deadly gæst at all,
to let the South-Danes themselves settle
their war with Grendel. I give thanks to God
that I might see you safe."

Beowulf matheled, bearn of Ecgtheow:

2000 "It is no secret, lord Hygelac,
that meeting renowned among many men,
what time of trial arose for me and Grendel
in the place where he had wrought so many
sorrows upon the Victory-Scyldings,
2005 unending miseries. I avenged all that,
so that none of Grendel's kinsmen need boast,
not any on earth, of that uproar at dawn,
whoever lives longest of that loathsome cynn,
enveloped in evil. There I came first
2010 to the ring-hall to greet Hrothgar;
at once the renowned son of Halfdane,
when he knew my mind,
assigned me a seat opposite his own sons.

1993. *I seethed with cares of heart, surging sorrows.* The chest, the seat of
emotional and mental activity, is portrayed as a container of liquid that is
heated and cooled, an image of the mind known as the "hydraulic model."
Longing, anxiety, and even love heat this container, resulting in seething
and boiling. Anger results in swelling (in his battles Beowulf becomes
ge-bolgen, rage-swollen, "bulging" with anger). The decrease of feelings
results in cooling. Ingeld's love for his wife is said to "grow cooler," for
example, after conflict arises with her people (2066).

The troop was in joy; never in all my life have I seen,
2015   under the vault of heaven, among hall-sitters
greater mead-drēam. At times the mære queen,
the peace-pledge of peoples, passed along the floor,
urged her young sons on, often gave a wreathed ring
to a warrior before she went to her seat.
2020   At times before the duguth Hrothgar's daughter
bore ale-cups, from end to end, to eorls,
whom I heard hall-sitters name Freawaru,
where she gave out studded treasure
to hæleths. She is promised,
2025   young, adorned with gold, to the glad son of Froda.   *Ingeld*
The friend of Scyldings, the shepherd of the realm,   *Hrothgar*
has agreed upon this, and accounts it good counsel,
that with this woman he might settle their share of deadly
    feuds,
hostilities. It is true that seldom anywhere
2030   after the fall of a people does the slaying-spear rest

---

2016. *mead-drēam* (OE *medu-drēam*), the joy of the mead-hall, the communal festivity associated with the *symbel*.

2022–69. *The Freawaru and Ingeld episode.* Here begins the fifth major inset episode. Ingeld, son of Froda, the king of the Heathobards, is betrothed to Hrothgar's daughter Freawaru. The purpose of this marriage is to secure peace between these two antagonistic groups. Beowulf predicts that the peace will not last, however, and that violence will again erupt as soon as Danes come to the Heathobard court wearing the weapons of slain Heathobard warriors. As with other inset episodes, the poet's reason for inserting this largely unrelated story is far from clear. The simplest explanation is that the Ingeld legend was known and loved by audiences (as Alcuin's angry letter about monks listening to tales of Ingeld instead of scripture makes apparent), and the hero Beowulf's description of the Danish court provided a natural point at which to insert it. These legends had value for Anglo-Saxons not merely for their story value, but because Ingeld and other legendary figures were their heroic ancestors; the names of Ingeld, Scyld, Heremod, Offa, Finn, and Hengest all appear in royal genealogical lists. Interweaving the story of Beowulf with other famous Germanic hero-stories would also allow the poet to elevate the lesser-known Beowulf to the pantheon of Germanic legend. Or, if Beowulf was a hero invented by the poet in order to have a blank slate on which to create an especially virtuous hero, linking this new hero to the most famous figures of Germanic legend would serve as an effective means of renovating the heroic tradition as a whole, which appears to be the poet's driving aim.

2030. *after the fall of a people.* The wedding of Freawru and Ingeld takes place after the Heathobards have been defeated by the Danes, in the hopes

but for a little while, though the bride be good.
It may then displease the lord of Heathobards
and every thane of that people
when one walks with that fæmne, the young virgin, upon
    the floor,
2035 a lordly son of Danes, splendidly attended;
on him glisten the heirlooms of their elders,
the hard, ring-patterned treasures that had belonged to
    Heathobards
while they were able to wield those weapons—"

FITTS 29–30. *Beowulf Speaks of the Heathobard Conflict
and His Two Fights*

....

"—until in the shield-play they led
2040 their close companions and their own lives to destruction.

---

of preventing further outbreaks of fighting. Although *Beowulf* does not
tell the larger story, the history of the Dane-Heathobard conflict can be
reconstructed thanks to references to it in Latin, Norse, and Old English
sources. Froda, the famed king of the Heathobards and father of Ingeld,
has been slain in a longstanding conflict with the Danes, which Tolkien
speculates was a war over control of Zealand and its political-cultic center
of Lethra (modern day Lejre), the holy site at which Hrothgar builds the
great hall Heorot: "Just as the story of Hoc and Hnæf and Hengest reflects
the incursion of Danes into Jutland and the peninsula, the Heathobard
story depicts their seizure of Seeland, the center of that world and the seat
of its cult [at Lethra]" (2014: 331). In any event, the peace between Danes
and Heathobards does not last. Following the wedding of Freawaru and
Ingeld, hostilities break out once more and Ingeld attacks Heorot, but is
defeated and killed by Hrothgar and Hrothulf. In the fighting the great
hall Heorot burns to the ground. A later version of the Ingeld legend is
told by Saxo Grammaticus, in which it is Ingeld (Ingellus) himself who
at the wedding feast is shamed for making peace with the slayers of his
kin and incited to take immediate bloody revenge.

    2033. *the Heathobards* (OE *heatho-beardan*, war-beards), a Germanic peo-
ple who inhabited the southern coast of the Baltic Sea, in what is now
northern Germany. They were perhaps related to the Lombards (Longo-
bardi), who had migrated to the south. They were destroyed or absorbed
into another people group during the Migration Age, so that little is now
known of them.

    2034. *fæmne*, virgin, maiden, young or unmarried woman. *Fæmne*, used
to translate Latin *virgo*, is the Old English term used for the Virgin Mary.

    Fitts 29–30 Synopsis. Beowulf speaks further of the proposed marriage,
predicting that it will end in bloodshed when some man of the Danes
who accompanies Feawaru to the Heathobards' hall is seen wearing the
weapons and ornaments of slain Heathobards. Beowulf then resumes the

Then at beer one will say, he who sees a bēag,
an old ash-warrior who remembers all,
the gar-killing of men—his spirit is grim—
he will begin, sad in mōd, to test the mind
2045 of a young fighter with the thought in his breast,
to awaken war-bale, and will speak this word:

'Can you, my friend, recognize that sword,
which your father carried to the fight
under his war-mask on his final journey,
2050 that dear iron, where the Danes slew him,
ruled the place of slaughter, when Withergyld lay dead,
after the fall of hæleths, the fierce Scyldings?
Now here the son of a certain of his slayers
walks upon this floor, exulting in his frætwa,
2055 boasts of the murder and bears the mathom
which you by right should possess.'

So on every occasion he urges and reminds him
with painful words, until the time comes
that, for his father's deeds, the fæmne's thane
2060 sleeps, blood-stained, after the blade's bite,
his life forfeit; from there the other man
escapes alive, he knows the land well.

---

narrative of his fights with Grendel and Grendel's Mother, which includes several details not mentioned previously by the poet. (Because of an error in fitt-number of the *Beowulf* manuscript, this section has been numbered as Fitts 29–30 to fix the problem.)

2043. *gar-killing*, spear-killing, the carnage of battle.

2044–45. *his spirit is grim . . . / he will begin, sad in mōd, to test the mind / . . . with the thought in his breast*. In Old English poetry the seat of emotions and of mental activity is not the head, but the chest cavity, hence "the thought in his breast." For this reason mental processes are not clearly distinguished from feelings of emotion, and as a result the vocabulary for heart/mind blurs together, as this passage shows. Here an old warrior, who is grim in *sefa* (mind, heart, spirit) and sad in *mōd* (mind, spirit, heart—also pride, courage, temper) begins to test the *hige* (mind, heart, soul) of a young warrior with the *gehygd* (thought) that is located inside his *hrethor* (breast, heart). (A related term, *ferhth*, meaning "mind," "spirit," "heart," does not occur in this passage.)

2051. *the place of slaughter* is the battlefield, which the Danes "rule" by winning the battle.

2054. *frætwa*, precious gear. The word can apply to both weapons and treasure, since the poem does not sharply delineate between them.

Then broken on both sides
are the sworn oaths of eorls; afterwards in Ingeld
2065   the deadly hostilities will seethe and his wife-love
will grow cooler, after those surging sorrows.
Therefore I do not consider the Heathobards' loyalty,
their part in the truce with Danes, to be without deceit,
nor their friendship fast.

                              I will speak further
2070   about Grendel, so that you may know for certain,
giver of treasure, as to what afterwards came to pass
in that hand-fight of hæleths:
                              After heaven's gem
had gone gliding over the ground, the angry gæst came,
terrible, evening-fierce, to seek us out
2075   where we, unharmed, inhabited the hall.
There the fight was fatal for Hondscioh,
deadly to the life of the fæge one; he was the first to fall,
the girded champion; Grendel became
the mouth-slayer of that mære young thane—
2080   he swallowed the entire body of the beloved man.
Yet no sooner for that would the slayer,
bloody-toothed, bent on evil,
go from the gold-hall empty-handed;
but he, strong of might, made a trial of me,
2085   grasped me with an eager hand. His glove hung,
broad and strange, fastened with cunning clasps;
it was all ingeniously devised
with the devil's craft and dragon fells.
The bold doer of evil deeds meant
2090   to put me, guiltless, inside it,

2069–70. *I will speak further / about Grendel.* The hero's narration of the
two monster fights seems somewhat redundant, but his retelling does
include several details lacking from the poet's earlier account: the name of
the slain warrior, Handscioh; Grendel's strange "glove"; and the scene of
Hrothgar's poetic performance.

2085. *His glove.* The details and context suggest that OE *glof* had the
meaning "pouch," alongside its ordinary sense of "glove." Whether bag or
glove, Grendel's *glof* is a wondrous, occult artifact, having been constructed
though the powers of the devil and formed out of the hides (*fells*) of dragons,
which may lend it further magical properties.

one of many; it could not be so
after I stood up in anger.
It is too long to recount how I repaid
that ravager of the people with his reward for every wrong;
2095 there, my theoden, I brought honor to your people
by my works. He escaped on his way,
possessed the joys of life a little while;
yet his right hand guarded his track
in Heorot, and he went from there humiliated,
2100 sad-minded, to the mere-bottom he fell.
The friend of Scyldings requited me
for the deadly combat with much plated gold,
with many mathoms when morning came
and we had sat down at the feast.
2105 There was song and joy; the aged Scylding,   *Hrothgar*
learned in many things, recounted from far back;
at times the battle-bold one touched the harp's joy,
the gomen-wood; at times he recited a gydd,
true and painful, at times a sellic spell
2110 that great-hearted king recounted rightly;
at times he began again, bound with age,
the old gūth-warrior, to lament his youth,
his battle-strength; his breast surged within him
when he, wise in winters, called to mind a great many things.

2115 So there all the day long within
we took our pleasure, until another night came
to men. Then swiftly in her turn
Grendel's mother was ready to avenge her griefs.
She journeyed full of sorrow; death had carried off her son,
2120 the war-hate of the Weders; the monstrous woman
avenged her bearn, boldly killed a warrior;
there the life departed from Æschere,
the frōd fyrn-wita—the wise old counselor.
Nor when morning came could the people of the Danes

2098. *his right hand guarded his track*, i.e., his hand remained behind.
2105. *There was song and joy.* Drawing upon a trove of stories and experiences, King Hrothgar recites poetic compositions to the harp, termed here the *harp's joy* and *gomen-wood*, the wood of mirth. The songs range in genre from elegies to tales of wonder (*sellic spell*, a wondrous story).

2125 burn him, death-weary, with fire,
      load him upon the pyre,
      the beloved man; she had carried his body away
      in her fiend's embrace beneath the mountain stream.
      For Hrothgar that was the most grievous of sorrows,
2130 of those which had long come upon the leader of the people.
      Then the theoden implored me by your life,
      troubled in mind, that in the tumult of the waters
      I should carry out eorlship, venture my life,
      achieve mærth; he promised me meed.

2135 Then I found, as is widely known, in the welling waters
      the guardian of the deep, gryreful and grim.
      There for a time it was hand to hand for the two of us;
      the holm surged with gore, and I cut off the head
      of Grendel's mother in that war-hall
2140 with the edges of an immense sword. Scarcely from there
      did I carry away my life; I was not then fæge,
      but the refuge of eorls, Halfdane's son,
      gave me a great many mathoms once again."

FITT 31. *Beowulf Becomes King*

      "So the people's king lived in accord with customs;
2145 in no way did I lose my reward,
      my might's meed, for he gave me mathoms,
      Halfdane's son, at my own choosing.
      These I wish to bring to you, warrior-king,

2134. *meed* (OE *mēd*), reward, or "meed" in archaic English (not to be confused with *mead*, the alcoholic drink!).

2141. *I was not then fæge.* This word (from which we get *fey*, "otherworldly," "marked by foreboding") originates in the belief that each person has an appointed time of death. But used casually here, it means no more than "it wasn't my time," or "my number wasn't up."

Fitt 31 Synopsis. Beowulf presents his lord Hygelac with the gifts he received from Hrothgar, and Hygelac in turn bestows on him wealth and lands; in the years that follow Hygelac and his son Heardred both die and Beowulf assumes the throne of the Geats. He has ruled for fifty years when a dragon is awakened.

2148. *These I wish to bring to you.* In yet another scene of gift-giving, Beowulf now presents to Hygelac treasures given to him by Hrothgar. As a tangible sign of one's honor, gifts of treasure provide a means of transferring honor to another, so that Hygelac can partake, in a manner, in

to present them with good will. On you
2150　all favors still depend; I have few
head-kinsmen apart from you, Hygelac."

He then bid a boar's head banner carried in,
a battle-tall helm, a gray byrnie,
a decorated war-sword; afterwards he uttered this gydd:

2155　"Hrothgar gave me this war-gear,
the wise fengel; he bid that I should first
speak a few words to you of his good will —
he said that King Heorogar had possessed it,
the leader of Scyldings, for a long while;
2160　no sooner for that would he give it to his son,
the breast-garment to bold Heoroweard,
though he was loyal to him. Use it all well!"

I have heard that four horses, each alike,
apple-fallow, swiftly followed that frætwe;
2165　he bestowed on him the gift
of mares and mathoms. So should a mæg do,
in no way weave nets of malice for another
with secret craft, prepare death
for his hand-companion. To Hygelac,
2170　hardy in hostilities, his nephew was most loyal,
and each was mindful of the other's benefits.
I heard he gave to Hygd the neck-ring,
the wrætlic wonder-mathom, that Wealhtheow had given
　　　him,

Beowulf's victory over Grendel. We can assume that the cycle will continue as Hygelac recirculates these gifts among his men for their deeds
of courage. Treasure only becomes problematic when it is hoarded (as by
the dragon) rather than given away.

　2151. *head-kinsmen*, close kindred, near relatives.

　2169–70. *To Hygelac, /... his nephew was most loyal.* An implied contrast
with those disloyal kinsmen who *do* in fact weave malicious nets and plot
the death of another—probably a reference to the treachery of Hrothulf.

　2173. *the wrætlic wonder-mathom.* This neck-ring, which Hygelac will wear
on his ill-fated raid in Frisia, is now labeled with the intriguingly elusive
word *wrætlic*. Translators usually settle for "wondrous," but "mysterious,"
"strange," "unique" are closer to the mark. Objects and animals marked as
wrætlic are riddle-like things that seem to belong to another, almost tran-
scendent order of existence.

the theoden's daughter, together with three horses,
2175 supple and saddle-bright; then was
her breast ennobled, after receiving that bēag.

So Ecgtheow's bearn proved bold,
a man well-known for battles, for good deeds;
he acted in accord with dōm, in no way slew drunken
2180 hearth-companions; his spirit was not harsh,
but with the greatest strength of mankind
he, brave in battle, guarded the ample gift which God had
    given him.
Long had he been lowly,
so that the sons of Geats did not account him good,
2185 nor had the lord Weders wished to put him
in possession of much on the mead-bench;
they thought rather that he was slack,
an unbold ætheling. Reversal came
to the glory-blessed man for all his troubles.

2190 Then the refuge of eorls, the battle-brave king, bid
Hrethel's gold-adorned heirloom fetched in;
among the Geats there was not then
a finer treasure in the form of a sword;
he laid it in Beowulf's bearm,
2195 and gave him seven thousand [hides of land],

2177. *Ecgtheow's bearn proved bold*. The verb *bealdian* (literally, "to bold")
occurs only here, so its exact sense is debatable: To be bold? To embolden/
encourage others?

2183. *guarded the ample gift which God had given him*. Beowulf's "super-
power," as we might put it, is his enormous strength—he has in his hand-
grip the strength of 30 men, according to Hrothgar (379–80). But Beowulf
never abuses this gift, using it rashly or selfishly. Instead he guards (*beal-
dan*, to hold, maintain, guard) it honorably as a gift from God.

2183. *Long had he been lowly*. Beowulf's glory and renown stand in
contrast to his earlier reputation. As a boy he was thought to be *slēac*
(sluggish, idle) and *unfrom* (feeble, inactive), until an *edwendan* (reversal)
comes and he is revealed as a mighty warrior. The sluggish-youth-turned-
hero is a common folktale motif.

2194. *he laid it in Beowulf's bearm*. Hygelac lays his father's sword in Beowulf's lap in what may be a formal investiture ceremony, which is followed by
the granting of territory, a hall, and a ruler's seat—effectively establishing
shared rule over the realm, although Hygelac retains supremacy.

2195. *seven thousand [hides of land]*. The words in brackets are implied. A
hide (OE *hīd*) is a measure of land, approximately 120 acres, based on the

a hall and brego-stol, a princely seat. To both of them alike
the land in that nation was hereditary,
the country as an ancestral domain—to the other more
    especially,
the wide realm to the one who was greater there.

2200 Afterwards it came to pass, in later days
through the clamors of war, after Hygelac lay dead,
and Heardred was slain by war-swords
behind the shield-covering,
when the hardy fighters, the Battle-Scylfings,
2205 sought him out among that victorious people,
violently assailed Hereric's nephew—
then the broad realm passed into Beowulf's
hand; he held it well
for fifty winters—the king was then frōd,
2210 an old ethel-weard—until one began
to rule in the dark nights, a dragon
who kept watch over the hoard in his high hall,
a stark stone barrow. A path lay under it,
unknown to men; into it there went
2215 a certain man, who *pressed forward*
near the heathen hoard. His hand *easily seized*
an *artifact* decked with treasure. Nor did he *conceal*
    it afterward,   *the dragon*
though he had been beguiled while he slept
by the thief's skill: the people *discovered*,
2220 the *beorns* of the neighboring folk, that he was enraged.

---

amount needed to support one family (*hīd* derives from a word meaning
"household"). Seven thousand hides would amount to an entire kingdom.
    2210a. *an old ethel-weard*, guardian of the homeland, an aged king.
    2210b. *until one began / to rule in the dark nights, a dragon.* Identical
language is used to introduce Grendel's incursions into Heorot (the men
dwell joyfully in the hall "until one began" to carry out attacks during the
night [100ff]). The language establishes a symmetry between the youthful
warrior and the old king. "It is essentially a balance," Tolkien says of the
poem's structure, "an opposition of ends and beginnings . . . a contrasted
description of moments in a great life, rising and setting."
    2215. *a certain man, who pressed forward,* is the thief who steals a cup
and arouses the dragon's wrath. At this point begins a damaged portion
of the manuscript. Words that have been restored on the basis of scholarly
conjecture are indicated by italics.

FITT 32. *The Robbing of the Dragon's Hoard*

Not of his own accord did he *break into* the wyrm-hoard,
by his own will, the one who sorely injured him,
but out of dire necessity a *slave*
of some one of the sons of hæleths had fled hateful blows,
2225   in need of shelter, and *made his way within there,*
a man beset by sins. Soon . . . time
so that grim terror arose in the visitor there,
yet the miserable man risked his life
                          . . .
2230   *afraid at heart,* when the sudden peril came upon him,
he sought a jeweled cup. There were many such
ancient treasures in that earth-hall,
as someone among men in days of old
had with careful thought hidden there,
2235   the immense legacy of an æthel race,
precious treasures. Death carried off them all
in earlier times, and he alone
of the hosts of his people — he who had roamed there longest,
a weard sad for friends — *expected* the same,
2240   that he would enjoy the long-accumulated treasure
for a little space of time. A barrow stood all ready
upon the ground near the waves of water,
new beside the ness, made fast with nearu-cræft.

Fitt 32 Synopsis. Although this portion of the manuscript is badly damaged (lines that have been reconstructed appear in italics), the storyline for the most part is clear: In his desperation a runaway slave seeking shelter enters the dragon's barrow and, discovering treasure, steals a precious cup which he hopes will win back the favor of his master. The treasure, we are told, was first placed in the barrow by the last survivor of a noble race, a man who speaks a lament over the treasure, a speech conventionally known as "The Lay of the Last Survivor." Later a dragon finds the Last Survivor's treasure hoard and takes possession of it; the dragon has possessed it for 300 years when the runaway slave steals the cup.

2221. *wyrm-hoard,* dragon's hoard. The basic sense of *wyrm* is "serpent," but in Old English texts it is applied to dragons and worms as well as reptiles.

2223. *a slave.* The specific identity of the thief is uncertain. All that remains in the manuscript is a *th-,* and *theow* (slave), *theof* (thief), and *thane* have all been proposed. Of these, "slave" makes the best sense of the narrative context.

2229 . . . . : The text of this passage is damaged beyond recovery.

2243. *made fast with nearu-cræft,* designed to be difficult to access. The treasure chamber has been specially constructed to protect the treasure

There the keeper of rings had carried inside
2245 a hoard-worthy portion of warriors' treasures,
of plated gold; he spoke these *few* words:

"Hold now, earth, now that hæleths may not,
the possessions of eorls. Hwæt, from you
good men once got it; war-death,
2250 fearful and deadly bale, carried off every one
of my people, who have left this *life*;
they saw their hall-joys. I have none who wears the sword
or *bears forth* the plated cup,
the precious drinking vessel; the duguth has passed elsewhere.
2255 The hard helm shall be stripped of hyrsted gold,
of its plating; the polishers sleep,
those who must burnish the battle-mask;
and the war-shirt, which in battle endured
the bite of iron over the clashing of shields,
2260 also decays after the warrior; nor may the ringed-byrnie
travel far and wide after the war-chief
at the side of hæleths. There is no joy of the harp,
gladness of the glee-beam, nor does the good hawk
swoop through the hall, nor does the swift steed
2265 stamp the burh-stead. Baleful death
has sent away a great many of the race of the living!"

So sad-minded, he spoke of his sorrow,
alone after all, passing unhappily
day and night, until the surge of death
2270 touched him at heart.

---

hidden inside it. Some have understood *nearu-cræft*, however, as a protective spell or curse.

2255. *hyrsted gold*, gold ornamentation. This passage that follows, a stirring litany of decay and dissolution, recalls similar moments in the Old English elegies *The Wanderer* and *The Ruin*. Here as in other elegies, the lament is less over the loss of material riches than that of the human community these items symbolize.

2263. *glee-beam*, joy-wood, the harp.

2268. *alone after all*. One theory imagines the Last Survivor as entering the barrow and there being transformed by his greed into a dragon, much like Eustace in C. S. Lewis's *Voyage of the Dawn Treader*. There are instances of humans becoming dragons in Norse literature, but such an interpretation of the dragon in *Beowulf* strains the evidence.

> The old dawn-ravager
> found the hoard-joy standing open,
> the burning one who seeks out barrows,
> the naked nith-draca who flies by night,
> engulfed in flame; earth-dwellers
2275 greatly dread him. He must seek out
> a hearg in the earth, where he guards heathen gold,
> frōd in winters; in no way is he the better for it.

2272–73. *the burning one who seeks out barrows, / the naked nith-draca.*
The *nith-draca* ("hostile dragon") is called "naked" on account of its smooth,
bare skin—it is a hairless, serpentine creature. As the present tense of this
sentence suggests, dragons were believed to exist by early medieval people,
which is why they "greatly dread him," although dragons came out only at
night. Place names provide evidence that this folk belief was once widespread.
Hills and earthen mounds found throughout the English countryside bear
such names as Drakelow ("Dragon-mound"), Wyrmelawe, and Drakenhorde,
"indicat[ing] the belief that these were inhabited by dragons" (Whitelock
73–74). There is also an entry in the *Anglo-Saxon Chronicle* for the year AD 793
that reports that "there were amazing sheets of lighting and whirlwinds, and
fiery dragons (*fyrenne dracan*) were seen flying in the sky," ominous signs that
portended the terrible Viking raids of that year. What exactly this creature
was thought to be is less certain. Based on the available literary evidence,
the dragon dreaded by Anglo-Saxons was a long-living, gold-hoarding,
fire-breathing, night-flying creature that inhabited ancient burial mounds.

2273-4. *who flies by night, / engulfed in flame.* Most dragons depicted in
medieval (Norse and Latin) literature are earth-dragons, essentially massive serpents with venomous fangs and poisonous breath. Flying, fiery
dragons are found in fully developed form only in Old English literature.
The fiery dragon may originate with lighting flashes in the dark sky; the
Dragon in the book of Revelation might also be a source (Rev 12:9: "the
great dragon . . . the ancient serpent, who is called the Devil and Satan").
The mechanics of dragon flight are never explained. We can assume the
dragon in *Beowulf* has wings, but they are never mentioned. This hasn't
stopped translators like Seamus Heaney from adding them, however.

2275 –76. *He must seek out / a hearg in the earth, where he guards heathen
gold.* The dragon's hoarding of gold, which might be found in ancient burial
mounds, was proverbial. "The dragon must dwell in the barrow, / frōd,
proud in treasure," declares the Old English *Maxims II* (26–27). This is
stated as matter-of-factly as the proverbs that follow it, which declare that
a fish must spawn in the water, a king must give out rings in the hall, and
water must flow downhill. In the same way, dragons seek gold and hoard it
in ancient burial mounds, which in the poet's imagination are merged with
heargs, heathen shrines. Tolkien notes that, while the dragon is depicted as
a flesh-and-blood creature, "with a bestial life and thought of his own," the
dragon is also "a personification of malice, greed, destruction (the evil side of
heroic life)." Calvert Watkins makes a similar point: "the dragon keeps wealth
from circulating: the ultimate evil in a society in which gift-exchange and
the lavish bestowal of riches institutionalized precisely that circulation" (300).

So for three hundred winters the ravager of peoples
held a certain hoard-ærn in the earth,
2280 eacen-crafty, until one man enraged him
in his heart. He brought to his man-drighten   *the thief*
a plated cup, pleaded for a wær of peace
with his lord. Then the hoard was laid open,
the ring-hoard diminished, the plea granted
2285 for the wretched man; his lord gazed upon
the ancient work of men for the first time.

Then the wyrm awoke, strife was renewed;
the stark-hearted one sniffed along the stone,
found the foot-track of his foe—he had stepped   *the thief*
2290 in his stealthy cunning too near the dragon's head—
so may an unfæge man easily survive
wrack and woe, he who holds the Waldend's
favor. The hoard-weard searched
eagerly along the ground, he wished to find the man
2295 who had sorely wronged him while he slept;
hot and fierce-minded, he often circled the mound
all around the outside; no man was there
in the wasteland—yet he rejoiced in the war,
in the work of battle. At times he turned back into the barrow,
2300 sought the treasure cup; he soon found
that some man had disturbed his gold,
the high treasures. The hoard-weard waited
impatiently until evening came;
then the barrow-keeper was swollen with rage;
2305 the foe would repay with fire   *the dragon*
the precious drinking vessel.
                     Then day had departed
to the wyrm's joy; he would wait no longer

2279. *hoard-ærn*, treasure house.

2280. *eacen-crafty*, exceedingly powerful, huge, or possibly "waxing strong" (Tolkien). The dragon remains powerful, or even grows more powerful, during the 300 years he occupies the barrow.

2305. *repay with fire / the precious drinking vessel.* Here we have the origin of Tolkien's Smaug with his fiery fury at the stolen cup in *The Hobbit*. Smaug's wiles and ability to speak, however, are indebted to Fafnir, a man-turned-dragon in the Old Norse *Saga of the Volsungs*.

within the wall, but went forth in a blaze,
ready with fire. The beginning was terrifying
2310 for the people in the land, just as soon
the ending would be painful for their treasure-giver.

FITT 33. *Beowulf Prepares to Fight the Dragon*

Then the gæst began spewing flames,
burning the bright dwellings—the burning leam came
upon men in anger; the loathsome sky-flier
2315 would leave nothing there alive.
The wyrm's warfare was widely seen,
his fierce hostility near and far,
how the war-ravager hated
and humiliated the Geatish people; to his hoard he went
shooting back,
2320 to his hidden dright-hall, before daytime.
He had engulfed the people of the land in flame,
in fire and burning; he trusted in his barrow,
his warfare and walls; his hope deceived him.

The terror was made known to Beowulf,
2325 swiftly and truly, that his own home,
best of buildings, had melted in the burning surge,
the gift-seat of Geats. For the good man that was
grievous within his breast, the greatest of heart-sorrows.
The wise one supposed that he had bitterly angered
2330 the Waldend, the eternal Drighten,

Fitt 33 Synopsis. The dragon begins to ravage the land with fire. When
Beowulf learns that his hall has burned, he prepares to face the dragon
by ordering the construction of a special shield made all of iron. He is
not afraid because he has survived many battles in the past, including the
disastrous raid in Friesland in which Hygelac was killed. Beowulf then supported Hygelac's son Heardred on the throne; when Heardred is killed in
a conflict with the Swedes, Beowulf becomes king, and eventually avenges
Heardred's killing.

2329–30. *supposed that he had bitterly angered / the Waldend.* When the
dragon destroys Beowulf's hall and gift-seat—the semi-sacral symbol of
his rule—the only explanation he can imagine is that he has offended God
in some way. Though God allowed Grendel to ravage Heorot, Grendel
was not permitted by God to touch or desecrate Hrothgar's gift-seat, the
throne from which he distributed treasure. Because Beowulf's own gift-seat

over the eald riht, the Law of Old; his breast within welled
with dark thoughts, as was not customary for him.
The fire-draca had destroyed the people's stronghold,
the outer coastlands, the earth-weard
2335 with his gleed. The gūth-king,
lord of Weders, taught him vengeance for that.
Then refuge of warriors, lord of eorls,
bid a wrætlic war-shield made for him
entirely of iron; he knew well
2340 that holt-wood could not help him,
linden against flame. The seafarer,
the good-of-old ætheling, had to endure the end of his days,
of his life in this world—and the wyrm with him,
though he had held that hoarded wealth a long time.

2345 Then the ring-fengel scorned
that he should seek that far-flier with a troop,
with a vast army. For himself he did not fear the fight,
nor did he make much of the wyrm's warfare,

---

has now been destroyed, he assumes it results from his loss of God's favor.
Nothing in the poem suggests that Beowulf has, in fact, angered God, and
this passage may simply indicate Beowulf's humility.

2331. *the Law of Old.* The identity of the *ealde riht* is left ambiguous; the
poet appears to have taken the concept of natural law, which is "inscribed
in the hearts" of all nations (Rom 2:14–15), and fused it with the language
of the Old Testament, found throughout the Psalms and prophetic books,
that speaks of God's punishment of his people for breaking his law ("Because
you have not . . . walked in his law . . . therefore this calamity has befallen
you, as it has this day" [Jer 44:23]). This explanation of *ealde riht* accords
well with the poet's depiction of Beowulf and Hrothgar as similar to Old
Testament figures.

2335. *gleed* (OE *glēd*), ember, fire; *gūth-king*, war-king.

2338. *wrætlic war-shield.* To face a highly unusual foe, Beowulf devises
a highly unusual weapon, a shield made completely out of iron in order
to withstand the dragon's flames. *Wrætlic* signifies the unique nature and
cunning of the shield. The special shield will in fact work, if not as well as
he hoped. It will preserve Beowulf's life long enough for him to defeat the
dragon, and will also protect the life of his kinsman Wiglaf.

2345–46. *the ring-fengel scorned / that he should seek that far-flier with a
troop.* A hotly contested sentence: Does the verb *ofer-hycgan* (to despise,
scorn, hold in contempt) indicate that Beowulf was prideful? Has he dis-
regarded Hrothgar's earlier warning to avoid *oferhyd*, "pride"? Or does it
merely convey that Beowulf was unafraid to face the dragon alone, as the
following lines seem to state? Whether Beowulf is being praised or criticized
is difficult to discern.

his strength and courage, because he had
2350   survived many hostilities, venturing narrow straits,
clashes of battle, after he,
victory-blessed, had cleansed Hrothgar's hall
and in combat crushed Grendel's kin,
the loathsome breed.
                                    Nor was it the least
2355   of his hand-combats where Hygelac was slain
in the storm of battle, when the king of Geats,
Hrethel's offspring, died in the sword-drinking
in Friesland, the frea-wine of the people,
beaten down by blades. Beowulf came away from there
2360   through his own strength, undertook a swimming feat;
he had the battle-armor of thirty eorls on his arm
when he pressed forward to the sea.
The Hetware had no need to exult
in that foot-battle, those who bore
2365   the linden against him; few came away again
from that battle-bold fighter to seek their home.
Then the son of Ecgtheow swam across the expanse of
            water,
wretched and alone, back to his people.
There Hygd offered him hoard and kingdom,
2370   bēags and brego-stol; she had no faith in her son,
that against foreigners he could
hold the ancestral seats now that Hygelac was dead.
Not for that could the bereaved ones
prevail upon the ætheling by any means
2375   that he should be lord over Heardred,
or accept the kingship,
yet he upheld him among the people with friendly counsel,

2358. *frea-wine*, friend and lord (literally, "lord-friend").

2360ff. *Beowulf came away from there*. In these lines we learn that Beowulf took part in Hygelac's disastrous raid in Frisia. Although Hygelac and
the Geats were defeated, Beowulf himself swam home carrying with him
the trophy of 30 warriors' armor, a triumph amidst tragedy. The *Hetware*
(Latin *Chatti, Chattuare, Attoari*) were a Frankish people inhabiting the
lower Rhine, part of the confederation of Franks, Frisians, and Hugas that
fought against Hygelac's forces.

2367. *the expanse of water*. Although the meaning of *sioloth* is uncertain,
context suggests "sea," "water."

graciously with good will, until he grew older,
ruled the Weder-Geats. Exiles sought him
2380 from across the sea, the sons of Ohthere;
they had rebelled against the helm of Scylfings,   *Onela*
the best of sea-kings,
of those who share out treasure in the Swedish realm,
a mære theoden. That marked his end:
2385 for his hospitality there Hygelac's son   *Heardred*
was allotted his death-wound from the strokes of a sword;
and Ongentheow's son departed again   *Onela*
to seek his home, after Heardred lay dead,
he let Beowulf hold the brego-stol, the royal seat,
2390 rule the Geats; that was a good king.

FITT 34. *The Tragedy of the Hrethlings*

In later days he was mindful of requiting
his prince's fall; he became a friend to Eadgils,
the wretched man; with his people he supported
Ohthere's son across the wide sea
2395 with warriors and weapons. Afterwards he took vengeance
in cold, sorrowful journeys, deprived the king of life.

So he had survived every struggle,
every dire onslaught, the son of Ecgtheow,
every work of ellen, until the one day
2400 when he had to fight the wyrm.
Then, one of twelve, he went swollen with anger,
the drighten of Geats, to look upon the dragon.

2379. *Exiles sought him.* Eanmund and Eadgils, the sons of Ohthere,
flee from their uncle, the Swedish king Onela, who had seized the throne.
They seek refuge from the Geatish King Heardred, but Onela then attacks
the Geats and kills Heardred for harboring his rebellious nephews. After
Heardred's death Beowulf becomes king.

Fitt 34 Synopsis. The slave leads Beowulf and eleven of his men to the
dragon's barrow. Sensing his end is near, Beowulf gives a speech that
recounts his history, how he was fostered by his grandfather, King Hrethel,
and raised with Hrethel's three sons, Herebeald, Hæthcyn, and Hygelac.
After Hæthcyn mistakenly slays his brother Herebeald with an arrow, their
father is overcome with grief and dies. His grief is illustrated by the scenario of a father who laments the death of his young son on the gallows,
a passage conventionally known as "The Father's Lament."

He had then learned how the feud arose,
that bale-nith of warriors; into his bearm had come
2405 the mære mathom-cup, through the informer's hand.
He was the thirteenth man in that company,
the one who had brought about the beginning of that strife,
the sad-minded captive, who, abject, from there
had to lead the way along the plain. Against his will he went
2410 to where he alone knew there was an earth-hall,
a hlæw under the ground near the sea's surge,
the striving waves; inside it was full
of wrætt and wires. A monstrous weard,
a ready fighter, held those gold mathoms,
2415 old under the earth; that was no easy bargain
for any among men to acquire.

The war-hardy king then sat upon the ness
while he bid hæl to his hearth-companions,
the gold-friend of Geats. He was sad in spirit,
2420 restless and ready for death, his wyrd very near,
that which must greet the gomel one,
seek his soul's hoard, divide
life from body; not for long after that
was the ætheling's life to be bound up in flesh.

2425 Beowulf matheled, bearn of Ecgtheow:

"In my youth I survived many storms of battle,
times of war; all that I remember.

2411. A *hlæw* is a man-made mound, usually a burial mound; here, however, it is used with reference to the open space inside the mound. Anglo-Saxons typically used this word for their own burial mounds, and used "barrow" (*beorg*) for the mounds of earlier cultures, although the distinction is not absolute, as is clear from the use of *hlæw* in this passage. Later *lowe/low* came to also mean a natural hill, and is common today in English place names.

2413. *wrætt and wires* (*wrætta ond wira*), jeweled ornaments and gold wire.

2418. *he bid hæl* (*hælo abead*), he saluted them (literally "bid them good fortune").

2420. *restless and ready for death.* Beowulf, sensing his death is at hand, experiences anguish. Some commentators see parallels in this scene to Christ's anguish in the Garden of Gethsemane. Despite his sorrow and restiveness, Beowulf is also *wæl-fus*, ready for death, or possibly "ready to be slain." Like Christ, Beowulf goes to his death willingly—but not easily.

2421. *which must greet the gomel one* is wyrd, the fated death that will soon approach the aged Beowulf and separate his soul from his body.

I was seven winters when the baldor of treasure,
frea-wine of the people, took me from my father;
2430 King Hrethel held and maintained me,
gave me treasure and symbel, remembered sibb;
while he lived I was no more hateful to him,
a warrior in the strongholds, than any of his own sons,
Herebeald and Hæthcyn, or my Hygelac.
2435 For the eldest, unfittingly,
a bed of murder was spread though the deeds of his mæg,
when Hæthcyn with his horn-bow
struck down his frea-wine with an arrow,
missed his mark and shot his mæg,
2440 one brother the other, with a bloody dart.
That was a fee-less fight, a deed wrongfully done,
thought-wearying to the breast; nevertheless
the ætheling had to lose his life unavenged.

Just so is it sad for an aged cheorl
2445 to endure—that his byre should ride,
young, on the gallows. He may then utter a gydd,
a painful song, when his son hangs
to the raven's delight, and he cannot,
old and very fröd, offer help to him.
2450 Each morning he is always reminded
of his offspring's ellor-sith, his journey elsewhere; he does
not care
to wait for another heir within the burhs,
when this one has had
his portion of deeds through death's necessity.
2455 Sorrowing, he sees in his son's dwelling
the desolate wine-hall, the windy resting place,
mournful, bereft; the riders sleep,
the hæleths in darkness; there is no harp's sound,
joy in the courtyards, such as there once was."

2441. *fee-less fight.* The killing was *feoh-leas*, unable to be compensated
with money (*feoh*) because it was inflicted by one brother upon another. The
system of wergild, payment to the kin-group, could not be applied in the
case of intrafamilial conflict. With no way to right the wrong, the wound
was left to fester in Hrethel's heart.

2445. *byre*, young son.

FITT 35. *The Dragon Fight Begins*

2460   "Then he goes to his couch, sings a sad lay,
        one after another. All seems too spacious to him,
        the grounds and dwelling place.
                               So the helm of Weders   *King Hrethel*
        carried surging sorrows
        in his heart for Herebeald. By no means
2465   could he settle the feud with the life-slayer
        any more than he could hate the warrior
        for the hateful deeds, though he was not dear to him.
        Then amid the sorrow that so sorely befell him
        he gave up the joys of men, he chose God's light;
2470   to his offspring he left—as a blessed man does—
        the land and stronghold, when he departed from life.

        Then there was hostility and strife of Swedes and Geats,
        a quarrel between them across the wide water,
        hard war-hostility after Hrethel died,
2475   until Ongentheow's offspring were
        bold, warlike, would hold no friendship
        across the sea, but around Hreosna Beorg
        they often waged terrible, malicious slaughter.
        My close kinsmen avenged that,

Fitt 35 Synopsis. The "Father's Lament" concludes and the death of King Hrethel is recounted. After his death hostilities arise once again with the Geats' perpetual enemies, the Swedes; Hæthcyn is slain in battle and the Swedish king, Ongentheow, is killed in revenge. Beowulf describes his courageous service to the king of Geats, including his slaying of Dæghrefn (Day-raven), a mighty Frankish warrior whom he crushes to death with his powerful grasp. Beowulf now seeks one final glorious contest, and asks his men to wait while he confronts the dragon alone. His shout rouses the creature, who comes spewing flame; when his shield proves less effective than he had hoped, and his sword fails him, Beowulf is forced to give ground. As he suffers in the flames of the dragon, his cowardly soldiers flee into the woods.

2469. *he chose God's light.* An expression for "he died," but according to Tolkien it also "would appear to refer to heaven." Tolkien explains that, in the *Beowulf* poet's conception, "good pagans . . . knew of the one God," and expressions like this are "evidence of the author's own view of the [heavenly] destiny of the just pagan." Indeed, "God's light" is used elsewhere in Old English literature to refer to the afterlife in heaven.

2477. *Hreosna Beorg* means "Hill of Sorrows."

2480 the feud and fyren, as it was well-known,
        although the other paid with his life,
        a hard bargain: for Hæthcyn,
        the lord of Geats, the war was fatal.
        Then, I have heard, in the morning one mæg
2485 avenged the other on his slayer with the edges of the sword
        when Ongentheow comes seeking Eofor;
        his war-helm split, the aged Scylfing fell,
        battle-pale; the hand remembered
        feuds enough, it did not withhold the death-stroke.
2490 The mathoms which he had given me   *Hygelac*
        I paid back with my bright sword in battle,
        as fate granted me; he gave me land,
        the joy of my ancestral home. He had no need
        to seek in the Swedish realm
2495 or among the Gifthas or Gar-Danes
        for a worse warrior, to buy one with wealth.
        I would always go before him in the foot-troop,
        alone at the front, and so all my life I shall
        do battle as long as this sword endures
2500 that has often served me well at all times
        since before the hosts I became the hand-slayer
        of Dæghrefn, the Hugas' champion —
        by no means could he bring that breast-ornament,
        the frætwe, to the Frisian king,

2486. *Ongentheow comes seeking Eofor.* The switch to the present tense is abrupt, but makes the scene more vivid. This battle between the Geats and Swedes will be narrated in greater detail later on.

2495. *The Gifthas* (Latin *Gepidae*) were an East Germanic people who, after migrating from southern Sweden in the 1st century, settled near the mouth of the Vistula River on the southern Baltic coast of what is today Poland. In subsequent centuries they migrated further south, where they fought successfully against the Huns. They disappear from history after the 6th century. In *Beowulf* they are portrayed as still occupying their ancestral homeland in Sweden.

2502. *The Hugas* were a Frankish people about whom little is known; the poet uses it synonymously with *the Franks*. In the poem they are said to fight with the Frisians and Hetware against Hygelac's forces.

2503-4. *that breast-ornament, / the frætwe.* Probably another reference to the wondrous neck-ring Beowulf received from Wealhtheow. Dæghrefn may have been the slayer of Hygelac, in which case Beowulf would be avenging his lord's death. He also takes from Dæghrefn a famous sword named Nægling (ln. 2680).

2505 but he fell in combat, the banner-keeper,
the ætheling with ellen; a sword's edge was not his slayer,
but my battle-grasp broke his bone-house,
his heart's surging. Now must my blade's edge,
my hand and hard sword fight for the hoard."

2510 Beowulf matheled, spoke bēot-words
for the last time:

                    "I braved many
battles in my youth; I desire still,
frōd guardian of my people, to seek this feud,
to achieve mærth, if the mān-scather, the wicked ravager,
2515 will come out of his earth-hall to seek me."

Then he addressed each of the men,
the bold helm-bearers, for the last time,
his beloved gesithas:

                    "I would not bear a sword,
a weapon against the wyrm, if I knew how else
2520 against the aglæca I might
grapple honorably, as before I did with Grendel.
But I expect hot battle-fire there,
breath and venom; therefore I have on me
bord and byrnie. From the barrow-guardian
2525 I will not flee one footstep, but in the fight
at the wall it shall be as the Metod of every man
allots us our fate. My mind is firm,
so that I will forgo a boast against the war-flier.

2513. *Feud*, with its negative connotations of illicit and uncontrolled
violence, is an imperfect rendering of OE *fæhth*, which is a licit and declared
state of hostility between two groups or individuals. Just as in modern
warfare it is considered legitimate to kill an enemy soldier, *fæhth* is a state of
sanctioned violence between two parties. Like many terms used in poetry,
however, *fæhth* is not always used with precision and sometimes simply
provides the poet with a handy word for fighting.

2526–27. *the Metod of every man / allots us our fate.* Once again, Beowulf
makes no promise to triumph over his foe, vowing only that he will not
flee the battle and entrusting the outcome to God. Some versions of these
lines make *Wyrd*, fate, the subject of the sentence ("as Fate allots, the Ruler
[Metod] of every man" [Donaldson]), but the OE grammar does not support
this interpretation.

2528. *so that I will forgo a boast.* A surprising assertion, given that this
statement comes in the middle of his heroic bēot. It is possible that the

Await on the barrow, protected by your byrnies,
2530   men in armor, which of us two may better
survive his wounds after the wæl-ræs,
the deadly onslaught. It is not your sith,
nor is it in any man's ability but mine alone
that he should share out his strength against the aglæca,
2535   perform eorlship. With ellen I shall
gain the gold, or battle, fearful and deadly evil,
will carry off your lord."

Then the bold warrior arose by his shield,
hard under helm, he bore his battle-shirt
2540   under the stone cliffs, he trusted in the strength
of one man; such is not the coward's way.
Then he saw by the wall—he who,
good in manly virtues, had survived a great many conflicts,
the crash of battles when the foot-troops clashed—
2545   arches of stone standing, out of which a stream
burst forth from the barrow; the burne's surge was
hot with battle-fires; near the hoard
he could not endure unburned for any length of time
in its depths, on account of the dragon's flame.
2550   Then, when he was enraged, from his breast
the Weder-Geats' leader let a word go forth,
the strong-hearted one shouted; his voice came
thundering, war-clear, in under the gray stone.
Hate was stirred up; the hoard-weard knew

---

scribe miscopied *gylpe* (boast) for *geoce* (help), in which case Beowulf would
be declaring that he will forego help from his troop to face the dragon alone.

   2533. nor is it in any man's ability but mine alone. Beowulf's decision to
face the dragon all by himself has occasioned endless debate: Was he right
to do so? Was it foolhardy, rash, or prideful? Or was he instead behaving
self-sacrificially? An important clue is provided in the word *ge-met.* Most
translators interpret *ge-met* as an adjective, "proper," "fitting," "meet" ("it is
not proper for any man but me alone"). But it is the noun form that is used
here, in the sense of "ability." Beowulf is explaining that since he alone has
the capacity—in his enormous strength—to battle the dragon, he must
do so alone. Tolkien's is one of the few renderings to get this right: "Nor
is it within the measure of any man save me alone" (2014: 87).

   2546. burne, stream. The dragon's fire makes the water of the stream
flowing out of the barrow unbearably hot. The image in the poet's mind
seems to be that of a hot spring.

2555   the voice of a man; there was no more time
        to ask for friendship. First there came
        the aglæca's breath from out of the stone,
        hot battle-sweat; the earth resounded.
        The beorn under the barrow swung his shield,
2560   the lord of Geats, to face the dreaded stranger.
        Then the heart of the coiled creature was roused
        to seek combat. The good war-king
        had already drawn his sword, the ancient heirloom,
        not slow of edges; for each of them,
2565   bent on destruction, there was a horror of the other.
        Firm of mind, he stood against the tall shield,
        the baldor of friends, when the wyrm quickly coiled
        together; he waited in his war-gear.

        Then in burning coils he came, scrithing,
2570   hastening to his fate; the shield defended well
        his life and body for less time
        than the mære theoden would have wished;
        there on that occasion, for the first day,
        he would have to wield it without wyrd granting him
2575   triumph in battle. He lifted his hand,
        the drighten of Geats struck the gryre-patterned one
        with the incge-heirloom so that its edge failed,
        bright upon the bone; it bit less mightily
        than its people-king had needed,
2580   hard-pressed by troubles. Then the barrow-weard was
        fierce-minded after the battle-stroke,
        throwing wæl-fire; far and wide sprang
        the war-flames.

  2569. *scrithing* (OE *scrithan*), gliding, moving in continuous motion. Grendel is said to move in the same fashion.
  2574–75. *he had to wield it without wyrd granting him /...glory in war.*
The translation is a speculative attempt to make sense of what even the
great Friedrich Klaeber admitted was "a perplexing passage" (216). Other
interpretations are possible.
  2576. *gryre-patterned* (OE *gryre-fah*). The dragon's appearance somehow
inspires terror, perhaps in its varied colors or flashing, gleaming scales, since
fah refers to a variegated, multicolored, or gleaming surface.
  2577. *the incge-heirloom* is Beowulf's sword. The meaning of *incge* is
unknown.

The gold-friend of Geats
did not boast of glorious victories; the war-blade failed,
2585 naked in the nith, as it should never do,
the good-of-old iron. That was no easy journey,
that the renowned son of Ecgtheow
should give up the open ground;
against his will he had to inhabit a dwelling-place
2590 somewhere else: so must every man
give up his loaned days.
It was not long then
before the aglæcas met again.
The hoard-weard took heart, his breast surged with breath
once more; he suffered dire distress,   *Beowulf*
2595 engulfed in fire, he who had ruled the people.
By no means did his hand-companions stand around him
in a band, with battle-virtue,
those athelings' bearns, but they turned back into the wood
to save their lives. In one of them the spirit
2600 surged with sorrows: nothing can ever turn aside sibb
in one who thinks well.

FITT 36. *Wiglaf Joins the Fight*
....

He was called Wiglaf, Wihstan's son,
an esteemed shield-warrior, a man of the Scylfings,
Ælfhere's mæg; he saw his man-drighten
2605 suffering heat under his war-mask.
Then he remembered the honors he had bestowed on him,
the wealthy habitation of the Wægmundings,

2600. *nothing can ever turn aside sibb.* The one warrior who refuses to
flee is Beowulf's closest relative. The ties of kinship prove stronger than
the bonds of fealty.

Fitt 36 Synopsis. Beowulf's kinsman Wiglaf takes up his sword and shield
to join Beowulf in the fight (the backstory of the sword is given) and bitterly
rebukes his comrades for their cowardice. Then he stands by Beowulf as
the dragon comes at them for a second attack. Wiglaf's shield is burned
up and he takes cover behind Beowulf's iron shield, while Beowulf strikes
at the dragon with his sword Nægling, but his strength proves too much
for it and the blade shatters. The dragon then comes on for the third time,
seizing Beowulf's neck in his jaws.

2607. *Wægmundings.* Both Beowulf and Wiglaf are called Wægmundings,
descendants of Wægmund. Yet Wiglaf and his father Wihstan are also

each of the folkrights his father had possessed.
Then he could not hold back: his hand seized the shield,
2610 the yellow linden, he drew the ancient sword—
among men of old it was the heirloom of Eanmund,
Ohthere's son; in that strife Wihstan
became the slayer of the friendless exile
with the edges of his sword, and to his kin he carried off
2615 the brightly burnished helm, ringed byrnie,
the ancient eotenish sword; Onela had given him that,
his gædeling's battle-garments,
ready war-gear—he never spoke of the feud,   *Onela*
though he had struck down his brother's son.
2620 For many half-years he kept the war-equipment,   *Wihstan*
the blade and byrnie, until his byre could
carry out eorlship, just as his forefather before him;
then among the Geats he gave him
countless war-garments of every kind, when he departed
    from life,
2625 frōd on his way forth. That was the first time
for the young champion that he had to carry on
onslaught in battle with his noble lord.
His spirit did not melt, nor did his mæg's heirloom
fail in war; the wyrm found that out
2630 after they had come together.

Wiglaf matheled, spoke many right and fitting words
to his gesithas; he was sad in spirit:

"I remember the time we drank mead
when we vowed to our lord
2635 in the beer-hall, he who gave us these bēags,
that we would pay him back for this battle-gear

---

identified as Swedes (Scylfings) rather than Geats. Bloodlines could cut
across tribal groups, and intermarriage further blurred ethnic designations.
    2611. *the heirloom of Eanmund*. Wiglaf's sword once belonged to Ean-
mund, one of the two sons of the Swedish king Ohthere who had sought
refuge among the Geats from their uncle Onela (lines 2379–84). We learn
here that Wiglaf's father Wihstan was Eanmund's slayer, and that Onela
had bestowed on Wihstan the sword and armor of his slain nephew, pleased
that his rebellious nephew was dead. Later the sword and armor were
passed down to Wiglaf.
    2617. *gædeling*, kinsman.

if such a need should befall him,
these helms and hard swords. For this reason he chose us
of his own will from among the host for this venture,
2640 thought us worthy of glory, and gave me these treasures,
because he accounted us good spear-warriors,
bold helm-bearers, even though our lord,
shepherd of the people,
intended to carry out for us this work of ellen alone,
2645 because he among men had accomplished the most mærth,
audacious deeds. Now the day has come
when our man-drighten has need of might,
of good warriors; let us go to him,
help our war-leader while the heat lasts,
2650 the grim gleed-terror. As for me, God knows
that I would much rather that the flame embrace
my flesh-garment beside my gold-giver.
It does not seem fitting that we should bear shields
back home, unless we can first
2655 fell the foe, defend the life
of the lord of Weders. I know well
that his deserts for deeds of old are not such
that he alone among the host of Geats should suffer affliction,
sink down in the struggle; to both of us two shall sword
      and helm,
2660 byrnie and battle-garment be shared."

Then he waded through the deadly fumes, bearing his war-helm
to the aid of his frea, spoke these few words:

"Beloved Beowulf, carry out all well,
as you said long ago in the time of your youth,
2665 that as long as you lived you would not allow
your dōm to decline; now, brave in deeds,
steadfast ætheling, with all your might you must
defend your life. I will support you."

After these words the wyrm came on in ire,
2670 the terrible inwit-gæst a second time,

2662. *frea*, lord.
2670. *inwit-gæst*, malicious spirit, hostile creature. The dragon is the
enemy of humans, "the hated men," though not described in such starkly

fierce with surging fire, seeking his foes,
the hated men. Fire came forth in waves,
burned the shield up to the boss. The byrnie could
provide no help to the young spear-warrior,
2675 but the young man went under his mæg's shield,
boldly, when his own was
consumed by flame. Then the war-king
was again mindful of courage; with great strength he struck
with his battle-blade, so that it stuck in the head,
2680 driven in by violence; Nægling burst apart,
Beowulf's sword failed in the fight,
ancient and gray-mæl. It was not granted to him
that the edges of iron could
help him in battle; too strong was the hand which,
2685 I have heard, overstrained every sword
with its stroke, whenever he bore it to battle,
the wondrously hard weapon; he was in no way the better
    for it.

Then for the third time the people's scourge,
the fierce fire-draca, mindful of feuds,
2690 rushed upon the brave man when the chance was given him.
Hot and battle-grim, he seized him all about the neck
with bitter fangs. He was besmeared   *Beowulf*
with his lifeblood; battle-sweat welled up in waves.

---

demonic terms as the Grendelkin. The reason the language describing
the dragon is less severe is not that, as some critics maintain, the dragon
is merely a dangerous but morally neutral creature like a rattlesnake, but
that the vice the dragon embodies—avarice—is less overtly destructive
than the violent aggression of Grendel and his mother.

2682. *gray-mæl*, gray- or silver-colored.

2689. *Fire-draca. Draca* is not a word native to Germanic; it is a bor-
rowing from the Latin *draco*, itself borrowed from Greek *drakon*. In this
respect it is unlike most other names for the mythical creatures in *Beowulf,*
which derive from Proto-Germanic and were apparently part of an earlier
mythology. The flying, fire-breathing *draca* was therefore not a feature of
early Germanic myth, although the other word used for the dragon, *wyrm*,
does derive from Proto-Germanic. It is probable that early Germanic belief
included an earth-dragon—a large serpent-like creature—especially since
Norse mythology, though considerably later, includes several such beings.
Calvert Watkins argues that a primordial dragon-slaying myth, from which
later tales descend, goes all the way back to Proto-Indo-European.

2693. *battle-sweat*, blood.

FITT 37. *The Slaying of the Dragon*

....

Then, I have heard, at the people-king's need
2695 the eorl at his side showed courage,
strength and keenness, as to him was cynde;
he took no heed of the head, but the hand
of the brave man was burned when he helped his kinsman;
for that he struck the nith-gæst a little lower down,
2700 the man in his armor, so that the sword plunged in,
gleaming and gold-plated, so that the fire began
to subside after that. The king himself still then
ruled his wits; he drew out the wæl-seax, the deadly knife,
bitter and battle-sharp, which he wore on his byrnie.
2705 The helm of Weders cut the wyrm through the middle.
They had felled the enemy—their courage had driven out
        his life—
and they had both destroyed him then,
those sib-æthelings: such should a man be,
a thane at need. For the theoden that was
2710 his last time of victory by his own deeds,
of his work in the world.
                                    Then the wound
which the earth-draca had inflicted
began to burn and swell; soon he found
that the venom seethed with baleful malice in his breast,
2715 the attor within. Then the ætheling went,
wise in thought, to sit by the wall
on a seat; he saw the work of ents,

Fitt 37 Synopsis. Wiglaf's hand is burned as he tries to help Beowulf. He disregards the fire-breathing head and strikes the dragon lower down, where the beast is more vulnerable, and the blow weakens the dragon, although Wiglaf's hand is burned. Wiglaf's blow allows Beowulf to pierce the dragon's midsection with his knife, finally killing him. But now the venom in Beowulf's wound has begun to take effect. Weakened, he sits against the wall and gazes upon the ancient barrow; there he utters a speech and requests Wiglaf to enter the barrow to bring out some of the treasure he has won.

2696. *cynde,* natural, innate (the source of ModE *kind*).

2708. *sib-æthelings,* kinsmen of noble blood, related warriors.

2715. *attor,* poison, venom.

2717. *the work of ents.* The massive stone structures and earthworks found throughout northern Europe were attributed to an ancient race of

how the stone arches, made fast with pillars,
held up the ageless earth-house within.

2720 Then with his hands the thane, immeasurably good,   *Wiglaf*
washed his wine-drighten with water,
the mære theoden bloodied from battle,
sated with war, and unstrapped his helm.

Beowulf matheled—he spoke over his hurt,
2725 his deadly wound; he knew well
that he had lived out his time of days,
his earthly joys; all departed then was
the number of his days, death immeasurably near:

"Now I would give my son
2730 these battle-garments, if it had so been granted
that there remained any heir after me
belonging to my body. I ruled this people
for fifty winters; there was no people-king
among the surrounding peoples
2735 who dared greet me with war-friends,
to threaten terrors. At home I abided
the occasions of fate, held well what was mine;
I did not seek treacherous quarrels, nor swore many
wrongful oaths. For all this I can
2740 have joy, sick with life-wounds,
because the Waldend of men need not reproach me

---

master builders, the "ents." Saxo Grammaticus writes in the 13th-c. *Gesta Danorum*: "The fact that the land of Denmark was once inhabited by a race of giants is attested by the huge boulders found next to ancient burial mounds and caves.... There is not enough evidence to decide whether those who devised these works were giants who lived after the influx of the Flood or were men of supernatural strength. Such creatures, our compatriots maintain, are reckoned today to inhabit the rugged and inaccessible wasteland ... and to be endowed with transmutable bodies, so that they have the wondrous ability to appear and disappear, to be present and then suddenly somewhere else" (Orchard 55).

2735. *war-friends* are either the king's warriors or his weapons.

2740. *life-wounds*, mortal wounds.

2741. *the Waldend of men need not reproach me*. Beowulf can face his Maker without fear since he has acted justly, according to what we might call natural law. He has not been false in his oaths or deeds, he has governed his people rightly, sought peace rather than fomenting quarrels, and he has patiently endured the ups and downs of fortune.

for the baleful murder of my kinsmen
when the life departs from my body. Now go quickly
to examine the hoard under the gray stone,
2745　beloved Wiglaf, now that the wyrm lies low;
he sleeps, sorely wounded, bereft of treasure.
Now be in haste, so I may see
the ancient wealth, the gold possessions, gaze eagerly upon
the bright skill-wrought gems, that I might more gently,
2750　for that wealth of treasures, give up
my life and people, which I long have held."

FITT 38. *The Death of Beowulf*

Then swiftly, I have heard, the son of Wihstan
obeyed his lord, wounded, war-sick, after these words;
he bore his ring-net,
2755　the woven battle-shirt, under the barrow's roof.
Exulting in victory, he saw then, when he passed by the seat,
that brave young thane, many bejeweled mathoms,
gold glistening along the ground,
wonders on the wall, and the wyrm's den,
2760　the old dawn-flier's —flagons standing,
the vessels of men of old, bereft of polishers,
stripped of ornaments; there was many a helm,
old and rusty, a great many arm-rings
cunningly twisted. Easily may treasure,
2765　gold in the ground, get away from
every one of the race of men, hide it who will!

　2748–49. *gaze eagerly upon / the bright skill-wrought gems.* The dying
hero's request to look upon the gold has surprised some readers. The
suggestion of some critics that Beowulf is overcome with greed in his
final moments has no support in the text; instead, the gold is a tangible
symbol of his victory and his earned glory. He also believes it will benefit
his people, as he will state in ln. 2797.

　Fitt 38 Synopsis. Wiglaf enters the barrow and returns with treasures to
find Beowulf dying. He revives him with water and Beowulf speaks his final
words, instructing that his men build him a burial mound overlooking the
sea. He then gives Wiglaf several treasures and dies, and his soul departs
from his body "to seek the judgment of the righteous."

　2765–66. *get away from / every one of the race of men, hide it who will!*
The verb *oferhigian*, here rendered "get away from," is a classic crux. The
word occurs only in this one instance, and its meaning is uncertain. Other

He also saw a banner, all of gold, hanging
high above the hoard, the greatest of hand-wonders,
linked by the craft of limbs; light came from it,
2770 so that he could perceive the ground's surface,
look upon the wrætt. Of the wyrm
there was no sight, for the sword had carried him off.
Then I have heard that one man in the mound
plundered that hoard, the old work of ents;
2775 into his bearm he loaded beakers and plates
at his own choosing; he also took the banner,
the brightest of beacons. The aged lord's blade—
its edge was iron—had earlier injured
the one who had been guardian of those mathoms
2780 for a long while, who had waged fire-terror,
hot before the hoard, surging fiercely
in the middle of the night, until he died by murder.

The messenger made haste, eager to return,
urged on by the frætwa; curiosity broke him,
2785 whether he, bold-hearted, would find
the lord of Weders alive in the place
where he had left him earlier, ellen-sick.
Then with the mathoms, he found the mære theoden,
his own lord, at his life's end,
2790 bloodied; he began again to sprinkle him
with water, until the point of a word
broke through his breast-hoard.
                    [The beorn-king spoke,]
the old one in grief, he gazed upon the gold:

---

proposed meanings include "overpower," "deceive," "get the better of," and
"outsmart." The sense of the sentence seems to be that wealth cannot be
kept to oneself, despite one's best efforts. The dragon hoarded immense
treasure, but lost all of it in the end to others. It is therefore better to dis-
tribute wealth rather than hoard it.

2771. *wrætt*, wrought jewels, treasures.

2782. *murder.* OE *morthor* can sometimes signify a violent death rather
than an illicit killing.

2787. *ellen-sick*, deprived of his strength and boldness, dying.

2792. *[The beorn-king spoke].* Lack of alliteration indicates that a half-
line is missing; the phrase "The warrior-king spoke" is no more than a
plausible guess.

"For these precious things I give thanks
2795   with these words to the Lord of all, King of Glory,
the eternal Lord, for what I look upon here,
that I was able to gain such things for my people
before my death-day.
Now that I have bought this hoard of treasures
2800   with the laying down of my old life, attend still
to the needs of the people; I can stay here no longer.
Bid men renowned in war to build a mound,
bright after the bæl, at the headland of the sea;
as a remembrance to my people
2805   it shall stand high upon Hrones Ness,
so that afterwards seafarers will call it
Beowulf's Barrow, those who drive the brentings, tall ships,
far over the darkness of the flood."

He took from his neck a golden ring;   *Beowulf*
2810   the bold-minded theoden gave it to his thane,
to the young spear-warrior, his gold-adorned helm,
bēag and byrnie, bid him use them well:

"You are the last remnant of our cynn,
the Wægmundings. Wyrd has swept away

2799–2800. *I have bought this hoard of treasures / with the laying down of my old life.* The language of this passage brings to light the poet's larger project in the poem: creating points of contact between the Germanic heroic tradition and redemptive history, in order to redeem and recuperate the heroic tradition. To do this, the poet links Beowulf's heroic actions with Christ's, not in simple allegorical fashion (which would ultimately diminish the character of Beowulf), but by discovering ways the hero's death recapitulates Christ's sacrifice. Beowulf remains a Germanic warrior; but at the same time he is *more* than a Germanic warrior. In Beowulf he fashions a hero who is glory-seeking and gold-winning, but also self-sacrificing. The poet accordingly stresses the voluntary nature of Beowulf's death, in which his life, like Christ's, is given rather than taken from him, as well as its redemptive results. Beowulf has bought the treasure with his own life, which is for the benefit of his people.

2802. *Bid men ... to build a mound.* Curiously, Beowulf's instructions to Wiglaf use the plural form of the imperative verb: "(You all) attend still to the needs to the people ..." (2800-1); "(You all) bid men ... to build...." Has the poet lost sight of the person addressed? Or are the instructions directed to Beowulf's men as a whole?

2805. *Hrones Ness,* Whale's Bluff.

2815 all my kinsmen to the Metod's decree,
eorls in their ellen; I must follow after them."

That was the old one's last word,
from the thoughts of his breast before he chose the bæl,
the hot battle-surges; his soul quickly went from him
2820 to seek the dōm of the sōth-fæst—the judgment of the
righteous.

FITT 39. *Wiglaf Rebukes the Cowardly Troop*

Then it was painful for the young man,
when he saw that most beloved man
faring piteously upon the ground
at his life's end. His slayer also lay there,
2825 the terrible earth-draca, deprived of life,
balefully afflicted. No longer could
the twisted wyrm rule over his ring-hoard,

2815. *the Metod's decree* (OE *meotodsceaft*) means "one's appointed end,"
"death." Terms such as *meotodsceaft* may indicate that *Metod* had an earlier, pre-Christian meaning of "ordaining fate," but this can no longer be
known for certain.

2819–20. *his soul quickly went from him / to seek the dōm of the sōth-fæst.*
The straightforward interpretation of this sentence is that Beowulf's soul
went to heaven. But the poet leaves some ambiguity, no doubt intentionally.
Dōm can mean "judgment" as well as "heroic glory," a rich polysemy that
allows the poet to meld the heroic and heavenly *dōm*, even implying that
one can lead to the other. *Sōth-fæst*, literally "truth-firm," is the term used
for the righteous, saints, and holy people in the Bible. In several passages
it refers to those who enjoy salvation as opposed to the sinful souls that
stand condemned. A few critics, on the assumption that the pagan Beowulf
cannot be saved, contort the meaning of *sōthfæstra dōm* to "the judgment
by those speaking the truth" (Mitchell and Robinson 147)—in other words,
Beowulf's soul will be judged by the righteous (and found wanting). But
the plain sense of the phrase is that Beowulf goes to his heavenly reward.
Tolkien remarks, "What precise theological views he held concerning the
souls of the just heathen we need not here inquire. He does not tell us, saying
simply that Beowulf's spirit departed to whatever judgment awaits such
just men, though we may take it that this comment implies that it was not
destined to the fiery hell of punishment, being reckoned among the good."

Fitt 39 Synopsis. Wiglaf looks sadly upon Beowulf's body, which is lying
beside the dead dragon. When the cowardly warriors return from the
woods, Wiglaf reproaches them and predicts that they will be forced into
exile once neighboring tribes learn of their cowardice. (The numbering for
Fitt 39 is missing from the manuscript; it has been inserted here by editors
to fix the scribe's mistake.)

for iron edges had carried him off,
the hard, battle-sharp leavings of hammers,
2830 so that the wide-flying one, stilled by wounds,
sank to earth near the hoard-ærn.
By no means did he turn, sporting in air
in the middle of the night, proud in his mathom-possessions,
show off his form, but he fell to earth
2835 through the war-leader's handiwork.
Truly, as I have heard, it has prospered
few among men in the land, those with might,
though they be daring in every deed,
to rush into the breath of a venomous ravager
2840 or disturb the ring-hall with their hands,
if they should find a watchful guardian
residing in the barrow. Beowulf paid for his share
of dright-mathoms with his death;
each of those two had traveled to the end
2845 of this loaned life.

It was not then long
before the battle-laggards left the woods,
the ten faint-hearted troth-breakers together
who before had not dared to sport with spears
at their man-drighten's great need;
2850 but with shame they bore their shields,
their war-garments, to where the gomel one lay.
They looked upon Wiglaf; he sat, wearied,
the foot-warrior near the shoulders of his lord,
rousing him with water; not a whit did he succeed.
2855 No matter how much he wished he could not
keep the life of his war-leader on earth,
or alter the Wealdend's will.
God's dōm would govern the deeds
of every man, as it still does now.

2860 Then it was easy to get from the young man

2831. *hoard-ærn*, treasure-house (the dragon's barrow).
2857. *the Wealdend's will*. This translation follows the emendation of *wiht*
to *willa*. If the manuscript is correct, however, it would read that he could
not "change anything [ordained by]" God—essentially the same meaning.

a grim answer for one who had lost courage.
Wiglaf matheled, Wihstan's son,
the sad-hearted man looked upon the unloved ones:

"Lā, he who will speak the truth may say
2865   that the man-drighten who gave you mathoms,
the eored-gear you stand in there,
when often on the ale-bench he gave
helm and byrnie to those seated in his hall,
a theoden to his thanes, the most mighty such
2870   that he could find anywhere, near or far—
that he utterly and senselessly threw away
those battle-garments when war came upon him.
That people-king had no need at all to boast
of his troop-companions; yet to him God granted,
2875   the Waldend of victories, that he might avenge himself
alone with his sword, when he had need of courage.
Little life-protection could I give him
in the battle, and yet I began
beyond my own means to help my mæg;
2880   ever the weaker was that deadly enemy
when I struck him with my sword, less forceful
was the fire welling from his wits. Too few defenders
thronged about our theoden when the time came.
Now treasure-sharing and sword-giving,
2885   all ethel-joys, beloved things,
shall cease for your cynn. Each man
of your kindred must wander
deprived of his land-rights, after æthelings
near and far hear of your flight,
2890   your dōm-less deed. Death is better
for every eorl than a life of disgrace!"

2864. *Lā*, interjection of emphasis and emotion (ah! oh! indeed! lo!).
2866. *eored-gear*, mounted-troop gear.
2890. *Death is better... than a life of disgrace!* Wiglaf's statement recalls
Tacitus's description of the code of loyalty of Germanic warriors to their
lord: "On the field of battle it is a disgrace to a chief to be surpassed in
courage by his followers, and to the followers not to equal the courage
of their chief. And to leave a battle alive after their chief has fallen means
lifelong infamy and shame. To defend and protect him, and to let him get

FITT 40. *The Messenger's Prophecy*
....

Then he ordered the results of battle announced
at the encampment up over the cliff's edge, where the troop
    of eorls
sat sad-minded the whole morning of the day,
2895 the shield-bearers in expectation of both
the final day and the return
of the beloved man. Little was he silent
about the new tidings, he who rode up to the ness,
but he spoke the truth to them all:

2900 "Now the joy-giver of the Weder people,
drighten of Geats, lies fast upon his deathbed,
dwells in a rest of slaughter from the wyrm's deeds;
beside him lies his life's enemy,
sick with seax wounds — with his sword
2905 he could make in the aglæca
no wound at all. Wiglaf sits
over Beowulf, Wihstan's byre,
one eorl over the other lifeless one;
weary-minded, he holds a head-watch
2910 over the loved one and the loathed one.

                           Now for our people
a time of strife is to be expected, once the fall of the king
becomes widely known to Franks and Frisians.
The hostility was begun,

---

the credit for their own acts of heroism, are the most solemn obligations
of their allegiance. The chiefs fight for victory, the followers for their chief."

   Fitt 40 Synopsis. A messenger brings the sad news to the soldiers'
encampment nearby and predicts a coming time of conflict with the Franks
and Frisians who inhabit the lands to the south of the Geats. He explains
how the conflict originated with Hygelac's disastrous raid on them, which
ended with his death. Conflict too is expected with the Swedes to the
north because of an earlier conflict, which began when the Geatish king
Hæthcyn raided the Swedes, capturing the wife of the Swedish king
Ongentheow. Hæthcyn is then slain in a counter-raid by Ongentheow,
who takes back his wife and pursues the surviving Geats into Ravenswood,
where they are besieged through the night. But at dawn they are rescued
when Hæthcyn's brother Hygelac arrives with reinforcements.

   2909. *head-watch,* a death-watch, a wake. Wiglaf sits reverently beside
the body of his fallen lord.

harsh with the Hugas, when Hygelac came
2915   traveling with an armed fleet on Frisian land.
There the Hetware assailed him in battle,
came on boldly with a greater force,
so that the byrnied warrior had to bow;
he fell among his foot-troop, by no means gave frætwe,
2920   the leader to his war-band. Ever since
the mercy of the Merewioing has been denied us.
Nor do I expect any sibb or truce with the Swedish people,
for it has been widely known
that Ongentheow deprived
2925   Hæthcyn Hrethling of his life at Ravenswood,
when for pride the Geatish people
first sought out the Battle-Scylfings.
Immediately the aged father of Ohthere,
old and terrible, returned the attack,
2930   cut down the sea-king, rescued his wife,
the aged woman of old, bereft of gold,
Onela's mother and Ohthere's,
and then pursued his life's foes
until they narrowly escaped,
2935   lordless, into Ravenswood.
Then with a great army he surrounded the survivors of
        swords;
wearied by wounds, he kept threatening woes
to that wretched troop all night long,
he said that in the morning with the edges of his sword
2940   he would spill them, [hang] some on the gallows-tree
as sport for birds. Relief came once more,
together with the dawn, for those sad-hearted men
when they heard the song of Hygelac's
horn and trumpet, when the good one came
2945   following the track of that people's host."

2918. *bow* (OE *bugan*), a visceral expression for being overpowered in
battle and being forced to give way, either through falling in battle or
by retreat.
    2920. *the Merewioing*, the Merovingian King, the ruler of the Franks—
unless this is a scribal error for *mere-wicing*, "sea-raider," i.e., Hygelac.
    2940. *[hang]*. This verb is missing from the text.

FITT 41. *The Battle of Ravenswood & the Feud with the Swedes*

"The bloody swath of Swedes and Geats,
the deadly onslaught of men, could be widely seen,
how the people had awakened the feud between them.
Then the good one set out with his gædelings,   *Ongentheow*
2950   old, full of sorrow, to seek his stronghold,
the eorl Ongentheow turned to higher ground.
He had heard of Hygelac's warfare,
the proud one's war-craft; he put no faith in resistance,
that he could withstand those sea-men,
2955   defend his hoard against the war-travelers,
his bearn and bride; he drew back from there,
the old one, behind his earth-wall. Then pursuit was offered
to the people of the Swedes; Hygelac's banners
overran the place of refuge
2960   after the Hrethlings thronged into the enclosure.
There with the edges of swords Ongentheow,
gray-haired, was brought to bay,
so that the people's king had to submit
to the dōm of Eofor alone. In anger
2965   Wulf Wonreding struck him with his weapon,
so that for the stroke blood spurted from the veins
under his hair. Yet he was undaunted,
the aged Scylfing, for he quickly repaid
the deadly blow with a worse exchange
2970   after the people's king turned to him there.
The swift son of Wonred could not   *Wulf*

Fitt 41 Synopsis. The messenger continues his account of the Battle of
Ravenswood: fearing Hygelac, Ongentheow retreats to his stronghold.
After this is breached, Ongentheow is attacked by a Geatish warrior named
Wulf, but Ongentheow strikes him down; Wulf's brother Eofor then kills
Ongentheow and strips him of his weapons. Later Hygelac richly rewards
the two brothers with land and treasure, giving to Eofor his only daughter.
Because of this feud, the messenger expects that now that Beowulf is dead
the Swedes will seek revenge on the Geats, and he predicts a coming time
of conflict and exile. After this speech the troop of Geats departs to look
upon the body of Beowulf; beside him lies the dragon as well as some of
the treasure, which is said to be bound with a curse.

2965. *the dōm of Eofor alone.* Ongentheow was at the mercy of Eofor.

give the old cheorl a return stroke
for he had sheared through the helm on his head
so that, stained with blood, he had to bow,
2975   he fell on the earth; he was not yet fæge,
but he recovered, though the wound hurt him.
Then the hardy thane of Hygelac,   *Eofor*
when his brother lay low, let his broad blade,
the eotenish sword of old, break the entish helm
2980   over the shield-wall; then the king bowed,
the shepherd of the people was struck in his life.
Then there were many who bandaged his mæg,
quickly raised him up after it was granted them
to control the place of slaughter.
2985   Then one warrior plundered the other:
he took from Ongentheow his iron byrnie,
hard-hilted sword, and his helmet too;
he carried the hoary one's armor to Hygelac.
He took the frætwe and with fair words promised him
2990   rewards among the people, and this he fulfilled:
he repaid them for the onslaught, the lord of Geats,
Hrethel's offspring, when he came to his home,
with over-mathoms to Eofor and Wulf.
He gave to each of them a hundred thousand
2995   in lands and linked bēags—no man on this middangeard
        could
reproach him for those rewards, since they won renown by
        fighting—
and then he gave Eofor his only daughter,
an honor for his home, as a pledge of fealty.

That is the feud and enmity,
3000   the deadly hostility of men, for which I expect

2988. *he carried the hoary one's armor to Hygelac.* Eofor presents the
plundered armor to his lord Hygelac, just as Beowulf had shared with
Hygelac the treasures he won from fighting Grendel. This action is a tangible means of imparting the honor won in battle to one's lord.

2993. *over-mathoms.* Hygelac repays Eofor and Wulf with an exceedingly
generous reward: treasure, land, and to Eofor his only daughter's hand in
marriage.

2994. *a hundred thousand [sceattas],* silver coins. The value of the land and
treasures comes to this amount.

the Swedish people will seek us out
when they learn that our lord
is lifeless, who before held
hoard and realm against those who hate us,
3005 after the fall of hæleths, the bold Scylfings.
He acted for the people's benefit, and further still
performed eorlship, heroic deeds. Now haste is best,
that we may look upon the people's king,
and bring him who gave us bēags
3010 on his way to the pyre. Not only shall one part
melt with the great-hearted man, but there is a mathom-
    hoard,
gold beyond counting, grimly purchased,
and bēags he has bought now at the last
with his own life; these must the brond consume,
3015 the fire enfold; by no means will an eorl wear
a mathom in his memory, or a bright maiden
have a ring-ornament upon her neck,
but sad-hearted, stripped of gold,
she must walk a foreign land, not once but often,
3020 now that our war-leader has laid aside laughter,
joy and gladness. Therefore many a spear shall
be grasped, morning-cold, in mund,
hoisted in hands; no sound of the harp
shall awaken the warriors, but the dark raven,
3025 eager over the fæge, shall speak many things,
say to the eagle how he fared in his feeding
when with the wolf he plundered the slain."

Thus the man was a teller of omens,
of hateful tidings; not much did he lie
3030 about fated events or words. The troop all arose;
they went unhappily under Earna Ness,
welling with tears, to look upon the wonder.

3014. *the brond*, the flame.
3022. *mund*, hand, palm (OE *mundum*, pl.).
3029. *not much did he lie*. In other words, the messenger was telling the truth about what would soon happen.
3031. *Earna Ness*, Eagles' Bluff.

Then they found him, soulless, on the sand,
holding to his bed of rest, who had given them rings
3035 in earlier times; the final day had then come
for the good one, so that the war-king,
lord of Weders, died a wondrous death.
They had first seen a stranger creature there,
the loathsome wyrm lying on the ground
3040 opposite him there; the fire-draca was
grimly gryre-patterned, scorched with gleed;
he was fifty foot-measures long as he lay.
For a time he had possessed the joys of the air
in the night; down again he went
3045 to seek his den; now he was held fast in death,
his use of earth-caves had come to an end.
Beside him stood beakers and flagons;
plates and precious swords lay
eaten away with rust, just as they had remained there
3050 in fæthm of earth for a thousand winters,
while that eacen-crafty inheritance,
the gold of men of old, was wound about with a spell,
so that no man could touch the ring-hall
unless God himself, the true King of Victories,
3055 granted one whom he wished
— he is the Protector of men — to open the hoard,
whatever man seemed fitting to him.

3047. *Beside him stood beakers and flagons.* An image of the futility of greed, the dragon's carcass lies motionless beside the pile of golden treasure. Though the monsters in the poem are creatures of flesh and blood, each of the three primary monsters also has a symbolic function, which is the inversion of an important social value. The gold-hoarding dragon is an image of greed, the opposite of the generous, treasure-giving kings extolled in the text. The outcast Grendel stands opposed to communal joy and the bond of the war-band. While Grendel's mother shares in this function, she also represents the excesses of unregulated blood vengeance. In their various ways, the monsters represent the forces of social disintegration.

3051. *eacen-crafty,* huge, mighty, "endowed with a mighty power" (Tolkien 2014: 102). The treasure is powerfully protected by a magic spell.

3054. *unless God himself.* The hoard is protected by a curse, but God can override the curse if He chooses to do so for one who is fitting. The poet makes this point to remind his audience that God is more powerful than spells and curses. He may also wish to explain why Beowulf was able to access the treasure — or why the thief who stole the cup was able to do so. It is debated whether Beowulf's death is the result of the curse or not.

FITT 42. *Wiglaf's Speech*

....

It was apparent then that the venture had not succeeded
for the one who had wrongfully hidden away
3060　the wrætt under the wall. The weard had slain
one of a few; then the feud was　　　　　　*Beowulf*
grievously avenged. It is thus a mystery where
an ellen-bold eorl will reach the end
of his allotted life, when he may no longer
3065　dwell in the mead-hall among his kin.
So it was for Beowulf, when he sought the barrow's weard,
treacherous quarrels. He himself did not know
by what means his parting from the world must come about—
so deeply had they declared that until the Day of Doom
3070　—the glorious princes who placed it there—
the man who plundered that place
would be guilty of sins, miserably tormented,
confined in heargs, held fast in hell-bonds.
By no means had he expected a curse on the gold
3075　but rather the Owner's favor.

Fitt 42 Synopsis. The curse is further discussed. Wiglaf tells the troop
what happened, and conveys Beowulf's instructions for his memorial. He
leads the men into the barrow and they load the treasure and Beowulf's
body onto a wagon.

3073. *heargs*, heathen shrines. Pagan gods were identified with demons,
and their places of worship therefore equated with hell.

3074–75. *By no means had he expected a curse on the gold / but rather
the Owner's favor.* The Old English text of this sentence is fraught with
difficulties, all of which significantly affect the interpretation of the poem,
and the translation above is only one of many possibilities. The meaning
of several of the words is disputed and ambiguous; the text itself may have
been miscopied by the scribe; and the references to "he" and "the owner"
are murky to say the least. Is "he" Beowulf or someone else, such as the
dragon, the thief, or the hypothetical man to be cursed? Is the "owner"
God, the dragon, or the previous owner of treasure who had cursed it?
Does *gold-hwæte* mean "gold-eager," "greedy," "gold-bestowing"; or, as in
the interpretation above, "a gold-curse"? A wide range of interpretations
have been suggested, condemning Beowulf, praising him, excusing him,
or not referring to him at all. Here's a small sampling: Beowulf only now
perceived the magnificence of the hoard. Beowulf had not previously
perceived God's gold-bestowing favor (but now realizes the treasure is
bestowed by God alone). Beowulf had never seen the gold-bestowing favor
of God more clearly than now. The man who plundered the hoard would
be cursed unless God's favor was shown to him. Beowulf did not expect
to have good luck. And on and on.

Wiglaf matheled, Wihstan's son:

"Often owing to the will of one man
many an eorl must endure misery, as has happened to us.
We could not persuade our beloved theoden,
3080 the shepherd of the realm, with any ræd
not to approach the keeper of the gold,
to let him lie where he had long been,
remain in his dwelling-place until the world's end.
He held to his high destiny; the hoard has been laid open,
3085 grimly gained; that fate was too strong
that incited the people's king to this place.
I was inside there and looked through it all,
the precious things of the hall, when a way opened for me,
a journey by no means pleasant was permitted me
3090 under the earth-wall. In haste I seized
in my hands a mighty burden
of hoard-treasures, bore it away here
to my king. He was then still living,
still had his wits and wisdom; a great many things
3095 he spoke, the old one in sorrow, and bid me greet you,
asked that, after the friend's deeds, you build   *Beowulf's*
a high barrow at the place of the bæl,
mighty and mære, just as among men
he was the warrior most worthy throughout the wide earth,
3100 for as long as he could enjoy the burh-wealth.
Let us now hasten another time,
to see and seek out the heap of wrought gems,
the wonder under the wall; I will show the way,
so that from near at hand you may gaze upon
3105 the rings and broad gold. Let the bier be made ready,
swiftly prepared when we come out,

3077–78. *Often owing to the will of one man / many an eorl must endure misery.* A rare expression of criticism toward Beowulf, all the more surprising since Wiglaf praises Beowulf's actions elsewhere. It has been suggested that this sentence refers to the thief or the dragon rather than Beowulf, though this seems unlikely. Yet it remains uncertain precisely what Wiglaf is criticizing Beowulf for, and what the consequences of this action might be. Is the "misery" the Geats' anguish at the loss of Beowulf? Or the social consequences of his death that they must soon endure?

3080. *ræd*, counsel, good advice.

and then let us carry our lord,
beloved man, where long he shall
remain in the Waldend's wær."

3110 Then Wihstan's son, the battle-brave warrior,
bid it made known to many hæleths, hall-possessors,
that they should bring bæl-wood
from afar, leaders of folk,
to the good one:

"Now shall fire devour,
3115 flame wax to black, the strengel of warriors,
who often endured the shower of iron
when the storm of arrows pressed on by strings
passed over the shield-wall, the shaft did its duty,
aided the arrow with its eager feather-gear."

3120 Moreover, the wise son of Wihstan
summoned from the troop of the king's thanes
seven together, the best;
he went as one of eight warriors under the evil roof;
one bore in his hands a blazing torch,
3125 he who went in front.
Then it was not decided by lot who should plunder the hoard,
when men saw any portion
lying unguarded in the hall,
wasting away. Little did any of them lament
3130 that they had hastily carried out
the precious mathoms; they also shoved the dragon,
the wyrm, over the cliff-wall, let the waves take him,

3109. *wær*, protection, keeping. The same phrasing is used for Scyld when he dies (27), and in other OE poems for saints at their deaths. "Germanic notions of the protecting lord and of lawfully guaranteed sanctuary were perhaps conflated with the Christian belief in the Almighty's protection" (Klaeber 1911–12: 33). At any rate, *wær* embodies a crucial Germanic concept. The Old Norse equivalent, *var* ("pledge"), appears in *Varangian Guard*, the elite guard unit comprised of Norsemen pledged to protect the Byzantine emperors. The word survives today only in *warlock* (OE *wær-loga*), which originally meant "pledge-breaker."

3115. *strengel*, chief; related to "strong" (OE *strang*).

3125. *not decided by lot who should plunder the hoard*. In other words, everyone plundered it. It was not a difficult decision, since treasure was lying about everywhere, free for the taking.

the flood embrace the keeper of treasures.

Then the wound gold was loaded onto a wagon,
3135   a countless number of everything, and the ætheling was borne,
the hoary battle-warrior, to Hrones Ness.

FITT 43. *Beowulf's Funeral*
....

Then the people of the Geats prepared for him
no small pyre upon the earth,
hung about with helms, war-boards,
3140   bright byrnies, as he had requested.
They laid their mære theoden in its midst,
the hæleths lamenting their beloved lord.
Then on the barrow the warriors began
to awaken the greatest of bæl-fires; the woodsmoke rose,
3145   black above the fire, roaring flame
wound about with weeping—the swirling wind lay still—
until it had broken the bone-house,
hot at the breast. With sad hearts
they mourned their cares of mind, their man-drighten's killing.
3150   A Geatish woman also sang a sorrowful mourning-gydd
for Beowulf, her hair bound up;
again and again she said
that she dreaded harsh invading armies,
a multitude of slaughters, troop-terrors,
3155   humiliations and captivity. Heaven swallowed the smoke.

Then the people of Weders made a mound
on the headland; it was high and broad,
visible from afar to seafarers,
and in ten days they built
3160   a memorial to the battle-bold man; around the remains
from the fire

Fitt 43 Synopsis. The Geats burn Beowulf's body on a pyre strewn with
weapons; as they mourn him an unnamed Geatish woman sings a fearful
lament. They then spend ten days constructing a great mound on a headland overlooking the sea in which they place the king's ashes and treasure.
Twelve warriors ride around the mound mourning their fallen king and
singing his praises.
    3147. *bone-house* (OE *ban-hus*), a kenning for "body."

they fashioned a wall, as worthily
as the wisest of men could devise.
In the barrow they placed gems and bēags,
all such ornaments as earlier
3165 hostile-minded men had taken from the hoard;
they let the earth hold the wealth of eorls,
the gold in the dirt, where it dwells now still,
as useless to men as it was before.

Then around the mound rode battle-brave men,
3170 sons of æthelings, twelve in all.
They wished to lament their grief and mourn their king,
utter a gydd with words and speak about the man.
They praised his eorlship, and his ellen-work
they deemed highly. Just so it is fitting
3175 that a man should praise his wine-drighten with words,
should love him in his heart when
from his garment of flesh he must be led forth.

So the people of the Geats grieved
the fall of their lord, his hearth-companions;
3180 they said that of the kings of the earth
he was the mildest of men and the most gracious,
the kindest to his people and most eager for praise.

3168. *as useless to men as it was before.* The buried gold is useless, not because it is gold, but because it is buried in the ground. The poet takes a dim view of gold when it is hoarded away. Treasure when circulated among warriors and war-leaders is an emblem of their worth and works of courage; only when hidden and hoarded does treasure become sterile and "useless."

3182. *most eager for praise.* The final word in the poem, and the last word on the hero, is *lof-geornost.* All major translations render it "most eager for fame" or "most eager for glory" to avoid the unfavorable associations of desiring "praise." But the root sense of *lof* is "praise"; a *lof-sang*, for example, is a hymn, a song of praise. Beowulf's longing for "praise," then, has led some interpreters to conclude that the poet ends the poem on a down note by pointing out Beowulf's fatal flaw. This is a misreading. It's true that *lofgeorn* can mean "boastful, vainglorious" in some Old English religious literature. Yet within the heroic world of the poem *lof* is wholly good and wholly to be sought, as made clear by lines 1534–36, and 24, in which the poet expresses obvious approval of seeking *lof*, as well as by the Old Norse equivalent, *lofgjarn*, which has only positive connotations. A warrior should seek *lof* the way an Olympic sprinter should seek a gold medal. It is simply the earned recognition for the worth of one's deeds.

ACKNOWLEDGMENTS

THE WORD-HOARD BEOWULF IS THE RESULT OF many years and many helping hands. I am deeply grateful to the friends and family who assisted and supported me in this endeavor, above all my wife Melanie, who along with my children—Aglaia, Juna, Peter Winter, Iris, Lazarus, Miriam, and Isaiah—put up with me through the ups and downs of this project. My parents, Tim and Nancy, offered encouragement and furnished a delightful study for my philological labors.

Instrumental as well was my closest circle of readers: Jon Schaff, Fr. Tom Anderson, Ken Blanchard, and Anthony Wachs. Their suggestions to an early draft resulted in many improvements. Patrick Whiteley was unstinting in his support and feedback. Expert assistance was generously supplied throughout the long process by Johanna Kramer. Ryan McDermott, with friendship and advice, helped to keep this project on track. Judy Raymo devoted many hours to correcting my manuscript.

Thanks are also owed to Mike Aquilina, Joseph Pearce, Joshua Cox, Kelvin Tan, Art Marmorstein, Stephen Pelle at the Dictionary of Old English, the librarians at Beulah Williams Library, the students in my *Beowulf* seminar, and my colleagues at the Northern Plains Conference on Early British Literature. I am also grateful to Northern State University for granting me the necessary research leave. Special thanks to John Riess and all the folks at Angelico Press.

Finally, I remain deeply grateful to John Miles Foley, who first introduced me to the Old English word-hoard of *Beowulf* and who taught me the meaning of *philologia*.

GLOSSARY

THE FOLLOWING GLOSSARY HAS BEEN DESIGNED for quick reference, with only minimal information provided. A more extensive discussion of each word can be found in the notes to the main text, as well by consulting the *Dictionary of Old English, Bosworth-Toller's Anglo-Saxon Dictionary,* and the *Oxford English Dictionary.* The pronunciations included below are only approximate. Old English speakers used several sounds that have long since disappeared from the English language. For example, the *h* sound in *wiht* and *drihten,* which linguists represent with a ʃ symbol, occurs in Modern German but not in present-day English, and in the pronunciations below, it is approximated with *k*. The same approach has been taken with other sounds no longer used in English (ɣ, x, ȳ and Y).

Note that, in the pronunciations below, Æ represents the *a* sound in *apple* and *cat*.

A

æl-wight (OE *æl-wiht,* ÆL-wikt): alien creature, monster.
ær-gōd (ÆR-gode): good-from-of-old, tried and true.
ærn (ÆRN): house, building.
æthel (OE *æthele,* ÆTH-ell-eh): noble, glorious, excellent.
ætheling (ÆTH-ell-ing): member of the warrior class, man of high birth and valor.
æthelu (ÆTH-ell-uh): (noble) ancestry; excellence of character.
aglæca (AH-glætch-ah): ferocious adversary, awe-inspiring opponent.
aldor (ALL-door; also spelled *ealdor*): chief, lord, figure of authority.
Alwalda (ALL-wald-ah; also spelled *eall-wealda*): All-ruling one, God, the Ruler of all.
Anwalda (ON-wald-ah): Ruler, one possessing power (God or human ruler).
attor (OTT-or): venom, poison.

B

bæl (BÆL): fire, funeral pyre.
baldor (BALL-door; also spelled *bealdor*): lord, ruler.
bēag (BAY-ogg; also spelled *bēah*): a ring-shaped treasure of any kind (ring, neck-ring, circlet).
bearm (BEH-arm): bosom, lap; also used figuratively.
bearn (BEH-arn): offspring, son, child.

beorn (BEH-orn): man, hero.

bēot (BAY-ott): heroic vow, the formal promise a hero declares aloud before battle.

bill (BILL): sword.

brego (BREG-oh): ruler, lord.

brenting (BRENT-ing): (high-prowed) ship.

brim (BRIM): sea.

brond (BROND; also spelled *brand*): flame; sword.

brūn (BROON): burnished, shining. (*Brūn* can also signify a dark color such as brown, black, or purple).

burh (BOORG; also spelled *burg*): stronghold, fortified place, town.

burne (BOOR-neh): stream.

byre (BIR-eh): son, boy, child.

byrnie (OE *byrne;* BIR-neh): chainmail coat.

C

cheorl (OE *ceorl*; CHEH-orl): man.

cynde (KYND-eh): natural, innate.

cynn (KIN): family, kin-group, kind, race.

cythe (OE *cythan;* KYTHE-an): to make known, proclaim.

D

dōm (DOME): glory; judgement.

draca (DRAK-ah): dragon.

drēam (DRAY-ahm): communal joy, festivity.

dright (OE *ge-driht*; yeh-DRICT): war-band, the troop led by the *drihten.*

Drighten (OE *drihten*; DRICT-IN): the Lord; also used for a human lord, the leader of the war-band.

duguth (DUH-guth): troop of veteran warriors, band of experienced troop.

E

ēacen (AY-ock-en): endowed with excellence, size, and strength — perhaps supernaturally.

ēam (AY-ahm): maternal uncle.

elf (OE *ælf;* ÆLF): a powerful, usually invisible, supernatural creature.

ellen (ELL-en): courageous daring, vigor, battle-zeal.

ellen-gæst (ELL-en GÆST): bold spirit.

ellor-gæst (ELL-or GÆST): alien spirit.

ent (ENT): mythological creature belonging to a vanished giant race of master builders.

eofor (EH-oh-for): wild boar.

eolet (AY-oh-let): a word whose meaning is now unknown; possibly signifying "sea" or "voyage."

ēorclan-stone (AY-orc-lan; also spelled *eorcnan*): precious stone.

ēored (AY-oh-red): mounted troop, cavalry.

eorl (EH-orl): man, warrior.

eormen (EH-orm-en): immense.

eoten (EH-oh-ten): a massive cannibalistic monster (such as Grendel).

ethel (ETH-ell): native land, home.

F

fæge (FÆY-uh): fated to die, marked for or near to death.

fæhth (FÆY-ah-th): state of open hostility, feud.

fæmne (FÆM-neh): virgin, maiden, unmarried woman.

fæthm (FÆTH-um): embrace. Also used figuratively to mean "grasp"
or "power."

fallow (OE *fealu*; FEH-all-uh): a color term ranging from pale yellow
to reddish brown, but as used in *Beowulf* perhaps signifying "pale"
or "glossy."

fengel (FENG-gell): prince, king.

fen-hop (FEN-HOPE): a remote and secret place in the fens.

fetel-hilt (FETT-ell-): perhaps a ringed or linked hilt. The precise meaning of *fetel* is uncertain.

fifel-cynn (FEEV-ell): race of monstrous creatures.

folm (FOLM): hand, palm.

frætwe (FRÆT-wah; *frætwa* is a plural form): precious gear or treasures.

Frea (FRAY-ah): Lord, applied to both God and human rulers.

freo-wine (FRAY-oh WIN-eh): lord-and-friend, noble friend (a term
applied to rulers).

frōd (FRODE): old and wise.

frum-cynn (FRUM-KIN): lineage, origin.

fyren (FI-ren): wickedness, sin, crime.

G

gædeling (GÆD-ell-ing): kinsman.

gæst (GÆST; also spelled *gast*): spirit.

gamol (GOMM-ol; also spelled *gomel*): aged, ancient.

gar (GAR): spear, pointed weapon.

gesith (yeh-SEETH; plural *gesithas*): troop-member, follower of a chief
who accompanies him on a military excursion (*sith*, "journey").

glædman (GLÆD-): cheerful, gracious, kind.

glee-beam (OE *gleo-*; GLAY-oh): joy-wood, the harp.

gleed (OE *glēd*; GLADE): flame, fire, ember.

gleeman (OE *gleo-*; GLAY-oh): singer, minstrel.

gomb (OE *gombe* or *gambe*; GAM-beh): tribute.

gomen-wood (GAM-en): the harp, the "entertainment-wood."

grim (GRIM): fierce, angry, grim, terrible.

grim-helm (GREEM HELM): war-mask, helmet with protective faceplate.

gryre (GRIR-eh): terror, horror.

guma (GUH-mah): man.

gumcynn (GUHm-kin): the race of men.

gūth (GOOTH): warfare, battle.

gydd (YIED; also spelled *gidd, giedd*): poem, song, or artful utterance of any kind, including a speech.

gylp (YILP; also spelled *gilp*): vow, boast, vaunt.

H

hæl (HÆL): safety, good fortune; health.

hæleth (HÆL-eth): hero, warrior.

hearg (HEH-arg): sacred pagan site, idol shrine.

hlæw (HLÆW): barrow, ancient burial mound.

hlith (HLITH): slope, hillside.

holm (HOLM): sea.

hwæt (HWÆT): an interjection that signals the start of a poem or speech.

hyrsted (HIR-sted): richly ornamented.

hythe (OE *hyth*; HIGH-th): harbor.

I

icge (IJ-eh): a word of unknown meaning.

incge (INJ-eh): a word of unknown meaning. "Shining," "mighty," "immense" are some of the scholarly guesses.

L

lā (LAH): an interjection (Indeed, Oh, Ah).

leam (OE *leoma*; LAY-oh-ma): light, luminary.

leod (LEH-odd): people, nation.

loath (OE *lath*; LOTH): despicable, hostile, hated.

lof (LOAV): praise.

M

mæg (MY): kinsman.

mægth (MYE-th): tribe, people-group.

mære (MÆR-eh): renowned.

mærth (OE *mærthu*; MÆRTH-uh): fame, glory.

mago (MOGG-oh): son, kinsman, young man.

mān (MONN): wickedness, crime (not to be confused with *man*, "man, person").

mathel (OE *mathelian*; MAHTH-ell-ee-on): to make a speech, speak in a formal manner.

mathom (OE *maththum;* MAHTH-um): precious object, treasure.

mead-settle (OE *meodu-setl;* MEH-oh-duh SETT-ell): bench upon which warriors sit to drink mead together in the hall.

meagol (MAY-ah-goal): firm, earnest, strong, hearty.

mearc-stapa (MEH-ark STOP-ah): a wanderer of the borderlands, one who haunts the fringes of human society.

meed (OE *mēd;* MADE): reward; not to be confused with mead (OE *medu*), the alcoholic beverage.

methel (METH-ell): council, meeting.

Metod (MEH-tod; also spelled *Meotod*): God, the Measurer of human fate, the Ordainer.

middangeard (MIDD-ann-yard): the world, the "middle realm" in the cosmos.

mōd (MODE): mind, spirit, heart, courage, pride.

morthor (MOR-thor): murder, slaying, violent assault.

mund (MUN-d): hand; figuratively, "protection."

N

ness (OE *næss;* NÆSS): headland, bluff.

nicor (NICK-or): water monster.

nith (NEETH): violence, hostility.

O

orc-neas (ORC-NAY-oss; plural): creatures of evil, possibly a kind of reanimated corpse.

R

ræd (RÆD): counsel, good advice, help, benefit.

Rædend (RÆD-end): the Ruler, God.

rand (ROND; also spelled *rond*): shield or the shield-boss.

rathely (OE *rathe;* also *hrathe:* RATHE-eh): quickly.

run (ROON): secret, mystery, or secret consultation; runic writing.

S

sark (OE *syrce;* SIR-cheh): shirt (of mail).

sceatt (SHEH-aht): silver coin.

scinna (SHIN-ah): evil spirit.

scop (SHOPE): court poet, singer.

scrithe (OE *scrithan;* SHREETHE-an): to move about in a gliding manner, to wander.

scucca (SHUCK-ah): demon.

seax (SEH-ax): a long, single-edged knife.

sibb (SIB): kinship, peace, friendship.

sith (SEETH): journey, voyage, military venture.

stapol (STOP-ohl): post, pillar, or large upright stone, perhaps serving as a pedestal.

strengel (STRENG-gell): chief.

symbel (SIM-bell): drinking banquet.

T

tide (OE *tid;* TEED): time, period of time.

thane (OE *thegn,* THANE): follower of a war-chief, a warrior.

thengel (THENG-gell): prince, chief.

theod (THAY-odd): people, nation, troop.

theoden (THAY-o-den): a lord, king, leader of the *theod* (people).

thing (THING): meeting, assembly, affair.

thole (OE *tholian*; THOLE-ee-on): to suffer, endure difficulty.

thrym (THRIM): power, force, glory, majesty.

thryth (THRITH): power, strength.

thyle (THIL-eh): orator, spokesman.

thyrs (THIRS): a giant and malicious creature.

W

wæl- (WÆL): slaughter, the slain in battle.

wær (WÆR): a covenant, such as a peace-pledge between two warring groups. Also one under the protection of such a covenant.

Waldend (WALD-end; also spelled *Wealdend*): God, the ruler.

warth (OE *waroth*; WAH-roth): shore, beach.

weard (WEH-ard): guardian.

wearg (WEH-arg): a criminal, accursed, or malignant person; a creature of evil.

wend (OE *wendan,* WEND-on): to turn.

wherve (OE *hweorfan,* HWEH-or-vonn): to turn, move about, wander.

wolcen (WOL-ken): cloud, sky.

wrætlic (WRÆT-litch): artfully or cunningly wrought; mysterious, wondrous, strange.

wrætt (WRÆT): ornament, precious or bejeweled artifact.

wyrd (WEIRD): fate, that which comes to pass.

wyrm (WIRM): dragon, or any serpent-like creature.

Y

ythe (OE *yth*; EYE-th): wave.

WORKS CITED

Barney, Stephen A. *Word-Hoard: An Introduction to Old English Vocabulary.* 2nd Edition. New Haven, CT: Yale University Press, 1985.

Blackburn, F. A. "The Christian Colouring in *The Beowulf.*" *Publications of the Modern Language Association* 12 (1897): 205–25.

Cardew, Philip. "Grendel: Bordering the Human." In Tom Shippey, ed., *The Shadow-Walkers: Jacob Grimm's Mythology of the Monstrous*, 189–205. Medieval and Renaissance Texts and Studies, Vol. 291. Tempe, AZ: Arizona Center for Medieval and Renaissance Studies/Brepols, 2005.

Chickering, Jr., Howell D. *Beowulf: A Dual-Language Edition.* Garden City, NY: Anchor, 1977.

Donaldson, E. Talbot. *Beowulf: A Prose Translation.* New York: Norton, 1975.

Fulk, R. D., Robert E. Bjork, and John D. Niles, eds. *Klaeber's Beowulf,* 4th edition. University of Toronto Press, 2009.

Gelling, Margaret. "The Landscape of *Beowulf.*" *Anglo-Saxon England,* 31 (2002): 7–11.

Green, D. H. *Language and History in the Early Germanic World.* Cambridge, 1998.

Green, J. R. *A Short History of the English People*, Volume I. London: Macmillan, 1902.

Heaney, Seamus. *Beowulf: A New Verse Translation.* New York: Norton, 2000.

Jack, George. *Beowulf: A Student Edition.* Oxford University Press, 1994.

Kaske, R. E. "*Sapientia et Fortitudo* as the Controlling Theme of *Beowulf.*" *Studies in Philology* 55 (1958): 423–56.

Klaeber, F. *Beowulf and the Fight at Finnsburg,* 3rd Edition. Boston: Heath, 1950.

———. *The Christian Elements of Beowulf.* Translated by Paul Battles. Kalamazoo, MI, 1996. (Originally published in German in 1911–12.)

Lapidge, Michael, et al. *The Blackwell Encyclopaedia of Anglo-Saxon England.* Oxford: Blackwell, 1999.

Leyerle, John. "The Interlace Structure of Beowulf." *University of Toronto Quarterly* 37 (1967): 1–17.

Mitchell, Bruce, and Fred C. Robinson. *Beowulf: An Edition.* Oxford: Blackwell, 1998.

Niles, John D. *Beowulf and Lejre. Medieval and Renaissance Texts and Studies* 323. Arizona Center for Medieval and Renaissance Studies, Tempe, AZ, 2007.

Orchard, Andy. *Cassell Dictionary of Norse Myth and Legend.* London: Cassell, 1997.

Robinson, Fred. *Beowulf and the Appositive Style*. Knoxville, TN: University of Tennessee Press, 1985.

Shippey, Tom. *Laughing Shall I Die: The Lives and Deaths of Great Vikings*. London: Reaktion, 2018.

———. *Roots and Branches: Selected Papers on Tolkien by Tom Shippey*. Zurich: Walking Tree Publishers, 2007.

Tacitus. *Germania and Agricola*. Translated by A. J. Church and W. J. Brodribb. London/New York: Macmillan, 1877.

Tolkien, J. R. R. *Beowulf: A Translation and Commentary*. Mariner, 2014.

———. *"Beowulf: Prefatory Remarks,"* in *Beowulf and the Finnesburg Fragment: A Translation into Modern English Prose*. Translated by John R. Clark Hall, with notes and an introduction by C. L. Wrenn, and prefatory remarks by J. R. R. Tolkien. London: Allen & Unwin, 1940. pp. vii–xli.

———. *"Beowulf:* The Monsters and the Critics." *Proceedings of the British Academy*, 22 (1936): 245–95.

Watkins, Calvert, ed. *The American Heritage Dictionary of Indo-European Roots*. 2nd edition. Boston: Houghton Mifflin, 2000.

Watkins, Calvert. *How to Kill a Dragon: Aspects of Indo-European Poetics*. Oxford University Press, 1995.

Whitelock, Dorothy. *The Audience of Beowulf.* Oxford University Press, 1951.

FURTHER READING

OLD ENGLISH LANGUAGE

Baker, Peter S. *Introduction to Old English* (Third Edition). Wiley-Blackwell, 2012.

The classic textbook for learning basic Old English grammar and vocabulary. Particularly helpful is the accompanying "Old English Aerobics" website: http://www.oldenglishaerobics.net.

Klaeber's Beowulf, 4th edition. Edited by R. D. Fulk, Robert E. Bjork, and John D. Niles. University of Toronto Press, 2009.

The standard edition of the Old English text of Beowulf. *Along with the authoritative text, the introduction covers much of the critical history of the poem, and the notes provide a detailed discussion of the text. An essential resource for any serious engagement with* Beowulf.

Videen, Hana. *The Wordhord: Daily Life in Old English.* Princeton University Press, 2022.

An introduction to the everyday vocabulary of Anglo-Saxon life, including the words for food and drink, work, learning, and animals.

CULTURAL AND HISTORICAL CONTEXT

Blair, John. *Building Anglo-Saxon England.* Princeton University Press, 2018.

The most up-to-date information about Anglo-Saxon halls and fortifications.

Crossley-Holland, Kevin. *The Anglo-Saxon World: An Anthology.* Oxford World's Classics, 2009.

A delightful sampling of Old English texts of all kinds—poems, riddles, chronicles, laws, letters—providing a glimpse into the culture that produced Beowulf.

Niles, John D. and Marijane Osborn, eds. *Beowulf and Lejre.* Tempe: Arizona Center for Medieval and Renaissance Studies, 2007.

A collection of essays, accompanied by photos and computer-generated images, offering archeological information about the hall excavations at Lejre (Lethra), the traditional location of the Scylding kings.

Shippey, Tom. *Beowulf and the North before the Vikings.* ARC Humanities Press, 2022.

Shippey presents an array of archeological, textual, and historical evidence, demonstrating that the legendary world of the poem has its roots in actual historical events.

EARLY PERSPECTIVES

Bede, *The Ecclesiastical History of the English People*. Ed. by D. H. Farmer, trans. by Leo Sherley-Price. Penguin Classics, 1990.

Written in AD 731, Bede's History *is the single most significant source for the history of early medieval England. Bede tells the story of the coming of the Anglo-Saxons and their conversion to Christianity. Written around the likely date of* Beowulf, *Bede's account of kings, saints, and the first Christian missions to England presents a vivid picture of early Anglo-Saxon culture.*

Saxo Grammaticus, *The History of the Danes*. Two volumes: *Books I-IX: I. English Text; II. Commentary*. Edited by Hilda Ellis Davison. Translated by Peter Fisher. D. S. Brewer, 1979-80.

Writing in Latin in the late 12th century, Saxo compiled earlier Scandinavian heroic legends. Though the inflated writing style is somewhat off-putting, the book preserves legendary materials that have otherwise been lost, including the earliest version of the Hamlet story.

Tacitus, *Germania and Agricola*, A. J. Church and W. J. Brodribb, 1877.

The first ethnographic account of the Germanic peoples, written c. 98 AD.

TOLKIEN AND *BEOWULF*

Carpenter, Humphrey. *J. R. R. Tolkien: A Biography*. Allen and Unwin, 1977.

The best biography available on Tolkien. Carpenter sheds light on Tolkien as an Old English scholar, Catholic, and imaginative writer.

Flieger, Verlyn. *Splintered Light: Logos and Language in Tolkien's World*. Kent State University Press, 1983. Updated and expanded in 2002.

An exploration of Tolkien's understanding of language as represented in his creative fiction, especially The Silmarillion. *Flieger applies the linguistic theories of Tolkien's fellow Inkling Owen Barfield to her interpretation of Tolkien.*

Shippey, Tom. *The Road to Middle-Earth: How J. R. R. Tolkien Created a New Mythology*. 1982.

An insightful study of the influence of medieval literature on Tolkien's fiction, with special attention to Beowulf, *written by a scholar with a deep knowledge of both.*

Tolkien, J. R. R. *Beowulf and the Critics*. Edited by Michael D. C. Drout. Revised 2nd edition, Medieval and Renaissance Texts and Studies, 2011.

Tolkien's famous essay, "Beowulf: The Monsters and the Critics," derives from an earlier, much longer text, Beowulf and the Critics. *Edited and annotated by Drout, this text elucidates Tolkien's interpretation of* Beowulf *as well as his own writing.*

ABOUT THE AUTHOR

PETER RAMEY is Associate Professor of English at Northern State University, where he teaches courses on medieval English literature, Latin, and linguistics. He has published articles on *Beowulf* and on Old and Middle English in *Modern Philology*, *Philological Quarterly*, and other scholarly journals, while also writing for a broader audience in his essays in *Public Discourse* and *Front Porch Republic*.

Made in the USA
Coppell, TX
17 March 2023